TECHNOCAPITALISM

TECHNO-CAPITALISM

THE RISE OF THE NEW ROBBER BARONS AND THE FIGHT FOR THE COMMON GOOD

LORETTA NAPOLEONI

Seven Stories Press
New York • Oakland

Seven Stories Press
140 Watts Street
New York, NY 10013
www.sevenstories.com

College professors and high school and middle school teachers may order free examination copies of Seven Stories Press titles. Visit https://www.sevenstories.com/pg/resources-academics or email academic@sevenstories.com.

Library of Congress Cataloging-in-Publication Data

Names: Napoleoni, Loretta, author.
Title: Technocapitalism : the rise of the new robber barons and the fight
    for the common good / Loretta Napoleoni.
Description: New York : Seven Stories Press, [2024] | Includes
    bibliographical references and index.
Identifiers: LCCN 2023027914 | ISBN 9781644213292 (trade paperback) | ISBN
    9781644213308 (ebook)
Subjects: LCSH: Technological innovations--History--21st century. |
    Capitalism--History--21st century. | Anomy.
Classification: LCC HC79.T4 N34 2024 | DDC 338/.064--dc23/eng/20231201
LC record available at https://lccn.loc.gov/2023027914

Printed in the USA.

9 8 7 6 5 4 3 2 1

For Davide,
Brilliant, Kind, and Caring

CONTENTS

ACKNOWLEDGMENTS

This is a pandemic book, conceived, researched, and written under the long shadow of the lockdowns. Technology is not only the main topic of the book; it is the instrument through which *Technocapitalism* has come to life. Though I could not visit my sources, those who advised and commented on what I was writing, technology brought them to my home as images on a screen.

My interaction with the Castelli family, on the contrary, was not virtual, it was very real because they were part of my bubble, i.e., the people I was permitted to see. As I developed the idea of the book, they became an unusual team of research assistants. Without their valuable contributions, I would not have been able to write *Technocapitalism*. I have very fond memories of the discussions during our lockdown Sunday lunches and long walks along the river, as well as of the inputs of the children, Davide and Matteo, about technology and social media. Davide's remarkable research under the supervision of his parents, Francesco and Serena, helped me understand the evolution of technology and the trajectory along which it is moving. To them I am deeply grateful.

My son Julian Gerson and his friend Andrea Idili, both scientists, have guided me in a field I was not fully acquainted with, helping me understand complex issues. Mary Nisse, a doctor and epistemologist, has enlightened me on the physical danger of space travel for the human body. Other friends, Sarah Freedman, Stefano and Silvia Mazzola, Stephen and Eleonor Creaturo, and Paola Pastoressa, have listened to my ideas and commented on how to present them to the reader. I am forever thankful to them for their support.

Thank you also to Lennart Carlsson, Tim Culver, and Andrew Seber for reading the book and commenting on it. A special thank you goes to my friend Miriam Cosic for editing the chapters while I was writing them.

As usual, my assistant Federico Bastiani has been an invaluable support, unveiling the mysteries of social media and virtual communication.

My US agent, Diana Finch, and my Italian agent, Marco Vigevani, have believed in the project right from the beginning and made it possible to realize.

Dan Simon of Seven Stories Press and Christer Sturmark of Fri Tanke, my publishers, bought the book on proposal and offered important inputs. To both of them, thank you for the trust in my work.

Life Is Full of Surprises

Over the last twenty years, disorientation has become a recurrent feature of our existence. The extraordinary often morphs out of the ordinary and life constantly surprises, shocks, or spooks us, demanding sudden, unexpected adjustment to astonishing changes: artificial intelligence writes summaries, articles, even books, and chats with us; solving complex mathematical formulas frees crypto wealth trapped inside software and enriches a new class of people; collectors and speculators pay millions of dollars to snatch up ownership of digital images, i.e., non-fungible tokens, which exist only in a universe of pixels; in the 2008 bailout the trillions of dollars printed by tapping on the keyboard of the US Treasury, far from avoiding foreclosures for thousands of people, ended up funding a new breed of serial capitalists, the Techtitans; space is the new frontier for mining precious resources and a handful of private companies owned by the Space Barons leads the race to harvest them.

At the same time, the living wages of working people have declined to less than what they were fifty years ago, the gig economy has stripped labor benefits, in many fields AI has already begun to replace humans, and the American dream is a distant memory. The very poor and the sick are no longer useless: far from it, they are a source of profits for Big Pharma and its cottage industry. Today an elderly person with terminal cancer might be kept alive for ten years longer than before, with Medicare delivering millions of dollars in revenue to private health care companies.

The Ukraine war may be a human tragedy of epic proportions, but it is a profit center for the hydrocarbon and arms industries. The war has led to the reopening of coal plants and allowed the United States and most European countries to modernize their aging weapons systems by sloughing them off on Ukraine. The unexpected reactivation of the Cold War arms race is breathing new life into the military industrial complex in Russia, in the US, and worldwide—at the expense of the Green Economy, which has been put on hold for the duration of the war, and at the expense of the global food supply, education, basic health care, and relief for all of society's neediest cases. Life itself is being devalued even as world leaders raise interest rates to combat people's number one economic enemy: inflation.

The list of out-of-the-ordinary, surreal events that hits us daily, altering our existence for good or ill, is endless. Every time, we are confused or baffled, even scared, and not necessarily because of the magnitude of the change—we have no time to evaluate it—but because of the speed and frequency with which life gets reshaped around us. Perhaps the best example to illustrate this condition is the set of consequences of the pandemic: as most nations went into lockdown, we were catapulted into the virtual world, a kind of reality video game where we began to live as avatars.

In *Technocapitalism*, I will seek to describe these phenomena as the genesis of a new paradigm, born in a period of extraordinary change in which the exceptional acceleration of time often causes the present and future to overlap. This unique era can be defined as the Present Future. Since technology and artificial intelligence determine the pace of transformation, the transition occurs at a speed that is mentally, emotionally, and existentially unbearable for most of us. Because everything changes so suddenly, any action appears useless: most of us sense that any achievement is destined to become obsolete in the blink of an eye. The futility of the present is so disconcerting that sometimes anxiety paralyzes us.

The coronavirus pandemic was one of a long litany of this type of events that triggered the pandemic of anxiety.[1] This mental illness could be defined as follows: a chain of negative thoughts prompted by fear of the unknown. Is fear of the unknown really the principal cause of the disease of the century? Or is what plagues most of us the speed at which current certainties are shattering and new horizons keep emerging? History could help us find the right answer.

At the dawn of any great transformation there are always some visionaries who embrace the unknown; these are people who perceive what is happening sooner than others and can, sometimes, contribute to create positive transformational change for society. It happened, for example, when the industrial use of steel led to the birth of modern cities. Although there is evidence that steel was applied to manufacture tools some four thousand years ago,[2] it was the invention of the Bessemer process,[3] a technique for creating steel using molten pig iron, in the 1850s, that turned steel into one of the biggest industries on the planet. Steel became widely used, from building bridges and railroads to the construction of engines and skyscrapers. It proved particularly influential in North America, where massive iron ore deposits helped the United States become one of the world's biggest producers—and the biggest economy in the world.

Andrew Carnegie foresaw the transformation which made him one of the richest men in American history. However, his intuition not only produced immense wealth for himself and his family but also improved people's lives. Far from the size of the wealth accumulated, successful visionaries' true achievement during great transformations is the magnitude of the leap forward in progress for humanity that they contribute to. Without it, most innovation is destined to harm society, either through impoverishment or oppression or even fraud, which is exactly what happened with FTX, the crypto exchange which collapsed in November 2022. Sam Bankman-Fried saw a gap in the market that nobody had noticed, i.e., prices of bitcoins were higher in Japan and South Korea than in the US; in a short time he closed the gap, arbitraging between them and pocketing the difference. He then built one of the biggest crypto exchanges, which he ran as a Ponzi scheme, and promoted himself as a philanthropist to save the planet and to shower politicians with donations. When FTX finally went bust, investors lost all their money, clients their accounts, employees their jobs. Behind Sam Bankman-Fried's philanthropic narrative, what motivated him was pure greed, not the common good.

If curiosity and intuition had not prevailed over our fear of the unknown, the human species would most likely not have survived. Curiosity about what was beyond one's habitat, and the perception that there lies our long-term survival, prompted our Stone Age ancestors to overcome their fears and to leave the security of the extended family and of the tribe to migrate in search of a better life. We are not different from them. Today, what fuels our anxiety is not fear of the unknown, but the speed at which the present morphs into the future and reality is altered and reinvented. We are ill-equipped to deal with a world in which certainties are continuously shattered and the pillars of advanced societies keep evaporating. For example, the currencies we use are no longer backed by any real asset; debt fuels monetary growth because financial engineering has morphed it into an asset. Fiat money is just an act of faith.

So what about our modern visionaries, those who are not overwhelmed by anxiety? A small group of high-tech-savvy entrepreneurs has indeed been able to embrace the velocity of change and rip benefits out of the Present Future thanks to their special knowledge of technological innovation. These people *understand* technology. Sadly, too often they abuse this unique advantage, damaging society. The genesis of Uber, for example, shows how control of technological innovation can flout the law, reduce the quality of life for workers, and trick municipalities into deregulating a vital transportation sector, discriminating against non-technologically-savvy companies. In October 2010, just a few months after Uber was launched in San Francisco, the company got a letter from the city's transportation authorities saying that what Uber was doing was illegal and that they would send the founders to jail if they did not stop the car service right away. The employees were very concerned—what to do? The answer came from cofounder and CEO Travis Kalanick: do nothing. While taxi companies filed complaints and regulators threatened legal action, Uber carried on, breaking the law without any consequence.

Too often, dismissing existing legislation is a feature of the work ethic, or lack thereof, of the Techtitans. Conscious of the exceptional speed of technological change and of the difficulties of the law to catch up with it, they have been exploiting this temporal gap to their own advantage. They have established and consolidated their businesses, often acting illegally, and, as in the case of Uber and Amazon, subverting existing labor market rules. Inside the gray, lawless area carved by the speed of change, the Techtitans have built their high tech monopolies. Unlike the Carnegie steel empire, most of their companies have not enriched society. On the contrary, some have stripped the state of its powers, and the workers of their rights, to enrich their founders and their investors. And yet we keep using their apps and services. Are we oblivious or unaware of the dire consequences of these disturbing facts for society as a whole?

In the past, to some degree, nature set the rhythm of great transitions even when the change has been man-made. Even during the Industrial Revolution, when against the backdrop of great exploitation, society was transformed across one generation, just in a few decades, the change was sufficiently slow to facilitate comprehension and adaptation across mankind. Society has always had enough time to conceptualize the consequences of innovation, to catch up with it, to regulate, and eventually to benefit from it. The unionization of the workforce, for example, advanced alongside the Industrial Revolution, and so did the study of the economy. Today we do not have such luxury. We live in a state of constantly accelerating time, to the point that life becomes like a speeded-up TikTok video. And everything appears infinitely complex, precarious, incomprehensible, even unreal to most people. Against this scenario we are constantly disoriented, easy prey to anxiety.

Having established that the pandemic of anxiety is linked to our inability to understand and adapt to the new, permanently fast-evolving reality, in other words, to exist today, one could argue that our brains are not able to process this high-intensity level of uncertainty. However, some anthropologists would assert that our very first ancestors lived in equally precarious and dangerous times, without certainties, with limited knowledge, and at the mercy of the whims of change. Those early people coexisted with permanently unpredictable transformation and their resilience is still an essential attribute of our species and part of our collective inheritance.

Of course, they lived in camps or even caves while we are surrounded by the comforts of modernity. More critically, their survival depended on banding together in clans and tribes, whereas we live either alone or confined to the nuclear family, and thanks to technology, we depend less and less upon each other. Whatever we need we can buy. What makes us weak, however, are not the accessories of modernity. Our lack of resilience has deep psychological roots which spring from the coexistence with a type of life our species has never experienced before.

Since the end of the Second World War, the West has enjoyed the fastest economic growth and the longest period of peace in history. Paradoxically, this exceptional time has been characterized by the anticipation of imaginary catastrophes, i.e., the nuclear threat of the Cold War or the menace of terrorism, and by consumerism. And it has been associated with hundreds of "small" real wars in far-off places, in which arms manufactured in the US, Russia, China, or Europe have been instrumental in killing millions and helping maintain the status quo of global power. Through the decades of imaginary fears, Westerners have come to the conclusion that the instruments our species has used until today, i.e., human solidarity, do not work anymore, that we have entered a new everyone-for-themselves phase of history. For nearly a century, we have let ourselves become almost constantly afraid, waiting for the inevitable end of our world at the hands of invincible forces, and each of us has been facing this nightmare essentially alone. Haruki Murakami is correct when he writes in *1Q84*: "Everyone, deep in their hearts, is waiting for the end of the world to come."[4] The politics of fear: this is the definition of the new state of permanent existential paranoia in which we coexist. It has eroded human resilience while projecting on the wall a darker and darker future, full of insurmountable and incomprehensible dangers. Our sole comfort has been unlimited access to the fruits of economic growth, i.e., a consolation prize: to consume, either in real life or virtually. But consumerism is nothing more than a quick fix.

In the collective imagination of the people, the politics of fear coupled with consumerism have corroded any possibility of transformation, morphing the present into a degeneration of the past, something to dread. Against this grim scenario, the most common reaction is to bask in nostalgia, to idealize the past and loathe the present and the future. For this reason, we are uninterested in understanding and controlling technology, a product of the Present Future, and are happy to just be users in a way that fits our immediate, self-centered needs—people dislike how Uber treats drivers, but they still punch their address on the app to call a ride. Even those who are willing to understand and embrace change fight their own anxiety produced by pessimism in the age of the Anthropocene.

The age of the Anthropocene is the era in which nature no longer drives change, when instead humanity and its Frankenstein creature, artificial intelligence, are at the helm of the planet. So far this transformation has mostly caused distress because we focus primarily on its negative impacts—the advent of AI comes at the same time as the loss of clean air, the shrinking of glaciers, the disappearance of beautifully colored coral reefs, the wholesale extinction of tens of thousands of animal species, the alteration of the four seasons—and so it is hard for us to discern any positive aspects of the technological transformation that is upon us. So we start to mourn change instead of welcoming it, instead of harnessing it to our own advantage, and take refuge in a nostalgic idyll of Nature, anything to help us cope with our anxiety. However, this nostalgia is another quick fix; it will not save the planet or its inhabitants from climate Armageddon. Nor will rejecting the age of the Anthropocene or rewriting the history of our species.

Even if we are part of it, Nature has never been a friend. The evolution of our species is the story of a long and spectacular conflict between humanity and Nature, a war fought on several fronts not by one individual alone, but together against predatory animals and natural disasters. Interestingly, during the Cold War, this narrative resurfaced and was used to justify the space race. Just before becoming the first man in space, cosmonaut Yuri Gagarin said, "to engage, single-handed, in an unprecedented duel with nature—could one dream of anything more?"[5] Fast forward to 2020, when we encountered a true example of how transformational modern science and technology can be in protecting our species against Nature's deadly microscopic viruses, when new vaccines were developed against COVID-19. But at the same time we witnessed an equally great failure of the human spirit as the very governments that had poured resources into that effort refused to give the new technology to poor nations, which would have eradicated the pandemic worldwide instead of enriching a few Big Pharma corporations.

Today, however, the real danger does not come from a feral Nature. Today our formidable enemy is the imbalance between the supply and demand of Earth's resources, an imbalance that paradoxically our extraordinary success as a species has triggered. Yes, we are the cause of the problem, but we are also the solution, or can be. Technology, the product of the age of the Anthropocene, can help us reach higher ground, providing we learn how to control and use it correctly, for the common good. Technology left alone in the hands of the Techtitans will, on the contrary, harm us and the planet. Just think of the technological revolution embodied in the electric car that consumes a fraction of the hydrocarbon energy of traditional vehicles, providing electricity is generated through renewable resources. And yet, very little—almost nothing—is being done to address the issue of the production and disposal of the batteries of electric cars, which have a considerable carbon footprint. Why? Because the final goal of those who control this technology remains profitability, not sustainability, i.e., greed, not the common good.

Electric vehicles—and, by extension, leading EV manufacturers like Tesla—are a good example of the dangers of technological innovation boxed inside profitability. A 2017 study on electric vehicles in China, published by the *Financial Times* four years later,[6] shows that the production of an electric car emits up to 60 percent more carbon dioxide than the manufacture of a traditional car, mainly due to the carbon footprint of the batteries.

We are at a point in our evolution in which technology makes it possible for us to rebalance the demand and supply of resources and achieve sustainability. One strategy is to look beyond the Blue

Planet, starting from the low Earth orbit (LEO). Colonizing LEO for resource exploitation, setting up space stations on the Moon, mining asteroids, who knows, even building artificial planets to meet our industrial needs and creating a system of cosmic railways to reach them: these projects no longer belong to science fiction, they may well become key components of the next volume of the history of our species. Why not? From the first migrations of the hunter-gatherers to the invention of the wheel to the first sea journeys around the globe based on the observation of the rotation of the stars in the sky, reaching new frontiers to discover novel lands has always been one of the shining characteristics of human beings. Interestingly, the adventurers were most often common people, not the rich and the powerful. Sometimes they were driven by religious persecution, or economic desperation.

Migration has saved humanity from famine, hunger, and wars. Early forms of globalization drove cultural and technological advances. Why should we stop now, why should we not look at the cosmos as our first ancestors looked at lands on the other side of the ocean? Why should we let the twenty-first-century robber barons, the Techtitans who own private space companies, steal our dream?

It is true that space terrifies us: it is the great unknown. The universe also presents major, possibly insurmountable obstacles to our survival on other planets, or even in near space in the foreseeable future. Biology is the biggest one. Our bodies cannot function without Mother Earth; without gravity, the rotation and the magnetic field of our planet, our bodies deteriorate. However, crossing the Pacific Ocean from Polynesia to Easter Island in a canoe around AD 300 was equally terrifying, dangerous, and involved overcoming similarly huge obstacles. Still, we made it!

If we cannot colonize space, perhaps our youngest creation—artificial intelligence, e.g., robots—can. We could direct and supervise their work from space stations on low Earth orbit. But the goal of such phenomenal effort must be to improve people's lives on earth and save our beautiful planet. This is not what has been happening; systems like ChatGTP[7] have been produced to boost profits of companies like Microsoft, hiding the potentially catastrophic consequences for humanity.

So far, the activity of the Space Barons and of the Techtitans has put the common good in jeopardy. For two decades, taking advantage of the speed of change, which they understand better than the rest of us do, they have been stripping the power of the nation state to turn our lives into commodities and us into consumers. More recently, to expand their high tech monopolies and enlarge their fortunes, they have targeted low Earth orbit. Nebulas of privately owned satellite labs are being constructed to achieve their goals. They have hijacked technological innovation and used it to dehumanize us to accumulate unimaginable wealth. While the politics of fear have prevented us from understanding the potential of this epic transformation, the Techtitans have blocked access to technology, and so we have been unable to reap its benefits for a much nobler cause: to heal the planet and the people. *This* is the unspoken true root cause of the pandemic of anxiety.

CHAPTER ONE

The Cypherpunks

In the early 1990s, a group of mathematicians, hackers, computer programmers, and activists gathered in a cottage north of San Francisco for a weekend of discussion about the future of computer science. Most of them had grown up in the shadow of the space race between the United States and the Soviet Union, had read the rich science fiction literature in vogue during those years, and regarded the cosmos as the next, natural frontier of humanity. In other words, they were "cosmic nerds." Back then, it wasn't uncommon for residents of the Bay Area to show up at parties wearing futurist costumes. Unsurprisingly, some arrived disguised as astronauts, others as Star Wars characters. Besides partying, they talked about a revolutionary new science and technology, born and bred in Silicon Valley—artificial intelligence—and the impact it could have on humanity.

Some of them believed artificial intelligence would finally make space travel and exploration feasible, bringing together two of the passions they shared: computer science and a science fiction approach to the universe.

In late 1992, several of the cosmic nerds who had participated in that cyber weekend north of San Francisco met at mathematician Eric Hughes's house in Oakland, California. Hughes, retired businessman Tim May, and computer scientist John Gilmore—considered the founding fathers of the cyber revolution that swept across North America in the 1990s—had organized the gathering.[8] For our story, it is worth revisiting their background.

After graduating in physics from the University of California at Santa Barbara in 1974, May had worked for Intel, where he succeeded in significantly improving the memory chips of computers. This major technological breakthrough allowed him to accumulate enough money to quit his job at the age of thirty-four. Since then, he had dedicated himself to the study of computer science, cryptography, physics, and mathematics, and to reading science fiction and political analysis. Gilmore had been the fifth computer scientist that Sun Microsystems, one of the first American companies to produce computer software, had hired. Like May, after earning several million dollars from his cyber inventions, he had quit his job and retired to further develop his ideas and cultivate his political views. In 1990 he had formed the Electronic Frontier Foundation (EFF), a nonprofit digital-rights group, together with John Perry Barlow and Mitch Kapor, to promote internet civil liberties. Hughes, a brilliant mathematician from the University of California at Berkeley, had worked in the Netherlands with David Chaum, at the time perhaps the most famous cryptographer in the world.

May, Hughes, and Gilmore believed that computer science would deeply affect the future of politics and of society, and worried about the role that the state was going to play in such a transformation. Unlike many West Coast liberals, for whom the dawn of electronics and computer science had heralded the birth of a new and liberating era, they feared that the web would ignite a golden age of state control and espionage. They believed governments could use digital surveillance of the internet to reduce individual freedom and limit people's privacy. Being committed libertarians, they had called the meeting in Oakland to expose to the Bay Area cyber community these fears and discuss strategies to block the state from turning the web into an instrument of repression. As a result, a study group was formed to deal with the issue. After a month of similar consultations, the cyber group concluded that a weapon was needed to prevent the internet from building the foundations of an Orwellian state. To protect the individual from government surveillance, therefore, a new software was required, one that would allow ordinary people to evade state control in cyberspace. The task of the group was to produce it.

During one of these meetings, Jude Milhon—an activist, programmer, and hacker, better known by the pseudonym St. Jude—referred to its members as "Cypherpunks." This was a play on the words "cipher," the most common cryptographic technique, and "cyberpunk," a genre popular among science fiction writers. Cypherpunks was also reminiscent of the antiestablishment punk rock music movement of the 1970s, so it captured well the subversive, anarchic nature of most of the cyber nerds.

The Cypherpunks decided to create an encrypted email list to serve as a cyber platform of exchange among themselves. They called it the "Cyphers Mailing List." The List not only contained political, economic, and philosophical messages and reflections, but it was also a theoretical and experimental platform for discussion. For example, if someone wrote a piece of software and sent it to the others, many would study and improve it—and then post it back for further comments, and so on. All exchanges were conducted using new cryptographic systems that ensured absolute secrecy and privacy among the participants.

During the late 1980s and early 1990s, it was common for online discussion to take place using mailing lists. Generally, members emailed an administrator who acted as a moderator. This was not how the Cypherpunks mailing list worked. In line with their rejection of any structure, which they believed always empowers single sources of authority, the List was unmoderated and organized by threads. Once posted, the emails were sent and received by everybody.

The logic behind this unorthodox methodology was to allow the ideas to move around freely, to be developed and to be shared without restrictions among the group. Naturally, the range of topics discussed in the threads was extremely wide; without a moderator, anybody could start a new thread at any time. This explains why threads on the List ranged from discussions of the use of Ritalin in children with ADD—some Cypherpunks considered it a violation of the First Amendment because the state should not chemically prevent anybody from expressing themselves—to strategies to block the Clinton administration's attempts to further regulate cryptography.

Lacking moderation, in time the List became overwhelming, especially once hundreds and hundreds of emails of no interest began arriving to all the inboxes. Sometimes members became so irritated that they replied with hostility. These heated exchanges were known as "flame wars," a precursor of modern trolling. Luckily, the unstructured system did not prevent the group from remaining focused on its fundamental goal: to secure and defend cyber privacy—in every shape and form—from the state.

Because of their firm rejection of any type of authority, the Cypherpunks have been described as libertarians, anarchists, and reactionaries. Libertarians believe that the most important political good is liberty, not democracy. They fear that when the majority is ignorant, democracy becomes just another form of tyranny. In line with this characterization, in 1994 Tim May wrote:

> Crypto anarchy means prosperity for those who can grab it, those competent enough to have something of value to offer for sale; the clueless 95% will suffer, but that is only just. With crypto anarchy we can painlessly, without initiation of aggression, dispose of the nonproductive, the halt and the lame.[9]

Not all Cypherpunks shared those views. For example, Julian Assange, who was one of the only non-American participants on the List, under the pseudonym Proff, disagreed with May and argued that targeting 95 percent of the population was a mistake. The real enemy, he wrote, was the 2.5 percent at either end of the "normal," meaning the elites in power, whether liberal or conservative.[10] Other Cypherpunks had a history of political activism and regarded themselves as activists rather than libertarians. The cryptographer Phil Zimmermann, for instance, was twice arrested for his involvement in antinuclear protests. Others included people like John Perry Barlow of the Electronic Frontier Foundation (EFF), who was an LSD junkie and friend of Timothy Leary, a libertarian anarchist who strongly believed that information wants to be free.

Describing the Cypherpunks either as radical right or radical left would be incorrect. They were a unique, heterogeneous political group that included a wide range of ideologies and creeds. Tim May said Cypherpunks were "anarcho-syndicalists, anarcho-capitalists, Neo-Pagans, Christian Fundamentalists, and maybe even a few unreconstructed Communists."[11] Politically, what they did have in common was a concern about Western democracies' looming crisis of freedom, the extensive and fast-growing control of state institutions over the private lives of individuals, and a deep mistrust of governments. The glue that held together the many factions of the Cypherpunks was the belief that technology, rather than laws, could protect individual freedoms, not necessarily because democracy was wrong, but because it was broken.

The Cypherpunks were children of the Cold War and at the same time, they were the first generation of the Present Future. They had grown up in the shadow of Hiroshima and Nagasaki, of the Korean and Vietnam wars, and of the dichotomy between the "free world" and communism. The advent of the nuclear bomb had traumatized them and they feared nuclear proliferation could lead to an apocalyptic outcome. Their anxiety was comparable to ours today. Stewart Brand, the visionary organizer of the first Hackers Conference, which was held in Marin County in 1984, recalls how the youth of the 1950s and '60s felt about the future: "We were the 'Now Generation' because we figured there would be no 'Then.' We were completely apoplectic; the sky was falling."[12] The Cypherpunks were also the first generation to witness the Space Race and the Moon landing. Their horizon was infinitely wider than that of their parents. Technology empowered them and technological innovation mitigated their deep pessimism and the anxiety produced by the Cold War's politics of fear. To the Cypherpunks, technology offered a way out of the existential crisis precipitated by the dropping of the nuclear bomb.

Technology was so drenched in positivism that it turned the Cypherpunks into visionaries. Over the years they envisioned, invented, and developed nearly all the techniques now applied by computer users to avoid government surveillance. For example, Tim May conceptualized the creation of cryptocurrencies, monetary instruments that would allow exchanges away from the eye of monetary authorities. In the List the Cypherpunks extensively discussed how to structure such a virtual means of monetary exchange to bypass state control, something similar to what Satoshi Nakamoto would create almost two decades later when he invented bitcoin. May also hoped for the birth of a tool to surf the web anonymously, in an unregulated market—which he called "BlackNet"—where everything could be bought or sold without tracking and surveillance. He equally anticipated an anonymous whistleblowing system that would expose the crimes of governments and states, exactly what Assange eventually produced with WikiLeaks.

The main obstacle to the implementation of all these initiatives was how to guarantee anonymity and secrecy inside the web, and that is the reason why the Cypherpunks dedicated most of their time to developing an unbreakable cryptographic code. The Cypherpunks email list soon became the virtual forum for a global community interested in using cryptography to empower individuals to communicate and conduct transactions over the internet privately, without interference from a central authority.

Cryptography is the art and the science to hiding secrets while transmitting data. From the time of the Roman Empire until the 1970s, cryptography has been based on a "single key" model: a single code used to send and to decipher encrypted messages. This is how, during the Second World War, the Enigma machine was able to decipher the Nazis' codes, having found their key.

The advent of modern computer science made cryptography much more complex, but it did not change the basic principle: to communicate secretly, people had to provide their correspondent with the code in which the message had been written. And messages continued to travel over unsecure channels where they could be intercepted before reaching the recipient, as was the case with the code the Nazis used during the war.

In 1976, two Stanford mathematicians, Whitfield Diffie and Martin Hellman, invented a new cryptographic system which they called "public-key cryptography." Here's how it works: each user is assigned a personal code system consisting of two "keys," which are different but mathematically related via a shared primary number. The math behind public-key cryptography is very complex, but the idea is simple: you can share the "public" key with everyone and they can use it to encrypt messages. But the messages can only be decrypted with a secret and personalized "private" key, a key that only the recipients possess.

To explain, let's imagine that the encrypted messages arrive in our mailbox. Inserting them is easy, everyone can do it. But only those who have the key, unique and personal, can open the mailbox. Without that key, the messages will lie in the mailbox forever; they cannot be extracted. Taking possession of the key is statistically very difficult; copying it is virtually impossible. This simple principle is at the root of the blockchain and bitcoin technology that is discussed in the following chapters.

Public-key cryptography revolutionized the potential uses of cryptography because it enabled the sending of encrypted messages without having to exchange a code and without having to meet in person. It is easy to understand why the American government did not want this invention to be disclosed; in a war, for example, it would be difficult to decode a public-key encryption and those who possessed such technology would be at a great advantage. If the Nazis had had such a system, the Enigma machine would most probably have been of no use and, who knows, the course of history could have been different.

Because of these considerations, Washington intervened to block the disclosure of public-key cryptography. Before Diffie and Hellman could publish, the National Security Agency (NSA) warned that to do so would constitute a federal offense. With the Arms Export Control Act of 1976, Congress had in fact outlawed the distribution and export of weapons to other countries without a license, and cryptography was classified as a "strategic weapon." The penalty for violation was up to ten years in prison or a fine of up to $1 million.

The Arms Export Control Act marks the beginning of the "crypto wars": the legal and public relations battle between the intelligence community and cyber privacy activists, including the Cypherpunks. The battlefield was the rights of citizens to use encryption for personal purposes, i.e., to remain anonymous online.

Until the early 1990s, public-key cryptography remained the exclusive domain of the US government, which built a series of legislations around it to guarantee government institutions access to citizens' crypto privacy. In early 1991, the United States Senate introduced a law that forced electronic communications service providers to hand over users' personal data to state authorities. Approval of the law was promoted by then Senator Joe Biden, now president of the United States. In 1993, the US government introduced the "Clipper chip," a standard encryption system for the internet—all the keys of which are held by the National Security Agency.

The response of the Cypherpunks was to create and publicize the public-key cryptographic system. This was done by antinuclear activist and computer programmer Phil Zimmermann. Zimmermann is the inventor of the Pretty Good Privacy software, better known as PGP, which he made accessible to everyone online, free of charge. From that moment onward, it became possible for two individuals to communicate without any risk that their messages would be intercepted and decrypted by anyone else. PGP opened the door to the future of e-commerce and was the grandfather of the cryptocurrencies. It also laid down the foundation of the dark web, a development that Zimmermann did not foresee and that, according to Tim May, years later led him to regret having divulged PGP.

In the early 1990s, the Cypherpunks were exclusively focused on the positive aspects of the anarchic, libertarian nature of the internet. They did not take into consideration the advantages that cryptography would offer to crime. For them, encryption technology was vital for the net to grow and privacy was fundamental to develop online commerce. The more the internet was perceived as free, the more reliable it was. Of course, the US government wanted to control the web, and this is why immediately after the online publication of PGP, Zimmermann was accused of exporting weapons and the US customs system started a criminal investigation against him. But Pandora's box had been opened and public-key cryptography was in the public domain.

After the release of PGP, the Cypherpunks began to look at online economic independence and even imagined the creation of cryptocurrency. The major obstacle was the total control that the state and its institutions exercised over all monetary movements. Online exchanges required bank transactions, credit cards, and wire transfers, all of which were traceable. Cash could not be used online. In 1993, Eric Hughes published "A Cypherpunk's Manifesto," in which he explained the importance of anonymity in online commercial transactions, one of the conceptual elements of future cryptocurrencies.

Here is a passage from the manifesto[13] explaining this concept:

> Privacy is necessary for an open society in the electronic age. Privacy is not secrecy. A private matter is something one doesn't want the whole world to know, but a secret is something one doesn't want anybody to know. Privacy is the power to selectively reveal oneself to the world.

And a couple of practical examples:

> When I purchase a magazine at a store and hand cash to the clerk, there is no need to know who I am. When I ask my electronic mail provider to send and receive messages, my provider need not know to whom I am speaking or what I am saying or what others are saying to me; my provider only need know how to get the message there and how much I owe them in fees.

Later in the text, Hughes adds:

> Therefore, privacy in an open society requires anonymous transaction systems. Until now, cash has been the primary such system. An anonymous transaction system is not a secret transaction system. An anonymous system empowers individuals to reveal their identity when desired and only when desired; this is the essence of privacy.

As canaries in the coal mine of technocapitalism, the Cypherpunks perceived how inadequate Western political, social, economic, and monetary norms would be in coping with the coming technological transition that the advent of computer science was going to set off. They envisaged the danger that the state monopoly of technological innovation would pose to individual freedom and to the safety of the entire world. In its place, they sought to imagine a future in which technological innovation would empower the individual and transform humanity into a cosmic species. They also understood that, in the extraordinary future awaiting all of us, there would be no place for nation states flirting with feudal behaviors—even if dressed in their best cloth, democracy. However, they still had no idea what a viable, successful alternative would look like. They lacked the instruments to conceptualize a new society. They were cyber and cosmic nerds, not philosophers. And perhaps there is even a further explanation for this blind spot in their thinking—even if it is one they share with other revolutionaries.

Some studies have shown the high incidence of Asperger's syndrome among computer geeks. People affected by this type of autism often have "limited social skills, a willingness to obsess, an interest in systems, and they love numbers." These characteristics can make people with Asperger's particularly good at coding—and encryption. Microsoft's cofounders, Bill Gates and Paul Allen, for example, were comfortable spending hours on end, day after day, coding software as young programmers. Their social life was clearly not what was important to them.

Another interesting trait of people affected by Asperger's is first principle thinking, that is, questioning and testing everything, never accepting society's or anybody's answer, never doing something because it is what everybody does, because of convention. Here is what Elon Musk says about first principle thinking:

> Rather than reasoning by analogy, you boil things down to the most fundamental truths you can imagine and you reason up from there. . . . This is a good way to figure out if something really makes sense or if it's just what everybody else is doing.[14]

People with Asperger's are often less interested in following the crowd and in conforming to social norms; they think independently. "Think different" is Apple's slogan, and it was a way of being that Steve Jobs embodied throughout his life. Think different is the encouragement to think individually. Asperger's syndrome may also shed some light on the Silicon Valley gender gap, since this type of autism is in fact more common in boys than in girls.

As foreseen by the Cypherpunks, the advent of artificial intelligence has produced major changes in our world, but not the egalitarian revolution that the activists among them had foreseen. Among the most relevant are the emergence of a new class of entrepreneurs with social skills that in the past would have been regarded as less valuable in managers, and the advent of the first computer-literate generation. Both these changes together have triggered a novel approach to society and politics, with less focus on the common good and more concentrated on individualistic needs.

The greatest contribution of the Cypherpunks to this new paradigm was the successful prevention of the formation of a state monopoly of technology, which they achieved using the weapons at their disposal. The most powerful one was cryptography.

CHAPTER TWO

Bitcoin

At the beginning of the 1990s, the Cypherpunks came to the conclusion that cryptography was the most efficient tool for preventing state access to people's online exchanges. To shield the individual from governments' digital surveillance, they developed a software and a peer-to-peer system of sharing information. However, as long as monetary transactions took place under the scrutiny of the state and of its institutions—for example, via bank accounts or credit cards—cyber freedom remained compromised. Though they understood the need to develop an independent, digital monetary system of exchange centered upon a new form of money, i.e., a new currency, the Cypherpunks never succeeded in producing it.

Money creation proved to be the biggest obstacle to the birth of a parallel digital reality, away from Big Brother, where the individual was completely free from surveillance and invisible to the state. It is ironic that the pioneers of computer technology, people who were at ease with highly sophisticated artificial intelligence, were unable to master mankind's oldest trick: the manufacture of money. One of the biggest obstacles was how to prevent double-spending. Because digitizing is easy and copying digital items is even easier, the Cypherpunks needed to find a way to prevent the replication of digital money in a peer-to-peer system in the absence of the monitoring and regulation of a centralized authority, the State. Another huge obstacle was security: how to ensure that the digital coin spent online was real, that it was not a counterfeit, and, therefore, that the transaction was not fraudulent. The Cypherpunks failed to create a digital currency with all these characteristics which cash possesses. Cash does not present the problem of double-spending; you cannot give two people the same banknote. And though counterfeit banknotes do exist, it is possible to minimize their impact, partly by making their production a high crime.

As the years passed and the digitization of life began taking shape together with e-commerce, the Cypherpunks' monetary failure became increasingly embarrassing. Then, unexpectedly, in 2008, in the midst of what would become a financial crisis of epic proportions, there was a reversal of fortune. In "Cryptography," another cypherpunk mailing list, a document arrived. The sender used the pseudonym Satoshi Nakamoto. The name Nakamoto was unknown to the members of this list. Had he, or whoever was behind the pseudonym, used a different digital name before? Or, had Nakamoto successfully hacked into their mailing list and nobody had noticed it? No one knew, but one thing was certain: whoever was hidden behind that name was well aware of the Cypherpunks' difficulties in money creation.[15] The document illustrated the functioning of a new, digital, totally independent monetary system, a system generated by a software the sender claimed to have designed. More shockingly, the document answered all the questions that the Cypherpunks had raised for years without a satisfactory answer, e.g., how to create and distribute money securely. And it provided a solution to all the technical impediments they had encountered previously, including double-spending.

Suddenly, activity on the Cryptography email list, which had been minimal for years, sparked back to life, and the members became engaged in frenetic email exchanges. After careful analysis and discussions, everybody agreed that Satoshi Nakamoto's document, "A Peer-to-Peer Electronic Cash System," and the cryptocurrency it referred to, the bitcoin, had the potential to make their dream of total digital independence come true.

The Cypherpunks did not know that several weeks before the arrival of the document on that list, on August 18, 2008, to be precise, someone had created the bitcoin.org domain in the name of Satoshi Nakamoto.[16] Naturally, nobody on the net had noticed it. Just a month later, on September 15, 2008, Lehman Brothers went bankrupt, triggering the most serious financial crisis since 1929. It was a crisis centered upon excessive debt. Within weeks, the US government began printing billions of dollars to bail out other banks and financial institutions, which were literally drowning in debt. People started losing trust in the financial system and in fiat currencies.

Nakamoto had contacted the Cypherpunks with a bulletproof plan for a cryptocurrency owned and controlled by the users at the exact moment when the global financial system was beginning to unravel. It was a currency with limited stock—only twenty-one million bitcoins would be produced over a period of one hundred and fifty years—issued by digital software. The element of scarcity proved to be particularly appealing, contributing to the idea that bitcoin could become a viable alternative to fiat money—money printed by central banks that was ultimately backed by nothing more than government debt and whose supply was therefore unlimited. A video from the *Financial Times* explains:

> The idea that there's a limit on bitcoin is really, really important because central banks, obviously to finance these huge interventions they've done really since the financial crisis [of 2008], have poured trillions and trillions of dollars into the financial system. Some people say, well we live in this world where there's all this fake money and I want to hold something that I know is limited.[17]

The release of Nakamoto's document was so perfectly timed, it could not have been coincidental. Satoshi Nakamoto, whoever he or she or they are, must be an insider in the financial world, someone aware of the impending collapse of the global financial system and of the subsequent worldwide crisis of confidence. Nakamoto knows how global finance works, is familiar with its weakest points, and these skills, together with innate genius, have made them a master of cyber money creation. Against this background there have been many rumors that he or she or they are central bankers, top ranking people from the Federal Reserve.

Although we cannot know Nakamoto's true identity, goals, and aspirations, it seems clear that the latter are aligned with the Cypherpunks' dream of digital freedom. This idea involves redesigning money and reinventing its source globally, producing a new monetary tool for a species on the verge of a technological leap, a species destined to live in a fully digitalized environment together with artificial intelligence, a task that the futuristic vision of the Cypherpunks had not yet addressed.

How does Bitcoin work? Open-source software, presumably designed by Satoshi Nakamoto, generates bitcoins in blocks. The software is accessible to everybody and can be downloaded on individual computers. Once downloaded, the computer becomes part of a global network and it is possible to extract the coins as the software produces them. This process is called "mining"— like the extraction of gold in mines—and requires the solution of mathematical formulas that the software generates. The allocation is based on the speed with which each individual computer solves the formula and in doing so separates, or extracts, the bitcoins from the software. The faster the computer, the more chances there are to win bitcoins.

To avoid the double-spending problem, i.e., to make sure that the same bitcoin is not spent twice, Satoshi Nakamoto resorted to the blockchain technology. The first miner who solves the mathematical formula receives the block of bitcoins, known as a block of information. Once released, the block is indelible and unalterable and it is automatically linked to all the others extracted before, forming a digital chain. As the block is mined, all the computers in the network receive the information that a new block has been issued; at this point the lucky miner must produce proof of work, i.e., must show how they have extracted the cryptocurrency. Once the network has verified that the procedure is correct, the new block is added to the chain and the miner pockets the bitcoins contained in the block.

Not only the extraction of each bitcoin, but all Bitcoin transactions, are recorded in the blockchain, which is a digital ledger; in this way they are accessible and visible to everybody in the network. This means that it is possible to trace back to its origin each individual bitcoin as well as to verify the digital identity of who bought it and sold it, when, how, and for what amount. The blocks are like the milestones of Roman roads; planted deep into the soil and engraved in stone, they cannot be moved or modified. As the milestones indicated to the travelers their position on the road, how far they had gone and how far they still had to go to reach their destination, so the blocks in the blockchain show to the computers in the network the journey of each single bitcoin from birth.

On January 3, 2009, Satoshi Nakamoto extracted the first block of fifty bitcoins, called the "genesis block" or "block 0."[18] Because the value of bitcoins is established through the transactions that take place within the network, initially it was minimal. In May 2010 one of these was the purchase of two pizzas in the United States from Papa John's in bitcoins; clearly the manager had a bitcoin account and accepted them as payment! According to Forbes, though, this isn't exactly what happened; in reality, the manager "spent 10,000 Bitcoin to purchase two Papa John's pizzas on May 22, 2010. Since Papa John's didn't accept Bitcoin as payment, he posted a 10,000 Bitcoin offer on Bitcointalk.org and Jeremy Sturdivant, a nineteen-year-old then, took the offer for an estimated $41, bought the two pizzas and delivered." However, since 2010 the value of bitcoins has soared exponentially and so has the volatility of the cryptocurrency.

Nakamoto knew that flooding the world with the new digital currency would be inflationary. He was also aware that the success of the new monetary system depended on properly pacing the release and distribution of bitcoins through time. Therefore, not only is the software designed to issue a fixed number of coins— as we have seen, 21 million in total in the next century and a half—but it does so at a given speed. To understand this concept, consider the latter as the heartbeat of bitcoins—which Nakamoto fixed at seven transactions per second. This means that about every ten minutes, a new block is added to the chain. Keeping this rhythm is vital to maintaining the correct scarcity of bitcoins, i.e., to prevent inflating the currency.

Naturally, the heartbeat of bitcoins is regulated by an algorithm which is built into the software. Its role is to make sure that miners do not produce blocks too fast or too slowly, which would decrease or increase their value, respectively. The algorithm, known as "difficulty adjustment," acts as a pacemaker; it makes sure that the new blocks are added at the designed speed, i.e., every ten minutes. If the blocks are mined too quickly, the algorithm automatically increases the difficulty of extraction, i.e., the mathematical formula becomes more complex, making it harder to solve. And if they are added too slowly, the opposite happens.[19]

At this point people will ask why the price of bitcoin has been so volatile, swinging at times 10 to 20 percent in a single day. The simple answer is that, like most commodities, assets, investments, or other products, the value of bitcoins depends heavily on their supply and demand. In addition, being a new product, with a limited number of people trading in it, bitcoin has attracted speculators. Also, due to the relatively small size of the market, lack of depth, and the novelty and ignorance of its functioning, media outlets, influencers, financial moguls, and well-known cryptocurrency fans have conditioned investors' behavior with their analyses and forecasts, contributing to the volatility of prices. These factors will play less and less of a role as the size of the market grows and its functioning is regulated. For now, however, the first crypto will almost certainly continue to be highly volatile.

Nakamoto set up another mechanism to guarantee scarcity: the halving effect. For every 210,000 blocks added, the miners' reward for mining a new block, i.e., the number of bitcoins in the blocks, gets halved. It currently takes about four years to extract that many blocks, so the halving has been occurring at approximately four-year intervals. The latest and third halving took place in May 2020. The next is expected in 2024.

The halving effect will continue until all 21 million bitcoins are released, which is expected in 2140. To understand how the halving effect works, let's look at how the number of the bitcoins in the blocks has changed since Nakamoto extracted block 0. As explained by John Caroline in Coinspeaker:

> In 2009, the reward for each block in the chain mined was 50 bitcoins. After the first halving, it was 25, and then 12.5, and then it became 6.25 bitcoins per block as of May 11, 2020. To put this in another context, imagine if the amount of gold mined from the Earth was cut in half every four years. If gold's value is based on its scarcity, then a "halving" of gold output every four years would theoretically drive its price higher.[20]

With the halving taking place at given times and resulting in decreased mining rewards, extracting new bitcoins becomes an increasingly more expensive proposition, and as time goes on, each coin becomes more and more valuable because of scarcity. This principle is in sharp contrast to how traditional currencies such as the US dollar or the British pound function. They invariably lose their purchasing power over time because of inflation.

If bitcoin is a deflationary currency, holding it for a long period of time becomes profitable. However, like any commodity that is traded, Bitcoin must have a business cycle; it cannot only rise in value, it must also fall, so Nakamoto used the halving effect to artificially create such a trend.

Since 2009, the halving effect has been correlated to an increase in the price of bitcoin when it takes place and with a softening of prices in anticipation of the halving, generally two years ahead of it. The first halving, which occurred on November 28, 2012, produced a price increase from $12 to $1,217 over a year. The second halving took place on July 9, 2016. At the time the price of bitcoin was $647. By December 17, 2017, it had reached $9,800. Two years into this cycle, on December 17, 2018, the price of bitcoin was down to $3,276, after falling for twelve months from its peak; however, it was still 506 percent higher than the pre-halving price of $647 on July 9, 2016.[21]

These price trends show that halfway through the four-year cycle bitcoins enter a bear market, what people call "crypto winter." The anticipation of the next halving softens prices, exactly as it happens in the traditional stock market when market sentiment changes due to events perceived as negative. So far, during the crypto winters the price of bitcoin never went below the level reached on the eve of the last halving, confirming the deflationary nature of the first crypto. Clearly, Nakamoto artificially reproduced market expectations and anticipations, some of the main components of any commodity business cycle, by conditioning miners' psychology through the halving effect. Possibly, the halving has also been conceived of as an instrument to curb speculation, making sure that speculators would not alter the steady, moderate trend of appreciation of bitcoins that Nakamoto envisioned.

Until 2019, when institutional investors entered the crypto world, the bitcoin cycle has not correlated with the business cycle. Miners sold bitcoins before the crypto winter and invested in stocks and bonds to buy back the cryptocurrency right before the halving. But as the market has grown—at the beginning of 2022 it stood at two trillion dollars—a correlation with the stock market has begun to emerge.

The most recent halving took place on May 11, 2020, when the price of bitcoin was $8,787. On April 14, 2021, the first crypto reached a peak of $64,507 (a 634 percent increase from its pre-halving price). Then the bitcoin price began falling. On May 11, 2021, it was $54,276; on January 19, 2022, it was $43,203; at the end of January it went below $34,000.[22]

Since May 2022, the price of bitcoin has fallen further, showing a correlation with the stock market business cycle, confirming that, at least for now, the first cryptocurrency has entered the world of finance and that, most likely, it is here to stay.

Is it possible that the halving effect has also been constructed to facilitate the penetration of the first cryptocurrency into the existing economic and financial system? To succeed, this process needs to be smooth, steady, and slow. Nakamoto knew the difficulty of transforming the global monetary system, and so he designed a mechanism of money creation with the necessary characteristics to merge, in time, into the existing system. And why not? Eventually, bitcoin may even replace fiat money. The same cannot be said for most of the other cryptocurrencies that have sprung up since the advent of bitcoins, almost 10,000 as of this writing.[23] The crypto crisis of the spring of 2022 has underlined their fragility. Some have ceased to exist. Many have lost almost all their value and will most likely disappear. Crypto supporters believe that the crisis has been beneficial, that the cleansing of the crypto world was necessary and therapeutic.

According to Satoshi Nakamoto, after the release of the twenty-one millionth bitcoin, the software will freeze its production and miners will start splitting the existing ones for a fee, that they will apply to each transaction they process. If you wonder who guarantees that this scenario will happen and that, once the limit of twenty-one million is reached, the system will not restart and carry on producing new bitcoins, the answer is: nobody. Like any form of money, bitcoin requires a leap of faith. You trust the software and the digital monetary system because you believe in the principles behind it, or maybe because you *want* to believe it. The trust in the traditional banking system rests on an identical act of faith. Here's a sentence from a video from the *Financial Times* which explains this concept:

> If you got a £5 note out of your pocket you will see it says on
> it "I promise to pay the bearer on demand the sum of £5,"
> signed by the Bank of England. The reason that you think
> it's worth £5 and I think it's worth £5 is that we trust the
> Bank of England. We trust the UK government.[24]

The invention of Bitcoin was clearly a political gesture to unmask what there is behind the faith in a political and financial system which Satoshi Nakamoto and the Cypherpunks loathed because they deemed it corrupt and inefficient. The legitimacy of the first digital currency springs from the network of miners and users, not from the state and its institutions which issue fiat currencies. The network is a peer-to-peer system, totally horizontal and egalitarian, and those who participate in it exchange the cryptocurrency internally without financial intermediaries. Bitcoin belongs only to, and is controlled only by, the people in the network. There is no board of directors, no owners or investors who benefit from fees levied at each transaction. The network gives bitcoins legitimacy by validating each block extraction with the proof of work and through the public ledger of the blockchain technology.

Yet, many would argue, banks perform functions that go well beyond collecting savings, disbursing loans, and supervising the use of money. For example, they monitor online payments not only to ensure that the same dollar is not spent twice but also to protect depositors from online fraud. In the introduction to "A Peer-to-Peer Electronic Cash System," Nakamoto points out that this form of security is faulty:

> Commerce on the Internet has come to rely almost exclu-
> sively on financial institutions serving as trusted third
> parties to process electronic payments. While the system
> works well enough for most transactions, it still suffers from
> the inherent weaknesses of the trust based model.[25]

In other words, frauds such as credit card cloning still do take place. Nakamoto explains that bitcoin is safer from this type of fraud than fiat money is, thanks to the public-key cryptography. To understand what this means, let's look at how the digital wallet works.

Let's imagine two sets of safes facing each other. Each set is composed of two safes, one in front and one behind; the former is the transit safe and the latter is the deposit one. The sets belong to two individuals, A and B. The deposit safes contain A's and B's respective accounts, or wallets, where their bitcoins are stored. Only A knows the key to open their safe and only B knows the key for their own. These are "the private keys."

Suppose A bought a bitcoin from B. This is how the exchange takes place. B will open their deposit safe, release the bitcoin, and deposit it in the transit safe. Once the deposit safe is closed, B will notify *A* that the bitcoin is ready, at which point *A* will open his own transit safe and *B* will deposit their bitcoin inside it, just like a letter in the mailbox. *B* will then close their transit safe and communicate to *A* that the bitcoin has reached its destination. *A* will open their transit safe, extract the bitcoin, and deposit it in their own deposit safe.

Public-key cryptography protects against fraud. Only the transit safes are accessible to members of the network; the deposit or wallet safes can be opened and closed only by the owners.

Unlike in the traditional monetary system, in the crypto world the individual takes full charge of their own money, which implies they are fully responsible for any exchanges. Once completed, bitcoin exchanges cannot be reversed, which means that managing a wallet requires a much higher degree of attention and responsibility when conducting transactions than what's required in our existing financial system. Here is an explanation from the *Financial Times* video:

> A bank account in many countries up to a certain amount is insured by the government. Banks have to go through stress tests. Send money to the wrong account, you can probably get that money back. Or if someone scams you, you can go to the financial compensation scheme. When you hold crypto, typically it's not protected in any way. There's no one to turn to. If your money is gone, it is gone, and you cannot get it back.[26]

Naturally, Bitcoin is not completely bulletproof from fraud. There are many stories of people who have lost vast amounts of money opening their wallet to fraudsters. Because everything is digital, particular attention needs to be paid to web pages and addresses. Fraudsters reproduce digital addresses, often altering a single letter or a number to mirror the web pages of investors.

They lure people to transfer bitcoins into their fraudulent wallets and disappear into cyberspace. There have even been cases in which fraudsters have reproduced the Twitter accounts of famous people, like Elon Musk, and used them to make suggestions about investing in accounts the fraud perpetrators have created.[27]

The danger of fraud persists because even bitcoins require a leap of faith. As explained before, people mine and buy bitcoins because they trust the software, the blockchain technology, and the peer-to-peer system of the network, even without knowing the identity of its creator. As more and more people and financial institutions enter this market, the system will feel more secure. However, one must remember, Bitcoin is constructed to encourage people to handle their own monetary transactions without intermediaries, like banks and other financial institutions that charge fat fees to perform these tasks, as well as to make investments on behalf of their clients. This enhanced personal responsibility for one's finances introduces a change that will lead to a new and more widespread understanding of the role of money as a means of exchange and as a store of value; it therefore demands an effort to educate oneself.

Finally, even if Bitcoin has survived its first decade and more, and weathered the cleansing crisis of spring 2022, and high finance is still holding portfolios in bitcoins decades from now, there is still no assurance that the system will remain intact. In the digital age, when dealing with money there is no certainty, just as there has never been any certainty in fiat money. Think of the hyperinflation in Germany in the 1920s, when entire fortunes vanished almost overnight, workers and employees lost all their savings, and the purchasing power of salaries evaporated, dragging working families into poverty as wheelbarrows of cash were used to buy a few eggs or a loaf of bread. The only difference is that in the 1920s one blamed the state; in the world of cryptocurrency, one can only blame oneself.

Crypto requires a high degree of knowledge, understanding,

and belief in a new system legitimized by the users, and it still demands an act of faith. Too many people have embraced the digitization of money without understanding these requirements, simply because every aspect of their real life is being digitized, from Apple Pay to the apps that regulate the central heating of their house to those to find a partner in life. They jump in, but they do not fully grasp the implications of such major changes in the patterns of living, or in money creation. They only sense that they must be part of it, that they must swim with the tide. Not even the Cypherpunks fully understood the implications of the digitization of money. They mostly believed it was essential to achieve total independence from a state they mistrusted. But self-regulating, highly functional cryptocurrencies like bitcoin are much more than that. As we advance into the third decade of the twenty-first century and beyond, we will discover several new tasks that cryptocurrencies can and will perform. In the Present Future, cryptocurrencies belong to the future and will continue to develop and be shaped in the present.

Interestingly, so far some of the most far-reaching applications of cryptocurrencies have taken place away from Wall Street. Crypto has shown the potential to provide poor countries in sub-Saharan Africa and elsewhere with the financial instruments they still lack, and helped them circumvent unfair banking and foreign exchange restrictions that weak or corrupt governments and institutions impose or do not prevent, as is the case in Nigeria, the second-largest user of bitcoins after the United States. Crypto has allowed people to take their wealth with them when escaping war—Ukrainian refugees and Russian dissidents alike carried the keys of their bitcoin wallets in their heads when fleeing their countries as refugees.

However, one needs to be careful before claiming that bitcoin provides a secure means of exchange by the people and for the people. As with fiat money, cryptocurrencies can perform good or bad tasks. They aren't inherently a force for good or evil, only an instrument, a means of exchange.

Historically, people have attached sentiments such as hope, revenge, or greed to money itself, and they still do. Cryptocurrencies attract an identical range of feelings, as the astonishing story of OneCoin illustrates.

Between 2014 and 2017, a Bulgarian lawyer named Ruja Ignatova, who called herself the "Crypto Queen," raised about $4 billion by pitching to small investors the idea that her virtual currency, OneCoin, would become the currency of the future. The money poured in from all over the world: from Pakistan to Norway, from Palestine to China, from Kampala to London. Then, suddenly, in the fall of 2017, Ruja Ignatova disappeared and no one ever saw her again.

OneCoin was a gigantic fraud; there was nothing behind it. Above all, it was not a cryptocurrency guaranteed by blockchain technology. It was a very well-orchestrated international scam which worked for one main reason: greed. Ruja Ignatova sold the dream of rapid wealth to regular people—small investors, pensioners, housewives—using the advent of cryptocurrency to rope them in, something that was sufficiently obscure but constantly in the news. She explained to them that cryptocurrencies would soon replace traditional currencies and that those who exchanged fiat money for her crypto, OneCoin, would profit from its rising value. To prove her point, she pointed at the climbing value of OneCoin against the US dollar. This was reported on the One-Coin web page, which was controlled and manipulated by her partners in crime.

Ruja Ignatova presented herself as a messianic figure. She held spectacular public events all over the world, often in large stadiums and parks, where she addressed vast numbers of people like the leader of a religious sect. Indeed, her rhetoric was not different from that used by the founders of the Church of Scientology or of the Mormon creed. She assured that those who joined OneCoin's revolution were the chosen ones, that they were the people elected to enjoy future affluence.[28]

Ignorance, dissatisfaction with one's own life, a sense of failure, mistrust of the state and its institutions, resentment against elites, hope, greed, revenge—all these were thrown in and became the ingredients of the toxic cocktail that Ignatova delivered to the masses to persuade them to believe in her. While manipulating these feelings during her rallies, she also instilled in people a sense of entitlement to great wealth. She told them that it was their destiny to become rich, to have stumbled onto her preaching, and that all they had to do was to convert their fiat money into OneCoin and wait for the crypto revolution to roll on. People handed over their savings, their severance payments, they sold their homes to invest more and more, and watched happily on OneCoin's web page as those funds, now stored in OneCoin, appeared to grow steadily in value every day.

Of course, Ignatova and OneCoin's propaganda was built on the ignorance of her potential investors, but it also fed on their mistrust and frustration with the world we live in, a world in constant, rapid evolution and therefore full of uncertainties. For many, the decision to turn their life savings and assets into OneCoin sprang from their anxiety around the inevitability of the advent of the digital future, a future they could not even begin to comprehend, and from the very human need to seek someone to trust to navigate the transition. They believed that Ruja Ignatova would look after them during the paradigm shift which was already reshaping every aspect of their lives. Against this existential destabilization, Ruja Ignatova locked in their trust and emerged as their rescuer, their savior. The leap of faith into OneCoin was nothing more than one more manifestation of the very human need to believe in a hero, a savior, in times of great anxiety over change.

What happened to all the money? Vanished. A BBC investigation found that Ruja had orchestrated the fraud together with the Eastern European mafia, the criminal organization to which she belonged. The crypto world can be like the Wild West.

OneCoin's fraud shows that people can be easily manipulated because they do not understand cryptocurrencies. Though they sense that crypto offers some solutions to certain problems, they also realize that so far only a small minority of the world's population has access to crypto and will benefit from its advantages. And most of the crypto elite seem more interested in using their knowledge to enrich themselves than in exploiting its real potential for finding ways that society can function more efficiently and even more humanely.

In the Present Future, the crypto world is still a mirror of the real world, a place where greed and power are paramount and where, often, those who have been empowered by technology leave all the others behind for their own advantage or for their own cause. When this happens, the risk of tremendous damage being done to society can be great.

CHAPTER THREE

Crypto World

In 1940, soon after the Germans invaded France, the former dean of engineering at MIT, Professor Vannevar Bush, approached the US president, Franklin Delano Roosevelt, with an unexpected proposal: the creation of the National Defense Research Committee (NDRC). The task of the new organization was to gather research of interest to the military and inform the armed forces about new technologies that could be applied to the war machine. Nobody knows if Professor Bush acted because he thought it was inevitable that the United States would be dragged into the European conflict or because he felt that it *should* get militarily engaged in preventing the spread of Nazism. In any case, he believed that fostering cooperation between the worlds of science, technology, and military defense would strengthen the United States. Roosevelt liked the idea so much that he nominated Vannevar Bush as chairman of the NDRC.[29]

A year later, as the war escalated, the NDRC was put under the wing of another, much more powerful institution: the Office of Scientific Research and Development (OSRD), and Bush became its chairman. The main task of the OSRD was to liaise with the Allies and to contribute to the success of the Manhattan Project—which is why by the end of the war its budget was a whopping $500 billion.

Bush, with his vast network of scientists, engineers, mathematicians, academics, and technicians, played a big role in the building of the first atomic bomb. He was so determined to see the project through that when a research team produced a report that doubted the viability of its construction, he ignored it and set up another research team. Eventually, he obtained the report he wanted: the atomic bomb was not only possible, but, most likely, the Germans were ahead of the Americans in building one. Naturally, a few years later, Bush participated in the decision to deploy it in Hiroshima and Nagasaki—an event that would convince the Cypherpunks decades later never to trust the US government. Shockingly, Bush never regretted it. On the contrary, in an interview for *MIT Science Reporter* after the war, he stated that the atomic bomb had shortened the war and saved lives. This is what he said:

> One, by ending the war abruptly, it saved 100,000 or more American casualties, it saved the lives of Japanese, for that matter. Then two, the bomb was bound to appear and I think it was well that it appeared in a dramatic fashion, so that civilization would face up to it. As it wouldn't have if it had come in some test way. And the world has got to live with it and had to learn to live with it.[30]

People believed Bush's justification because they had no knowledge or understanding of what the new weapon really was. The technological and information gulf between ordinary people and scientists and politicians at the time was unbridgeable. The American people were not informed that Japan was trying to find a way to end the war before the dropping of the two bombs, as is still often debated today. But Vannevar Bush would have been aware of this and the US administration certainly was when the decision was made to drop the two bombs to achieve a goal considered more important than the truth: asserting America's military supremacy. This is an example of how dangerous technological innovation can be for society when information does not flow freely. And it is a stark example of how warring nation states which have resumed some feudal behaviors can be the wrong model for society, since it means that when the interests of the people for peace are in conflict with the hegemony of one state seeking world dominance, it may be the latter that triumphs. And the world has lived with the consequences ever since. Far, far beyond even the waves of destruction they caused and the hundreds of thousands of tragic deaths of innocent civilians, and the trauma experienced by Japan, the bombing of Hiroshima and Nagasaki became the clay used to mold the politics of fear of the Cold War. And today it provides a justification to the hegemonic desires of Russia; Putin has already said that if he were to use nuclear weapons in the war in Ukraine, he would not be the first world power to do so.

Though Vannevar Bush is one of the key figures responsible for this tragic outcome, it is not what he is known for, especially within the cyber community. With chilling irony, he is considered the father of the personal computer. In the 1930s, while teaching at MIT, he produced the first analog computer, which he used to solve complex engineering problems related to electrical power supply.[31] In the 1920s and 1930s, anticipating the electronic revolution of the second half of the century, Bush had focused his work on designing electronic devices for the coming electricity-based society. The analog computer was his most significant invention.

After focusing on the war effort for several years, Vannevar Bush returned to his futuristic vision of industry and society towards the end of 1945, when he wrote a seminal article in *The Atlantic Monthly*, titled "As We May Think." In the article he voiced concern that all the information available to mankind was scattered around the world, that it was not properly organized and, therefore, not easily accessible. Imagine how much faster progress would be, he argued, if a machine could overcome all these shortcomings? This machine was Memex—an indexed, archival microfilm machine for cross-referencing and retrieving information. Memex, which may well be regarded as the prototype of modern computers, allowed readers to annotate and create links between articles and books recorded on microfilm, similar to the links that are today called hyperlinks. In effect, in 1945, Bush anticipated the advent of the internet and of the World Wide Web.[32]

Returning to crypto history, like Vannevar Bush, Satoshi Nakamoto is a first-rate visionary, someone who can foresee the next big technological jump, but the similarities between the two individuals end there. Nakamoto appears to have been eager to provide the multitude with the necessary tools to bypass the power of the elites in creating money and controlling its usage, i.e., to bridge the technological knowledge gap. His objective was to empower people and improve their lives, not to promote one country's supremacy over the others or to enrich an elite or himself and his company. Therefore, he produced bitcoin by merging two separate fields: money creation and technology, which traditionally have been the domain of the state and of the few. The software provided the first digital currency with all the necessary attributes of a successful means of exchange, superior even to gold, as stated by JPMorgan:

1. "Bitcoin cannot be destroyed nor does it perish. It will survive as long as the network survives, which given the network is decentralized makes bitcoin very hard to destroy. When comparing gold to bitcoin, both are durable."

2. "Bitcoin is particularly easy to store and transport. Large quantities of Bitcoin can be transmitted all over the world nearly instantly and can be stored on a cell phone. Gold is far harder and more expensive to store, transport and insure."

3. "Bitcoin is fungible and is interchangeable with all other Bitcoin. Gold is generally fungible and can be readily seen as better than diamonds, which can have different qualities and shapes that impact value. That said, gold comes in different measures of purity with 24k gold and 14k gold of different values. The edge goes to Bitcoin."

4. "Bitcoin is divisible out to eight decimal places, out to 1/100,000,000, which today is worth $0.0005. Gold is divisible, but not easily accurately."

5. "Bitcoin has a finite number of tokens, capped at 21mn, which will be mined by ~2140. Gold is difficult to mine and there is expected to be a finite amount. However, as the price of gold rises, so does the supply."

6. "Bitcoin is readily verifiable with transactions recorded on the blockchain, which is publicly available for all to view. Gold too is verifiable, but can also be forged and its purity can be diluted, making value more questionable."

Unlike Vannevar Bush, Satoshi Nakamoto is profoundly anti-establishment. He does not trust the state. He believes that the technology behind his invention is better placed in the hands of ordinary people than in those of state institutions or an elite. Collective action, to him, is a superior guarantee than the supervision of central banks, especially when dealing with the standard value of everything: money. Is he a socialist? A crypto socialist? For sure he is an activist.

Some believe that the decision to hide his identity springs from Nakamoto's desire to remain an outsider to politics and to the financial elites that he or she or they—whoever is behind this pseudonym—loathe. According to this interpretation, he could be regarded as a sort of crypto Robin Hood, who gives bitcoin to the people and in doing so diminishes the power of the monetary elites. Despite how appealing this interpretation sounds, it is unlikely to be the sole reason for his anonymity. For a start, as we have seen in the previous chapter, the timing of the launch of bitcoin proves that Satoshi Nakamoto was an insider to high finance and, who knows, maybe he or she or they still are. Most likely, technical and security issues lie behind Nakamoto's choice of anonymity. It is worth analyzing some of them.

Nakamoto's public involvement with bitcoin would have affected prices and damaged the smooth global development of the first cryptocurrency. The main pillar of any monetary system is trust, whether this be towards the tribe, the baron who mints the coins for those living under his protection or, in modern times, the nation state and democracy. For instance, during the gold standard era, people put their trust in their own elected governments, and believed that the banknotes they held corresponded to a certain amount of gold and could be always converted. In 1971, when Nixon declared on TV the end of the convertibility of the US dollar, Americans and the world learned the hard way that such trust can be violated easily.

With Bitcoin, people trust the software—a new technology— and the network of people linked to it. Nakamoto understood that this formula was infinitely more trustworthy than himself, even if he was the inventor of the new system. The reason? Whoever is behind this pseudonym is human, subject to passions such as rage, anger, greed, and revenge like anybody else, as proven by the OneCoin scam. This would not be a good start for any new currency. Instead, bitcoin's money creation is collective; it transcends individuals and their feelings—even if it is the product of human ingenuity. It also transcends state institutions. In the ultimate analysis, it belongs to the people. And as people trust society because it is the expression of their community, so they will trust bitcoin. This is the first time in modern times that, at a global and highly sophisticated level, individuals have been put in the driver's seat of money creation.

Nakamoto's anonymity also provides protection for the system. Money is the monopoly of the state, and anybody who threatens that monopoly risks being punished. He must have been aware of what had happened to Bernard von NotHaus, a resident of Hawaii, who in 1998 created and launched a private currency, the Liberty Dollar. The currency flourished, but in 2007 the FBI and the Secret Service started criminal proceedings against him. Eventually, in 2009, the Liberty Dollar was shut down. Von NotHaus was found guilty of creating a "private coin or currency system to compete with the official coinage and currency of the United States." However, on his web page von NotHaus had defined the new currency as follows: ". . . the Liberty Dollar is a private voluntary barter currency. It is not government money, so it is not intended to be used as 'Legal Tender,' 'Current Money,' or a 'Coin.'"[33]

Something similar happened to the digital currency e-Gold. Between 1996 and 2009, e-Gold allowed the instant transfer of gold ownership. In 2009, transactions were suspended and e-Gold was outlawed. It was regarded as a monetary instrument that fostered illegal activities because the system could not collect enough information about its customers. Those who had launched it were arrested and prosecuted.[34]

Like e-Gold, bitcoin is available to anyone. This includes people who conduct both legal and illegal activity, as happens with fiat currency. However, when dealing with fiat money the state has in place its own system of controls, enforced by institutions that prevent and punish criminal activities. People trust systematic law and order. Bitcoin is not part of that; blockchain technology provides the security system.

Satoshi Nakamoto's anonymity, the blockchain technology, and the network's collective management have prevented the bitcoin system from being shut down. Law enforcement and the state cannot put an anonymous software or a technology on trial, let alone a global network of computers. Nakamoto's anonymity has not, however, prevented the proliferation of criticism and mistrust towards the new system from both institutions and people. Interestingly, most of the criticism refers to the situation created by the time lapse between the launch and usage of bitcoin and the enactment of legislation to regulate it, that same gray, unregulated area where Uber, Amazon, and all the Techtitans carved their high tech monopoly.

Initially, the anonymity of the bitcoin digital wallets appealed to criminal organizations, and the first crypto seemed an excellent means of payment for illegal and criminal activities. Bitcoin also became a popular payment method on the darknet, gaining notoriety on the now-defunct Silk Road. However, in 2013, Ross Ulbricht, the man who created and managed this infamous marketplace, was arrested and given two life sentences for facilitating the trade in drugs and other illegal materials.[35] His activity was traced thanks to the blockchain technology of bitcoins.

It took some time for criminals and law enforcement officers to understand that blockchain provides a public ledger of all transactions and that every exchange is immutable, transparent, and, therefore, traceable, in spite of the anonymity of digital wallets. Not only can illegal transactions be traced but blockchain also makes it possible to prove when and how such activities have taken place. In February 2022, the US government seized $3.6 billion in bitcoin from the 2016 Bitfinex hack and arrested two individuals, Ilya Lichtenstein and Heather Morgan, on charges of money laundering. The successful operation was made possible by tracing the bitcoins' movements on the blockchain. As soon as the money laundering process began, the perpetrators were spotted.[36]

Today, criminal organizations have reverted to fiat money because cash remains the best form of payment for activities conducted outside the law, especially for money laundering. Here are some numbers to show that criminals today aren't so keen on using bitcoin. A study conducted by the University of Oxford in 2017 reported that 44 percent of bitcoin exchanges were associated with illegal and criminal activity.[37] By 2022 the crypto criminal report from Chainalysis, an American blockchain analysis firm headquartered in New York, put the figure at less than 1 percent.

Though the report concludes that crime has become a small part of the cryptocurrency world,[38] the bad reputation gained by bitcoin at its outset has stuck and a vast mythology has been constructed around it, to the point where many still believe that the bulk of bitcoin exchanges involves illegal activity. Some people are even reluctant to purchase old bitcoins, those mined in the early days, for fear of being associated with criminal activities.

Another myth refers to tax evasion and avoidance through bitcoins. Like any other assets, earnings from bitcoin must be declared; it is the responsibility of the individual to do so. And as with fiat money, the tax authorities can and do investigate people and companies which they think are not properly filing their taxes. Thanks to blockchain technology, however, they can verify if the correct amount of bitcoin earnings has been declared. It is true that the digital wallet does not carry the name of the owner, but just as tax authorities can require proof of bank transactions, they can demand proof of bitcoin transactions if they suspect that earnings from them have not been declared.

In recent years, bitcoin production has also been condemned for its big carbon footprint, which makes it bad for the environment. The media has deemed the proof of work to legitimize the extraction of each new block as a high energy activity, leading several people to suggest its replacement with the less energy intensive proof of stake[39] technique. While proof of work requires the validation of the entire network of computers linked to the software, proof of stake uses a much smaller network of "validators" who contribute—or "stake"—their own crypto in exchange for a chance of getting to validate new transactions, update the blockchain, and earn a reward.[40] As discussed towards the end of this chapter, proof of stake is a much better validation process for the many applications of blockchain, such as smart contracts; however, for money creation, e.g., the production of a universally accepted store of value such as bitcoin, proof of work remains the best possible consensus mechanism. Why? Because it requires the consensus of everybody, a bulletproof process against manipulation.

Of course, nobody can dispute that mining bitcoins consumes energy and that proof of work is energy intensive; however, so is the functioning of the traditional monetary system. According to the Cambridge Bitcoin Electricity Consumption Index, bitcoin's current greenhouse gas emissions are half the emissions from gold mining.[41] In 2020, the carbon footprint of the gold industry, which includes mining, refining, and recycling, was 144 million tons of CO_2. The global banking system, which includes the production of physical money, i.e., cash and the running of bank branches and ATM machines, has a much higher carbon footprint, 408 million tons of CO_2.[42] And Bitcoin? It is estimated to produce 70 million tons of CO_2 annually.[43] High energy consumption is the price we pay for a universal store of value. The idea that fiat money is green, or greener than cryptocurrency, is a fantasy.

Miners have an incentive to reduce energy costs because those costs represent their single most significant expense related to bitcoin extraction. In recent years, therefore, miners have been actively exploiting energy inefficiency, tapping into sources that otherwise would go to waste. For example, renewal power plants are built to meet the demand of the future, not of the present, and consequently large amounts of the energy they generate are wasted. Miners obtain this energy at discounted prices and use it because unlike other industries, bitcoin can be mined anywhere. During the wet season in Sichuan and Yunnan, for example, enormous quantities of renewable hydro energy go to waste. Why? Because production capacity exceeds local demand and we do not yet have the technology to save energy and transport it where it is needed, e.g., to cities in coastal areas. This explains why, until China banned bitcoin mining, these provinces were responsible for almost 10 percent of global bitcoin mining in the dry season and 50 percent in the wet season.[44] The Cambridge Bitcoin Electricity Consumption Index shows a 14 percent drop in estimated emissions from 2021 to 2022, which the research team attributes to a more efficient usage of the hardware. It also estimated the share of sustainable energy sources in Bitcoin's electricity to a mix at 37.6 percent (26.3 percent renewables and 11.3 percent nuclear).[45]

The high energy costs of bitcoin mining also encourage miners to conduct a sort of energy arbitrage, which can be beneficial for the planet. How? By capturing natural gas. Oil production, for example, releases natural gas that ends up being burned off, a phenomenon known as gas flaring, because pipeline infrastructure lacks the capacity to take it to market. For traditional industries to leverage such energy is very difficult: most oil production takes place in remote locations, for example, in North Dakota or Siberia. The decentralized model of bitcoin mining allows miners to place their computers anywhere, including next to oil production fields, and to tap into gas flaring. Some companies, like Denver-based Crusoe Energy, have even come up with new technology to lower CO_2 emissions from gas flaring by using it to directly power computers which mine cryptocurrencies. In early 2022, Crusoe Energy operated data centers in Montana, North Dakota, Wyoming, and Colorado, and its technology reduced emissions by as much as 63 percent compared with continued flaring.[46]

Could Bitcoin and cryptocurrency end up helping us to lower CO_2 emissions? This is not an absurd question. The technology to capture gas flaring is already here, it is only a matter of time before it is applied everywhere. Will this new source of energy be sufficient? Some estimates suggest that it will; there is enough flared natural gas in North America to power the entire Bitcoin network.[47]

Most people believe that Satoshi Nakamoto's greatest contribution is Bitcoin. But they are mistaken. His outstanding innovation is the blockchain, a revolutionary technology powerful enough to potentially redesign everything, including human relationships, for a simple reason: the core principle of blockchain technology is trust.

Trust is the social junction where humans interact with each other, for good and for ill; trust is also at the essence of the survival of our species. The trust in the extended family and in the tribe made it possible for our first ancestors to protect their young and their elderly from the perils of the world. Protection of the young contributed to prevent the extinction of a physically weak species while the elders instilled in the young the wisdom of how to do so, so this passing along of accumulated wisdom would continue through the generations. Trust transformed a species destined to be the prey of larger animals into powerful survivors by shaping an extraordinary division of labor: women stayed with the children and the old, and collected gatherable foodstuffs, while men went hunting for high-protein meat for everybody. At the very outset, well before the development of language, our ancestors forged alliances among themselves which allowed for the fulfillment of the specific tasks of survival; this very basic social contract gave birth to the tribe. Such a remarkable development took place because they trusted each other and, through this trust, learned that together they had better chances to survive. One could argue that trust is, and always has been, more precious than love. Love comes and goes; trust is there forever.

Today, trust continues to regulate human interactions both between individuals and within and between the entire population and societal institutions. In post–World War II America, a big feature of the American dream was that housewives trusted that their spouses would look after them financially, so they stayed at home to look after the children and the family, a modern version of the prehistoric division of labor; in today's democracies, citizens trust that their vote will count, and consumers trust that, when they buy an apple with the label organic on it, the fruit will not be covered in pesticide. It is very difficult to think of any human transaction or interaction that does not require trust.

Trust is not passive; it implies responsibility. Trusting the wrong people can have disastrous consequences, as happened to those who handed over their savings to Ruja Ignatova to purchase OneCoin. They did it because she had stolen their trust using her powers of persuasion. Trust can also be instinctive: it is not uncommon to trust somebody simply because we believe that they are trustworthy, without hard proof that our judgment is correct. In other words, trust can be spontaneous and natural—and thus easily manipulated. Since trust is an act of faith, fraud is plentiful.

To prevent fraud and protect the individual, society has created institutions and professions that function as trust exchanges or regulators. In the US, for example, title companies verify that the property you want to buy is owned by the seller and that there are no mortgages or liens attached to it. In the UK, specialized lawyers carry out title searches for the same reason. Institutions keep records for the community. If I lose my UK driving license, the Driver and Vehicle Licensing Agency will replace it.

Dealing with this type of mediation takes time and can be costly, but it is necessary because we do not have access to this documentation, even if it refers to us, even if it is ours. Institutions also protect society against fraud and other criminal or illegal activities. I am not allowed to issue a duplicate of my driving license myself because the state does not trust me to do this. It needs proof that I passed the test and obtained my driving license through the proper channels, and it has designated the Driver and Vehicle Licensing Agency to provide such proof.

Unlike our ancestors, we live in highly bureaucratic communities because our societies are so large that it is impossible to trust each other individually. Institutions are needed to guarantee everything: that we went to school and earned a degree, that we own a car, that we are voters, that we have been vaccinated. We even need institutions to prove that we exist.

In 2008, when banks and financial entities began to fail, the world realized that these institutions, which act as trust-junctions, are not perfect. Of course, it had happened many times before throughout history, but over the centuries we have forgotten these incidents and come to look at institutions as infallible, especially in the rich West. The collapse of Lehman Brothers made people realize that banks can be corrupt, that they can fail, that they can take your trust and your money with them. It was a shocking discovery that came precisely at a time when a new, alternative, potentially more trustworthy system had just been introduced: blockchain technology.

Blockchain technology is more secure than the banking system. For example, while a criminal bank employee could tamper with your bank account by striking a few keys on the bank's computer, it would be impossible to do that with blockchain. The distributive ledger is more secure and transparent than bank accounts because everybody can see what is happening in real time and presumably send cyber alarms and protests about any tampering.[48]

Blockchain provides an unalterable public record of what has happened in the past, so it contains memory. Memory was another important tool of survival for our early ancestors: hunters had to memorize and remember the way home to get back from the hunt. Within the tribe, individuals' reputations were built upon the collective memory of their actions. And so was their wealth.

For centuries, on the Pacific island of Yap, the inhabitants have used stones that they named Rai as a symbolic form of money. Because they cannot be easily moved around from sellers to buyers, the community has kept a record of transactions, i.e., of who owns what, by memorizing the story of each stone and passing it down from generation to generation. The distributive ledger is in the minds and memories of the people. The value of the stones is not linked to their size but to the collective oral history that is attached to each of them. As everybody knows who owns each stone, how much each is worth, and trusts the collective memory, there is no need for an institution to keep a record.[49]

There are two other elements that Bitcoin shares with Rai: production and scarcity. The island of Yap has very few stones and no precious metals. Centuries ago, some of the inhabitants began a long and perilous sea journey to a neighboring island, about three hundred miles away, in search of something rare to use as a store of value. They brought back stones they had hacked out, smoothed, rolled down to the shore, and transported to Yap on canoes or rafts. It took about a year, a long time to complete these tasks, and the true value of the stone came from the work that went into each individual piece, from its story not from its size.

Even the stones that had been tossed overboard during the journey because of bad weather have a value. They remain at the bottom of the ocean but have been shared by the tribe and used by the owners as a store of value, and their ownership has been passed from generation to generation. They remained part of the system of exchange because the community trusted those who had thrown them overboard. The stones are so heavy, so hard to move, that it does not make any difference if they are stored in front of someone's house or at the bottom of the ocean. What really matters is the collective memory of ownership, the ledger, and the trust in people and in the system.

As conceived by Satoshi Nakamoto, blockchain technology is the modern version of communal recordkeeping that does not need an intermediary institution. It provides efficiency, transparency, security, speed, and savings. It could make our life easier, lighter, less expensive, and faster. In this way, blockchain could be bigger than the internet.

It can be applied everywhere: in the insurance sector, in the health system, in education, even in the electoral sector, cutting out the institutional middlemen and making everything cheaper. It can allow you to track the money you give to charity to verify if it is going where you want it to go, or to check that the diamond you buy for your engagement does not fund warlords in Africa. Blockchain could save money and lives at the same time.

Blockchain could improve food security, partly by managing contamination and waste much faster and more efficiently. From the farm to our table, food takes a long journey. The organic apple you are about to eat has been handled by many hands: it was picked, packed, shipped, repackaged, driven to its final destination, and placed on shelves. Each of these steps—the farm, the pickers, the shipping, the packaging, the label, the grocery store—needs to be recorded and mistakes can happen. Information can be misfiled or falsified. Imagine if that apple could be tagged at the farm and tagged by blockchain as it passes through all those points. New blocks of information could be created and attached to the previous one. You could track back through the blockchain the apple to the farm where it came from and verify that it is indeed organic in a matter of seconds. This could be applied to fair trade coffee or organic chocolate—why not?—to whatever you want.

Blockchain technology could quickly identify the source of a bad batch of vegetables or fruit, and allow suppliers to recall the product quickly, before people buy it and get sick. It would do so with minimal disruption to the supply chain. Today in the United States, the average time required for such a process is six days; in a pilot experiment with blockchain technology at Walmart, it took 2.2 seconds.[50]

As with products, all information relating to people could be contained and stored in blockchains and be accessible online, making passports and identity cards superfluous. Digital identity would also become obsolete. Everything from medical history to bank details to the tax code could be recorded in a blockchain, which is hacker-proof. These precious data, including vaccinations and health history, would be controlled by the individual, not by the government or other state institutions. As with bitcoins, people could store them in their deposit safe, in a digital wallet, to which they alone possess the private key. When they want to share some data, they could use the public-key cryptographic system to send that information only to whomever they want to view it and only for a specific period of time. Since every access is automatically logged, people would immediately know if someone unauthorized had seen it.

Another application of blockchain technology is smart contracts. These are contracts for future events that do not need certification from a notary or a lawyer. The contract establishes that by a certain date, in specific situations that both parties agree upon, the contract becomes valid. A self-driving car, for example, could become an autonomous maintenance vehicle. The machine will know when to go to the workshop to have the oil changed and any other maintenance checks, at which point the service will be paid for by the activation of the smart contract that refers to the fulfillment of these specific tasks. This would be possible by applying blockchain technology to artificial intelligence.

In the not-too-distant future, blockchains will also make many professions and institutions obsolete. Why have a land registry if every purchase and sale is registered in blockchains? What use are drivers if the cars do everything themselves? And notaries? Lawyers? Let's imagine the savings for the user. But the most revolutionary effect would be the flattening of the functions of the state, which would be reduced to . . . well, I would say to a sorting system for virtual transactions, an online traffic light.

On the flip side, blockchain technology will put many people out of work, replacing them with artificial intelligence. This is risky if technology remains in the hands of the few and if the final outcome is an increase in unemployment. But if the fruits of technological innovation are equally shared, the higher efficiency and productivity of AI could improve goods and services and reduce the length of the working week and the time we dedicate to work during the day. If so, the benefits of AI will free a considerable amount of the workforce and cut costs of production. People will be able to spend more time with their family, to care for the elderly and the sick, to be better members of society, or to cultivate their interests and hobbies.

Another fear refers to energy consumption. If proof of work is applied as a consensus mechanism, redesigning society according to blockchain would require a phenomenal, impossible-to-produce amount of energy. Each little entry, alteration, and smart contract would in fact need the validation of the entire network, something intuitively impossible but also unnecessary. Why must a smart contract in Alabama be verified and approved in South Africa? Much better to apply a localized, proof of stake version. These validators will perform some of the role that state institutions execute in modern society; they are the trust junctions between the individual and the community. Proof of stake is indeed the consensus mechanism applied by Ethereum, the crypto online platform discussed in the following chapter.

The decentralization of the state, the empowering of the individual, who paradoxically becomes the ruler of himself inside the online multitude, was the dream of the Cypherpunks that Satoshi Nakamoto may well have made possible. Blockchain technology, coupled with AI, could redesign the interaction of individuals, alter the social traits that we have had since the dawn of our species, and make the institutions of the state and the state itself, as we know it, obsolete. But let's remember that many of these institutions have been created not to make our lives more difficult but to protect us from human error and prevent oppression. If we are not careful, removing them completely, entrusting our future into the hands of an artificial intelligence technology controlled only by a select group of people who are familiar with it, could open the door to the dystopian world described in the movie *The Matrix*.

To illustrate this concept, let's use the brief history of OpenAI. In 2015, a group of investors that included Sam Altman, Greg Brockman, Wojciech Zaremba, Ilya Sutskever, John Schulman, and Elon Musk (who left in 2018 when it became apparent that he could not control the company) founded OpenAI.[51] Other vintage tech investors such as Peter Thiel, Reid Hoffman, Jessica Livingston, and Olivier Grabias soon joined in because they all understood the revolutionary potential of the product OpenAI was working on: a large language model (LLM), essentially a technological replica of the human brain. LLMs are based on "neural network" architecture[52] and since the end of 2022 have literally taken the world by storm, not only on social media platforms but also inside of businesses and places of education.

OpenAI was funded as a nonprofit with the "humanitarian" goal of developing safe and open artificial intelligence tools to empower people everywhere.[53] These were big words and noble intentions, which vanished as early as 2019 when the company partnered with Microsoft and ended its philanthropic mission, embracing the quest for fat profits.

Microsoft invested $1 billion in OpenAI's new ChatGPT, an artificial intelligence chatbot,[54] which was publicly launched at the end of 2022. By January 2023, Microsoft had invested an additional $10 billion for exclusive access to GPT-4, whose task is to power Microsoft's Prometheus model for Bing.[55] ChatGPT could not only put Google Search out of business and open that vast field to Microsoft but it also has the power to erase a vast array of jobs and carriers by replacing them with AI and, in a not distant future, to redefine civilization. For now, ChatGPT is still a parrot which produces outputs based on data it has seen before on the internet;

however, certain neurons in the human brain have also been found in OpenAi, i.e., there are possible common mechanisms between this technology and our own human brains, i.e., it gets better with experience, and with that it shows an inclination to misinformation and bias. OpenAI admits to not be able to understand all the inner workings of neural networks, i.e., such evolution, so it exercises a manual control, i.e., humans, to rectify the mistakes.[56] This process is known as "reinforcement learning with human feedback," where the GPT system learns to become less biased and more friendly by talking to real humans, which inevitably raises the question of whose bias the GPT will end up assimilating.

Another big question refers to the development of consciences. What if the human brain at some point on the evolutionary ladder developed enough parameters to surpass some threshold and display the emergent phenomena of human intelligence? It would therefore be reasonable to say that neural networks could one day match the human brain (and become "artificial general intelligence") if they managed to reach the same parameters. However, it is becoming harder and harder to scale up LLMs—we are running out of data on the web to train larger neural networks—but we are only in the infancy of the techno brain.

The founders of OpenAI are well aware of these existential issues, and to continue to pursue their goal they have hidden the dangers of LLMs behind a façade of philanthropism. Many have been vocal in their support for universal basic income, a good tool to prevent social revolts against a technological innovation that has the potential to make work obsolete for large segments of the population. A common mantra is that AI will generate so much wealth that the state will be able to pay people not to work. In reality, this would be the first brick of technocapitalism, i.e., the removal of human labor from the equation of growth, a capitalism based solely on capital.

Without jumping into science fiction, one could envisage,

within a decade, personalized AI, products which will enhance the knowledge and cognitive capabilities of the new elite. In the wrong hands, such tools could also be used to keep the masses ignorant, to enslave them through lack of or false knowledge. Because the stakes are so, so high, it is imperative to empower the multitude. And this can only happen by unmasking the current oppressive nature of technology. Satoshi Nakamoto's gift as well as LLMs will truly benefit humanity when everybody will be able to use and enjoy them.

CHAPTER FOUR

Non-fungible Tokens

On March 11, 2021, Mike Winkelmann, known online as the digital artist Beeple, and his family gathered to watch the last hours of the Christie's auction of his digital collage, *Everydays: The First 5000 Days*. The auction had started nearly two weeks earlier, on February 25. By the time Beeple and his family had switched on the video link, the bidding was already at $20 million. An hour and a half later, Vignesh Sundaresan, a Singapore-based blockchain entrepreneur, coder, and angel investor, known online as MetaKovan, bought *Everydays: The First 5000 Days* for the whopping sum of $69.3 million. The sale propelled Mike Winkelmann into third place among the highest-selling living artists, after Jeff Koons and David Hockney.[57]

What was so special about Beeple's digital collage? He had started it on May 1, 2007, by posting the first image online. It was a very simple drawing of his uncle Jay, whom he nicknamed Uber Jay, presumably because he drove an Uber car. Since then, he had posted a new digital image daily, without missing a single day, including when his wife gave birth to their first baby.

Everydays: The First 5000 Days is a digital window into Beeple's personal life as it took shape over a period of over fourteen years. In the background is visible the socio-political tapestry of the United States. Recurring themes include society's obsession with and fear of technology; the desire for and resentment towards the quest for wealth; and America's recent political turbulence.[58] Many artists deal with these topics. However, a close look at the individual images of the collage reveals Beeple's extraordinary ability to capture and communicate the grotesque aspects of today's life, the absurdity of politics, the degradation of democracy, the omens of dystopian nightmares, the overwhelming presence of a state that has morphed into a farcical dictatorship of the super-rich and super-privileged.

Beeple's unique artistic signature springs from the evolution of his technical skills, sharpened over two decades spent in a separate reality: the digital world. This explains why *Everydays: The First 5000 Days* seems to move in parallel with cyber technology in a relationship so close that traveling from picture to picture, one can almost visualize the evolution of the digitization of life, the anxiety it has generated but also the hints of hope for a better future it has unleashed. From that initial simple drawing of Uber Jay in 2007 to the more and more sophisticated, surreal, grotesque, and fantastically effective images of 2009, the digital collage transcends Beeple's experience and becomes a representation of the current existential turmoil of Western societies. Because the work offers a unique historical record of how cyber technology has advanced during those 5,000 days and of how Beeple has managed to apply it artistically, almost in real time, *Everydays: The First 5000 Days* is a visual testimonial to the era of the Present Future. The extraordinary speed of technological change, which in individuals triggers overwhelming fears about the transition, in the hands of the artist becomes a powerful instrument to undo the present in order to show its futuristic nature. Instead of doing sketches, Beeple used the most advanced 3D tools to make comments on current events, almost in real time.[59]

Mastering technological innovation in real time opens new digital frontiers for artists like Beeple. This, however, is not the unique characteristic of *Everydays: The First 5000 Days*. Technology has made it possible to smash a major commercial barrier in the art world. Beeple's digital collage was sold as a non-fungible token, better known as an NFT, i.e., a cyber certificate of authenticity. And it was paid for in Ether (ETH), the cryptocurrency of the digital platform Ethereum.

So far NFTs are the most popular commercial application of the blockchain technology, which should not come as a surprise. Non-fungible means not exchangeable. Money is fungible: five one-dollar bills can be exchanged with any other five one-dollar bills or with one five-dollar banknote. Gold is fungible: a gram of 18-karat gold can be swapped with another gram of 18-karat gold. Artwork is the most universally recognizable non-fungible item. I cannot exchange one piece of art for another; each work of art is one of a kind, it is unique. However, until NFTs were invented, digital art, unlike traditional art, had been easily replicated and distributed as the original.

From the outset of cyberspace, digital artists have been battling for ownership of intellectual property, to prove digitally what was their own creation. How to prevent someone replicating artistic work? How to distinguish the original from the copy? Sounds familiar? This was the main dilemma of the Cypherpunks. The answers came at the end of 2008, when Satoshi Nakamoto solved the identical problem for digital money by boxing bitcoin inside a blockchain. As with bitcoins, the blockchain technology gives digital proof of ownership and, therefore, unique originality.

A non-fungible token is a token attached to a blockchain that guarantees its authenticity. Beeple used it to transform his original digital drawings into a collage. He took the five thousand JPGs stored in his computer, images that millions of people had already seen and downloaded, put them together in a single piece, and created or minted an NFT, a unique piece of art. Essential information about the artwork, which includes the digital fingerprint of the artist, the token name—Beeple named his collage *Everydays: The First 5000 Days*—and a specific symbol, are stored and locked in the blockchain. The artist becomes the owner and can sell it.

Each time an NFT changes hands a new block is added to the chain. As with bitcoins, the blockchain technology for NFTs provides a ledger of transactions and a guarantee that nobody can tamper with it. People can track who is the current owner of the token and how much has been paid to acquire it through the blockchain. However, unlike bitcoins, NFTs cannot be divided or exchanged with other NFTs. Bitcoins are fungible; one bitcoin can be exchanged for another bitcoin in exactly the same way as cash. But the opposite is true of an NFT. Like any original work of art, the *Mona Lisa*, say, an NFT is one of a kind and non-fungible.

The NFT stores the ownership, i.e., the fingerprint or hash of the file; however, the token name and its symbol do not contain the actual work of art. Unlike traditional art, NFTs are intangible: they are made of pixels and live in cyberspace, and the images are available to everybody to see and enjoy on a computer screen. So MetaKovan does not possess the physical piece of art produced by Beeple—how could he if it physically does not exist? MetaKovan paid $69.3 million for a certification to prove that he, and he alone, owns the original digital work of art, a bunch of colored pixels. Does that seem absurd?

Clearly the purchase is a form of investment: anybody can look at *Everydays: The First 5000 Days* simply by switching on a computer. Most likely, MetaKovan's purchase was motivated by the anticipation that digital art will take off and that in the future people will be willing, as has happened to traditional art, to use it as a store of value and as an investment. Several people shared these expectations. In October 2020, Miami-based art collector Pablo Rodriguez-Fraile spent almost $67,000 on a ten-second NFT video artwork that he and everybody else could have watched for free online. The author was Beeple. A few months later Rodriguez-Fraile resold it for $6.6 million, netting a very handsome profit.[60]

Rodriguez-Fraile and MetaKovan's behavior is reminiscent of

the practice of big investors and art collectors who purchase the work of the great masters to keep them locked in their vaults, without enjoying their beauty, as a secure way to store their wealth. NFTs have widened this segment of the art and investment market to include digital artists, like Beeple, who until the marriage of digital art and blockchain could not become part of it. The two largest parts of an NFT's value are (i) pride in holding the NFT and ability to show off your ownership, and (ii) the possibility of selling it in the future.[61]

Until the sale of *Everydays: The First 5000 Days*, the digital and traditional art worlds had only marginally overlapped. Though Beeple had 1.8 million followers on Instagram and his work had been shown in two Super Bowl halftimes and at a Justin Bieber concert, no art gallery had shown or sold his work, and no auction house was interested in it. The Christie's auction of Beeple's collage was the first time a traditional auction house had put an NFT on sale and the first time cryptocurrency was accepted as form of payment. Clearly, for auction houses, art galleries, and art dealers, NFTs open new business opportunities with almost unlimited potential. On November 28, 2021, the one-of-a-kind *Quantum* artwork by digital artist Kevin McCoy sold for more than $1.4 million in a Sotheby's auction. *Quantum*, a pixelated octagon filled with different shapes that pulse in a quite hypnotic way, was the first NFT ever minted: McCoy created it on May 2, 2014.[62]

The above examples place the NFT among the techno trophies that the cyber nouveau riche buy with their crypto wealth. And once again, we are confronted with the fact that technology has been bent to satisfy the narcissistic need of the few instead of serving humanity, i.e., instead of improving our lives. In sharp contrast with this paradigm, the founder of Twitter, Jack Dorsey, sold his first tweet as an NFT for $2.9 million to Sina Estavi, the chief executive of the Malaysia-based blockchain company Bridge Oracle, and donated the entire amount to charity.[63] Although his gesture was noble, society cannot rely upon the charity of those who understand and control technology. Technology must be put at the service of humanity. And indeed, this is possible.

As we shall see in the second part of this chapter, however, the trajectory at the moment is to widen the commercial horizons of NFTs. Though for now this is limited to a small segment of the techno-savvy population that has minted wealth from technology and thus can afford to buy digital art, potentially it can enlarge the market reach of many sectors from sports to merchandising, even to social media. Following this path, NFTs will likely remain a product of consumerism, and their contribution to humanity will remain confined to charitable donation and taxation.[64]

At the moment, like any other financial and crypto product, NFTs are subject to the market swings and ups and downs of the economic and speculative cycles. These changes can result in huge losses in value, as stated by Sundaresan, who has warned that those trying to profit off the tokens are "taking a huge risk."[65] NFTs are risky because they are a new product, with a very limited market— data from the analytics firm Chainalysis shows that at the end of April 2022, there had been 9.2 million NFTs sold, which were bought by 1.8 million people, a tiny elite. This explains why, in the midst of the crypto crisis of spring 2022, demand for NFTs quickly dried up, prompting prices to collapse. In April 2022, Sina Estavi put on sale the NFT of Jack Dorsey. The highest bid was $14,000. He decided not to sell.[66] Even Beeple is concerned about the speculative nature of NFTs. He compared the NFT market to the dot-com bubble and predicts that only parts of the NFT market will thrive while others will wither. This is what he told CNBC: "I'm very, very bullish on the technology and space long-term. . . . I just think people need to be careful right now because there's a rush and it's so new. It is quite speculative."[67] It was not coincidental that *Everydays: The First 5000 Days* was bought with Ether. Between 2014 and 2015, non-fungible tokens took off thanks to Ethereum. A blockchain-based software platform with its own cryptocurrency, Ether, Ethereum offers the possibility of minting and commercializing the tokens. The supply of Ether is not fixed and no halving effect has been built into the software. The halving of Ether takes place whenever the community of holders decides to halve its value. However, the fundamental difference between Ether and Bitcoin is the role they play. The latter has been designed as an alternative to fiat currencies, so it is a medium of exchange and store of value. Ethereum is essentially an online platform which offers a programmable blockchain with applications in many areas and fields, for example NFTs. Bitcoin does not offer these services.

Ethereum was originally launched to facilitate transactions online using its own cryptocurrency, which until September 2022 was mined in the same way as bitcoins. After the so-called "Merge," proof of stake replaced proof of work.

Unlike bitcoin, Ethereum allows people to publicly create and maintain their own secure digital ledgers on its platform, which means that they can mint and trade their own NFTs. The advent of Ethereum literally opened up a universe of possibilities in cyber commerce and beyond because, potentially, it makes it possible to apply the blockchain technology to everything from art to sports images and videos to any material or immaterial item, providing there is proof of work, i.e., authorship, or, after the Merge, proof of stake. The platform is intuitive, easy to navigate, and has detailed instructions on how to create, issue, and deploy new tokens.

Initially, NFTs were used as digital trading cards representing memes. The first major successful set was the CryptoPunks, a series of ten thousand unique digital characters generated on the Ethereum platform. The images celebrated the Cypherpunks, considered the fathers of the cyber revolution. In 2017, the CryptoPunks were given away for free to anyone who had an Ethereum wallet. To the surprise of their creators, John Watkinson and Matt Hall, people rushed to claim their own and soon began trading them on the secondary market, where prices started to climb, eventually reaching seven figures.[68] It is rumored that, in October 2021, one of the CryptoPunks cards was sold for $532 million—much more than Beeple's *Everydays: The First 5000 Days*—which would make it the highest NFT sale ever.[69] There have been rumors that the sale was manufactured for publicity; however, Christie's is adamant that it did take place in full. Daniel Van Bloom, a Senior Writer at CNET, says that even if largely manufactured, the sale was still a remarkable turning point because it showed the potential of NFT.

In 2017, the Vancouver-based company Axiom Zen launched *CryptoKitties* on the Ethereum platform. Its unexpected success offered a sneak preview of the shining commercial future of NFTs. *CryptoKitties* is a blockchain-based virtual game that allows players to adopt, breed, and trade virtual cats from the safety of their own wallet. Digital breeding mimics biological breeding: all crypto cats possess unique and common genomes and have DNA with different attributes, some of which can be passed on to their offspring and some of which cannot. Interestingly, the digital cats do not have a permanent assigned gender and can act as male or female in the breeding process.

Though the game has no other goal than creating and trading feline digital images, it went viral as soon as it was launched. Players became hooked on breeding virtual cats. Clearly, *CryptoKitties* had struck a chord in the digital community. Conceptually, the game is a cross between *Neopets*—the website of the virtual pet community—and trading in futures. It captured people's imagination and creativity on one hand and, on the other, it offered the possibility of betting on the future value of the cats. That cocktail literally exploded on the Ethereum platform. This is how Dan Finlay of MetaMask, one of the cryptocurrency "wallets" that

allows users to access the game, describes the initial response to
CryptoKitties:

> When *CryptoKitties* finally happened, they were launched
> on a Friday, and we had scheduled a Consensys design
> thinking retreat for that week. We were all in New York,
> basically checked out, with no one on staff. While we were
> there, people kept talking about *CryptoKitties*, showing us
> their collections, and very quickly things escalated to the
> point that people we met were paying off chunks of their
> college debt by flipping cats. Myself, I was just trying to
> breed a funny looking cat! Right when that mania started
> happening, we began getting reports of major congestion
> problems, nothing working.[70]

The network started to get seriously clogged and for a short
time people feared that the crisis would bring down much more
than the game itself. They feared it would break the Ethereum
platform, which at the time was considered one of the most
remarkable applications of the blockchain.[71] But it didn't. The
platform survived the sudden surge in transactions and soon after
was strengthened to withstand the next big digital success. But
the experience taught a lesson on the technological limitation of a
consensus system based upon proof of work. Clearly, the platform
could not properly process all the transactions.

The popularity of *CryptoKitties* prompted the surge of crypto
collectibles: digital puppies, pandas, bunnies, and tiny monsters
all linked to the various blockchain-based collectibles. And people
spent millions of dollars buying them. Many of these collectibles
will most likely end up like the Beanie Babies, whose markets and
valuation have plummeted after their soaring popularity during
the 1990s.[72]

Unlike bitcoins, NFTs are fashionable items. They are a product, not a means of exchange, and therefore NFTs are subject to changes in people's desire and taste and are conditioned by the ups and downs of their disposable income. Therefore, the NFT craziness that swept through the market in 2021 came crashing down in 2022 when the tech industry, by far the sector with the highest number of NFT buyers, took a major hit.

After reaching new heights in November 2021, by the beginning of May 2022 the NASDAQ Composite, which is heavily influenced by tech companies, had fallen by 23 percent; bitcoins had shed 43 percent of their value while the value of thousands of cryptocurrencies had gone down to zero, flattening the NFT market. The website nonfungible.com shows that, in the first week of May 2022, sales of NFTs fell to 19,000, a 92 percent decline from the peak of 225,000 in September 2021.[73] Prices have literally crashed and at the time of writing they have not yet recovered. As Paul Vigna writes in the Wall Street Journal:

> [An] NFT buyer purchased a Snoop Dog curated NFT, titled Doggy #4292, in early April for about $32,000 worth of the cryptocurrency ether. The NFT, an image of a green-skinned astronaut standing on what looks like a Hollywood Walk of Fame star, is now up for auction, with an asking price of $25.5 million. The highest current bid is for 0.0743 Ether—about $210.[74]

Though regarded as fashionable items, non-fungible tokens are not themselves works of art, though they can be assigned to artworks, as in the case of Beeple's collage. They are essentially smart contracts that live in the blockchain and could be used by society in every industry and field, for example, to cut red tape and costs of bureaucracy. For now the most extensive usage has been in the art world. And it has been beneficial to artists; for example, their flexibility has allowed some artists to retain the copyright and reproduction rights of their work, which means that although the original digital artwork has been sold, the artist can still sell prints of it. NFTs can also include royalties for resale, i.e., each time an NFT changes hands, the artist receives the percentage negotiated and incorporated in the original smart contract.

In April 2021, Yuga Labs, a secretive outfit led by pseudonymous founders—Gordon Goner, Emperor Tomato Ketchup, No Sass, and Gargamel—minted on the Ethereum blockchain 10,000 NFTs, collectible digital images of uninterested-looking apes, which they named Bored Ape Yacht Club. From an initial price of $300 each, the cost of the digital images soared to more than a million dollars on the secondary market. In September 2021, a single Bored Ape NFT went for 740 ETH, equivalent to $2.9 million. The buyer was the developer of the Ethereum game *The Sandbox*. Because in the smart contract underlying the NFTs of Bored Ape Yacht Club, Yuga Labs has retained a royalty percentage; each time one of the images changes hands, Yuga collects a cut from the resale.[75]

In a not too distant future, however, NFTs could be applied to everything from the sale of concert tickets to the domain of rare digital names to real estate to anything that requires proof of ownership and that can be traded. Therefore, NFTs are one of the fastest-expanding segments of the digital asset realm.[76] From the beginning of 2021, major brands in sport, fine wine, art, and fashion have all launched dedicated NFTs, hoping to capitalize on their cyber boom despite the incidences of fraud and price manipulation as well as hacks and counterfeits. In 2021, before the big crash of 2022, the NFT market had reached $40 billion.[77]

The easiest way to use NFTs is still in relation to non-fungible items. Like works of art, memorable sports moments are universally recognizable as non-fungible because they are unique, exceptional, and cannot be replicated. So, it comes as no surprise that the other major field in which NFTs are being used is sports.

Sport NFTs are much more than digital trading cards, sports

memorabilia, or even investment items where wealth can be stored. They are a new class of products that have become available in "fandom," the universe where sports fans interact with athletes, clubs, leagues, and sponsors. Rich Kleiman, cofounder of Thirty Five and manager of superstar basketball player Kevin Durant, claims that new ranges of NFT contents, e.g., personalized videos, will give Durant's fans more direct access to him. Kleiman also believes that NFTs will help athletes to further monetize their abilities. Rob Gronkowski, the first professional athlete to launch his own range of NFTs, made over $1 million auctioning his digital trading cards online. The buyer of the rarest card was given the chance to meet him in person, come to one of his games, and receive VIP access at one of his other franchises. Bored Ape Yacht Club follows a similar marketing strategy and grants the owners access to exclusive events and sought-after merchandise.

Potentially, sport NFTs could redesign the commercial landscape of fandom, generating a new stream of revenues that could end up dwarfing all others. In 2021, a video that highlighted basketball superstar LeBron James's dunk was minted into an NFT and sold for $200 million. Before the crash of spring 2022, NFTs for sports media were expected to generate $2 billion in transactions in 2022, about double the previous year.[78]

The National Football League (NFL), the biggest and wealthiest sports league in the US, has also engaged with NFTs. The NFL does not need the money, nor does it need to rush into an unproven market for new revenues. Its involvement with NFTs springs from a long-term view of fans' expectations. The NFL believes that younger generations will prove to be very responsive to NFTs and so the league is willing to enter this new market. For Joe Ruggiero, senior VP for consumer products for the NFL, NFTs may even give new generations of fans a novel way to interact with athletes and teams through collectible video games and social media, well before they get engaged in real-life games.[79]

It is unquestionable that gaming is the new frontier of NFTs, especially financially. The involvement of the sport industry in this new digital tool could facilitate the marriage of non-fungible tokens and digital games. People could earn tokens in the form of NFTs in one game and take them to another platform, helping to unlock the metaverse. Fans could build their own avatar, sell merchandise, i.e., their NFTs, and even attend games online with their friends. Though nobody knows what the metaverse can or will be, as Joe Ruggiero said during an interview with the *Financial Times,* we all know that it is going to change things. In a not too distant future, fans may go to a digital stadium with other digital fans and enjoy a game; the tickets may come in the form of NFTs.[80]

Unlocking the metaverse is much more than replicating the internet. It is opening another dimension, possibly much bigger than virtual reality. People could lead several digital lives through their avatars, experience different genders, professions, lovers, or religions. And these lives will be conducted alone, wearing virtual life googles. Perhaps Facebook's metaverse project is the best example of the commercialization of technological innovation for the sole purpose of enriching those who control it and entertaining through escapism those who use it. This is indeed the dark side of the Present Future.

Stripped of the key elements of humanity, which made it possible for a weak species to survive against all odds, the metaverse strengthens our new identity as unhappy loners, mere consumers and commodities. Not only does it increase our isolation and individualism but it also encourages the proliferation of "pretend" lives, fake versions of ourselves and of reality, that we can buy as we purchase new clothes, often to avoid confronting our failures, our low self-esteem, our existential malaise. The metaverse offers escapism as the cure for the pandemic of anxiety, a potent virtual opioid that shuts out the real world. And as with all drugs, addiction and its consequences are very serious. As we plunge deeper into virtual reality, our distance from the truth itself increases, our avatars become more and more disconnected from politics, economics, true human passions, activism, heroism. All the things that make us human become distant memories that fade away.

Unsurprisingly, the multi-personality dimension that the metaverse offers is particularly appealing to those whose goals are purely commercial, for example, celebrities. The metaverse allows them to alter their images to meet the taste of their fans. In doing so, the metaverse could multiply the followers of movie stars, great athletes, or influencers, by simply duping their fans into believing that they are who their fans want them to be. Naturally, to achieve such a goal their relationship with the wealthiest and most devoted fans needs to be even more intimate and special, and this enhancement is what NFTs could help achieve.

Along these lines, Bored Ape Yacht Club gives owners access to an exclusive Discord server where other owners, including celebrities like Gwyneth Paltrow, Eminem, and Snoop Dogg, hang out and chat. Apes also tend to flock together on social media, where familiar avatars form a digital brotherhood. One of the reasons for the success of Yuga's NFTs is the popularity of the Bored Apes among celebrities who use their digital ape as their picture on social media. In other words, Bored Apes has become a symbol of exclusivity, the digital tattoo of a superior cyber tribe. Because NFTs are tradable items, NFTs are about signaling wealth.

All one has to do to get into such a tribe is to be very rich and spend one or two million US dollars buying a digital drawing of a fed-up primate. Should we be surprised? As the process of dehumanization proceeds at the hands of the high tech elite and our new identity of consumers and commodities evolves, wealth and materialistic possessions become our primary objectives. Hence the rush to conquer the new virtual frontier. As envisioned by Facebook, commercially the metaverse could easily deliver a new generation of billionaires and of clueless people, and this is all that matters to those who master the new technology. From celebrities to hedge funds, from auction houses to individual graphic designers to merchandisers, everybody wants a piece of the digital pie. Some are even openly admitting that is their aim. In 2021 Yuga Lab tweeted: ". . . Our ambition is for this to be a community-owned brand, with tentacles in world-class gaming, events, and streetwear."[81]

Contrary to what many believe, to profit from everything from NFTs to the metaverse is not going to be a smooth ride. Look at the story of the video game *Axie Infinity*. The game is played using characters knowns as Axies, which are NFTs, and their ownership is documented on a blockchain, which means that they can be traded like cryptocurrencies. Owning Axies allows players to breed more Axies—exactly like *CryptoKitties*—which can be sold. The aim of *Axie Infinity* is not entertainment but profits; the game is what Sky Mavis Inc., the start-up that created it, defines as a "play-to-earn game."[82] Earnings are collected in tokens, Smooth Love Potion (SLP) and Axie Infinity Shards (AXS), or cryptocurrencies, in large tournaments.

Though the actual game is fast and not particularly exciting, *Axie Infinity* was very successful and became almost instantly popular because of the play-to-earn characteristic and the breeding activity. Gamers from all over the world flocked to play it and invested heavily in purchasing and breeding Axies. Owners of Axies could also rent them to people who play the game to learn about the crypto market.

When the crypto crisis broke in the spring of 2022, the economics of *Axie Infinity* crashed. AXS, which had been worth $165, dropped below $20, and SLP, which had traded as high as 40 cents, was worth half a penny.[83] NFT is just one application of the blockchain technology and the metaverse is just a step up for our current virtual life, like a more sophisticated version of Second Life.[84] So it is worth finding out what ever happened to Second Life. In 2003, Philip Rosedale, an internet entrepreneur who owned Linden Lab, a San Francisco company, created a 3D virtual world which he named Second Life. He describes the site as "a world of endless reinvention where you can change your shape, sex and even your species as easily as you may slip into a pair of shoes at home."

The virtual world of Second Life is still there, in cyberspace, offering an alternative life, one that people can manufacture themselves, their ideal life. But no matter how rich, powerful, or beautiful the avatar of your choice is, it is still subject to the full spectrum of human passion, the good and the bad of real life. Second Life has been plagued by criminality, terrorism, and war, and the moderators have found it difficult to contain and restrain, even while it has also provided love, friendship, and companionship to its inhabitants. The experience of Second Life proves that the metaverse is just a copycat of real life on Earth, and perhaps this is why the membership of Second Life has remained small.

Imagination and scarcity are the boundaries within which the avatars interact; they are no different from the limits that our first ancestors faced in their quest to survive. Boom and bust mark the evolution of cyber economics as they are the heartbeat of the real economy. Art and beauty are still symbols of wealth. Biology is still the engine of life. Finally, as in real life, the metaverse is conditioned by money creation, the overwhelming terrestrial boundary of wealth.

Bitcoin and Ether constitute new wealth, which is produced in cyberspace by software, i.e., by algorithmic, mathematical formulas, codes, and numbers. Cryptocurrencies have flooded the digital world and produced wealth that has been spent and invested in digital products, e.g., NFTs. Digital money creation has taken place outside the traditional monetary system, in cyberspace, away from the monetary monopoly of the state. But unlike what the Cypherpunks envisioned and Satoshi Nakamoto predicted, the digitization of money has not broken the monopolistic monetary mold, and it has not weakened the traditional monetary and financial establishment. The opposite has happened! Big Brother has embraced the digitization of money and has even used it to shore up its public and private institutions during a time of great financial upheaval.

CHAPTER FIVE

Financial Meltdown

Hyman Minsky, the American economist, once summarized in a sentence the fundamental role that trust plays in the use of money: though anybody can create money, he wrote, the real problem is to get people to accept it. If you can't convince someone to use it, money is worth nothing.[85]

Even during the gold standard, which was in force from 1870 to 1920 and partly from 1930 to 1932, the belief that banknotes were certificates of ownership of a set quantity of gold was essentially an act of faith. The value of paper money was based upon the so-called golden parity; for example, one US dollar was equivalent to one five-hundredth of an ounce (0.0567 gram), because the price of one ounce of gold had been set at $500. Theoretically, anyone could have gone to the central bank and exchanged their banknotes for the corresponding amount of gold. Where did the gold come from? From the central bank's reserves, which means that the value of the stock of banknotes in circulation was equal to the value of gold held in the reserves. However, nobody bothered to convert paper money into gold: it was impractical. People could not buy a bus ticket or pay for a meal in a restaurant with gold dust. The population had faith that the state would always honor the golden parity and the banknotes circulated freely, retaining their value as if they were grams of gold.

It turned out that such trust was ill placed. Governments manipulated the data and printed banknotes well in excess of their reserves, eroding the gold parity. They did it to finance expansionary wars against their neighbors and to fund their appetite for colonization to control strategic natural resources which belonged to poorer nations. This fraudulent behavior greatly contributed to the First and Second World Wars.

After the Second World War, when it became clear that a return to the gold standard was impossible, a new system was invented and put in place: the gold exchange standard. With the Bretton Woods agreement, it was decided that only one currency, the US dollar, would maintain the golden parity, which was set at $35 an ounce.[86] All the other currencies were pegged to the dollar's value through a fixed exchange rate. Every nation that joined the new monetary system agreed to monitor and maintain the US dollar exchange rate within a margin of fluctuation of 1 percent. How did they do it? By buying and selling US dollars with their own currencies on the open market as needed. The Bretton Woods agreement, therefore, created a new fixed exchange rate system aimed at minimizing the volatility of exchange rates, a task that for a very short time greatly helped international trade relations.

Fiat money officially entered the global scene with the gold exchange standard. Fiat money is a government-issued currency that is not backed by a physical commodity, such as gold or silver, but rather by the government that issues it. Fiat derives from Latin and refers to an act of determination by an authority, e.g., the system of fixed exchange rates pegged to the value of the US dollar.[87] In the gold exchange standard all banknotes, apart from the US dollar, ceased to be a certificate of ownership of another asset, such as gold, and became an act of monetary faith in the new system. Washington took advantage of the trust of the other nations and financed the Korean and Vietnamese wars by printing banknotes well above the level of its gold reserves and, in doing so, it devalued, together with the US dollar, all the other currencies pegged to it. Because of that, in 1971 Richard Nixon was forced to end the convertibility of the US dollar.[88]

From that moment onwards, everything changed. Currencies ceased to be anchored to a real asset, even if only indirectly, through a fixed exchange rate to the US dollar, and became exclusively an act of faith in the issuer, the state. People did not understand the significance of this change at the time, mostly because they had never comprehended how the monetary system created at Bretton Woods really worked in the first place. For example, they attributed the inflationary wave which the US dollar's failure to maintain the gold parity had unleashed, to other economic factors. When in 1973 the oil shock came, after the boom of the 1960s, they blamed the energy crisis exclusively for the rise in prices. Their monetary faith in the issuer remained unshaken. Even when double digit inflation ate away people's monetary wealth, they carried on believing that the banknotes they had in their pockets were anchored to the wealth of their nation, a wealth now under attack from Middle Eastern oil suppliers.

The biggest menace to fiat money is inflation. It erodes the value of currencies, eating away at it. Inflation is like an infestation of moths inside a closet full of woolen clothes: you need to fumigate it several times to kill the eggs as they hatch and you must dry clean the clothes for the same reason. However, you can never fix the holes left in the fabric; what has been eaten is gone forever.

Without the anchor of gold, inflation accelerated. In 1973, with the first oil shock, it literally exploded. No one could escape it. During the second half of the 1970s, industrialized countries suffered double digit inflation which, combined with the slow or zero growth that the oil crisis had triggered, produced a new economic abomination: stagflation.[89] Governments, central banks, international organizations, economists: nobody really knew how to deal with the new economic monster until Margaret Thatcher, in the United Kingdom, and Ronald Reagan, in the United States, came to power. They embraced the idea that the market economy could heal itself, providing that the many financial restrictions that the state had imposed after the Great Depression were lifted. Thatcher and Reagan firmly believed that free from the shackles of financial regulation, the market economy could and would recover. Their motto might as well have been: Let the market be, let it be free to perform its marvels.[90]

Though identified with the two terms of Ronald Reagan, financial deregulation actually began at the end of the presidency of Jimmy Carter, in 1979, when the chairman of the Federal Reserve, Paul Volcker, raised interest rates. It was a smart move to fight inflation. Inflation discourages savings and incentivizes spending, which in turn pushes prices up. If today I save $100 which can buy a new coat and in a year's time, when I need that coat, it will cost me $120, I will be better off buying the coat today. To curb spending and encourage people to save, the US Congress lifted legislation introduced after the Great Depression that limited the interest that banks were allowed to pay to depositors. In doing so, it freed the interest rates of high street banks, which also began incentivizing saving.

Financial deregulation unleashed a battle within society, a conflict fought between the inflation and interest rates. As long as the latter were higher than the former, people would be prone to spend less and save more—the necessary behavior for restoring the trust in the value of fiat money. The logic is simple: if instead of buying the coat today, I deposit $100 in the bank, and in a year's time I will have $122 and the coat will cost $120, I will be better off saving and buying the coat next year. As interest rates on deposits climbed to double digits, above inflation, money started to flow back into the high street banking system in the form of savings. This is the same blueprint that Western governments followed to weather the inflationary economic storm which began in 2022.

Back in the early 1980s, flush with this liquidity and freed from financial restrictions, high street banks began acting as brokers, intermediaries marketing financial products and mortgages among themselves. Demand for real estate was buoyant because during the decade-long inflation and stagflation, people had learned that properties insulated their savings from inflation; as a result, everybody wanted to own a piece of the real estate pie.

Since the Great Depression, in the United States the mortgage market for affordable housing had been in the hands of two government institutions: Fannie Mae (Federal National Mortgage Association) and Ginnie Mae (Government National Mortgage Association). The latter was founded in 1968 with the specific aim of expanding affordable housing, a goal achieved by guaranteeing mortgages and lowering financing costs, i.e., interest rates on loans. In the post–World War II era, both institutions became instrumental to the fulfillment of the American dream, funding the sprouting of residential suburbs where American families bought their homes and settled down.

In 1970, Ginnie Mae produced the first mortgage-backed security (MBS), a new financial instrument de facto backed by the US government. The MBS was one of the first successful attempts at financial engineering; that is, to transform a product, house loans, into a new financial instrument, essentially a stock.[91] How does it work? A large group of mortgages are aggregated and packaged together into a bond or stock that is then sold to investors. The value of the resulting mortgage-backed security is the stream of money attached to the repayment of the mortgages which are packaged inside the bond, a stream of revenues that the investors who have bought the MBS pocket monthly.

Ginnie Mae created the first MBS to raise money to fund more affordable housing. The idea was to sell the MBS and to use the money to invest in additional affordable housing. However, the financial market saw the transformation of a group of mortgages into a new security, i.e., a bond, as a new opportunity to profit from house loans, essentially making money from a debt. In 1977,

Lew Ranieri of Salomon Brothers developed the first private residential MBS, which was backed by the mortgage providers rather than by the US government.

MBSs established a financial link between high street and Wall Street banks, making it possible for both entities to profit from it. With the lifting of the restrictions introduced after the Great Depression, local banks found themselves in a position to transform the housing loans on their books into new, very profitable financial products, which they marketed to the big investment banks for a fee. It was a very easy and profitable business that turned high street banks into brokers. Suddenly, high street bank managers and their employees, who had for decades been cautious and diligent, had a taste of how their risk-prone colleagues on Wall Street lived. And they liked it. They enjoyed the profits, the lifestyle, the power, and the sense of entitlement that spring from managing huge sums of money.

Initially, the mortgages pooled into the MBSs were low risk. But soon, banks and other private lending institutions began running out of "good mortgages" to repackage into MBSs, so high street banks aggressively marketed and sold more and more "less good" mortgages. Working with real estate brokers, they came up with the idea to use adjustable mortgages—house loans with an initial period at a very low interest rate—to lure into buying houses with mortgages people who could not afford the market rates and did not qualify for housing loans. And voilà, they created subprime mortgages. The housing market literally took off.

In his book *The Big Short,* Michael Lewis describes the web of deception and stupidity that inflated the real estate bubble as a sort of non-declared conspiracy of dunces. Real estate agents prepared mortgage applications leaving blank the sections referring to salaries and down payments for borrowers, without even bothering to check if they had a job. They suggested that buyers opt for adjustable mortgages, assuring them that before the initial period of low interest rates expired, they could refinance the mortgage and get another adjustable rate with an initial low interest rate period. Banks approved these mortgages and immediately piled them up in new MBSs which contained thousands of them, "wrapping" the subprime mortgages with the less risky ones, essentially hiding the bad mortgages inside the MBSs.

Rating agencies automatically stamped them AAA, fearing that their clients would go to their competitors if they objected and believing that the risk was sufficiently spread across the MBSs, i.e., that even if some of the "bad mortgages" defaulted, all would never fail together. The big investment banks in Wall Street bought them and sold them to investors, among them pension funds, which were not allowed to invest in mortgages, but could buy MBSs. No one read the conditions of the thousands and thousands of mortgages piled up in each MBS; nobody noticed that the bulk of them were bad loans, i.e., subprime; so nobody really paid attention to the fact that the percentage of subprime mortgages in the MBS was disproportionately high. Financial engineering was the new money mantra.

In the film *Margin Call*, a young risk assessment officer with a degree in rocket science discovers that a small movement in the market, for example, defaults in mortgages, could create losses from his investment bank's MBS portfolio bigger than the whole capitalization of the bank. When he is asked to explain how this is possible, he replies that MBSs are kept in the bank's portfolio for more than a month while the actual mortgages inside them are checked. But as often happened at the time, the MBSs were resold before these checks had been completed. Because of the speed of buying and selling, the banks and the market did not detect the percentage of highly risky loans in the MBSs. Nobody bothered to check the solidity of the mortgages because demand was strong and reselling MBSs was not a problem; on the contrary, the business was very lucrative because demand outstripped supply. As a result, at any given time banks held in their books large amounts of highly risky MBSs—financial products that were worthless and potentially lethal—without knowing it. If house mortgages started to default, the losses for most banks would be much bigger than their assets. Which is exactly what happened in 2008.[92]

Before the big crash, however, the extraordinary success of MBSs proved that financial engineering was the instrument of the future, a magic wand in the hands of the private sector to turn any debt into profits. So on the blueprint of MBSs, financial engineering was applied to produce other, similar products, such as collateralized debt obligations (CDOs). CDOs are made up of a diverse set of debts linked to assets, from corporate bonds to mortgage bonds, to bank loans to car loans to credit card loans. These loans, ranging from those considered very safe to those regarded as high risk, are bundled together in one new bond for sale to investors. The various types of debt packaged inside the CDOs are known as tranches. As in mortgage-backed securities, the percentage of risky loans wrapped together with the good ones inside the collateralized debt obligations was excessively high; however, as had happened with MBSs, they easily got AAA ratings.

And here is how, in the film *The Big Short*, chef Anthony Bourdain describes the creation of CDOs. It is Sunday afternoon and the chef is setting the menu. He has left-over fish that was ordered on Friday but it did not sell. What to do? Throw all the fish, which is no longer fresh, in the garbage and take the loss? No way the chef will do that. Instead, he creates a seafood stew. The chef has made a new dish that people order from the menu without knowing that they are eating three-day-old fish. The old fish is the risky loan and the stew is the CDO.

In the fairy tale "The Emperor's New Clothes," nobody has the courage to say that the emperor is naked, even though everybody can see that he has no clothes; in the years running up to the 2008 crash, the opposite happened: everybody believed that the housing market was rock solid when in fact it was crippled. Nobody could see the nakedness of the emperor. Lewis attributes this illusion to the herd mentality of the financial sector. Mortgage-backed securities and collateralized debt obligations spread the risk inside the market as a child spreads Nutella on a piece of toast; the certainty that absolutely everybody is involved in the business is reassuring; people believe that everyone can't be wrong. Financial engineering cemented the herd mentality because it provided the market with a new, very powerful source of wealth for the entire sector by spreading the risk of default across the entire financial industry. And in this way to feed the financial industry's insatiable greed.

Is the world of politics today suffering from the same illusion? In 2022 nobody seems to realize that the shunning of Russia, the confrontation with China, and the disinterest in the impact such policy has upon the less privileged segments of the world is suicidal. The same herd mentality that Lewis described has taken hold of Western politicians, the media, and the world's elites. Blinded by the false security of the herd, nations are convinced that they will succeed in reestablishing their supremacy and in redesigning the world order. As in 2008, in 2022 and 2023 such behavior is pure hubris.

Financial engineering institutionalized greed. Each time a new product was created, and each time it changed hands, a fat fee was applied, paid, and pocketed. MBSs, CDOs, and many other, similar products were bought and sold, repackaged into new products, and sold and bought again, over and over for a couple of decades, never ceasing to generate unimaginable sums of money through fees. It was an insane circus, where a bank sold in the morning a product that by the afternoon would be repackaged into a new one, which the same bank bought in the evening.

After the gold exchange standard collapsed, financial engineering became a source of money creation out of debt for the private sector. It replaced the classic banking multiplier. And here is the proof: before the 2008 crash, the CDO market pooling mortgages was estimated to be twenty times the actual mortgages' market. Financial engineering products used leverage as a powerful multiplier. Banks and financial institutions also used leverage to buy more MBSs, CDOs, and any other new financial instruments. They borrowed against their own assets in the repo market, which can be defined as a reservoir of liquidity or a very sophisticated short-term pawnshop for the finance sector.

Repo stands for repurchase agreement, or short-term collateralized loan. In the repo market, one financial institution borrows from another that has un-utilized short-term liquidity. Government bonds and debt obligations, e.g., MBSs or CDOs, are deposited in exchange for cash as collateral with the promise to rebuy them in a very short time at a higher price. The difference between the selling and the repurchase price is the repo rate. How big is the repo market? It is big, very big. It is estimated to be between $2 trillion and $4 trillion.[93] During the housing boom of the late 1990s and early 2000s, activity in this market literally exploded. John Mullin, of the Federal Reserve Bank of Richmond, explains: "In just four years, between December 2003 and December 2007, the asset-to-equity ratio of US broker-dealers ballooned from 24:1 to 35:1. And this balance sheet expansion relied heavily on repo borrowing."[94] Leverage had become the magic word and everybody wanted a slice of the debt-cake, so people began betting on the performance of loans. How? By creating a new synthetic product: credit default swaps (CDS). CDSs are essentially insurance contracts that protect against the risk of the default of a collateralized debt obligation, a CDO. In the late 1990s, the London office of American International Group (AIG) came up with the idea of profiting from the popularity of MBSs and CDOs. For a small fee, hedge fund managers were offered a guarantee that in the "unlikely" event of a CDO collapse, they would still receive a certain return. AIG judged that the chances of having to pay out on this insurance were slim. Why? Though a big chunk of the insured CDOs came in the form of bundled mortgages, with the lowest-rated tranches comprised of subprime loans, AIG believed that defaults on these loans would be insignificant.[95]

A small group of people, however, anticipated the bursting of the housing bubble and bought CDSs, i.e., the insurance contracts, without owning any CDOs or MBSs. In other words, they bought only the insurance against the failure of mortgages without ever owning any mortgage-backed securities or CDOs. Some have compared this move to owning theft insurance on someone else's home in which you only get paid if they get robbed. In reality what this group of people did was bet on the collapse of the housing market, and they were right. In 2008, the house of cards of financial engineering imploded, and those insurance contracts became extremely valuable; everybody caught in the crash wanted them and was willing to pay huge sums to own them.

Once again, the US banking system was on the brink of the abyss, and, once again, the world economy was heading for a great depression. Luckily, those at the helm of the monetary system remembered the lessons of 1929: instead of letting the market punish excessive leverage, the US Federal Reserve and the White House put together a rescue package. Soon the European Central Bank and the European Commission followed suit. The package was essentially open-ended: nobody really knew how big the hole in global finance was, so central banks began printing money not knowing when they could stop. This scheme is called quantitative easing.

Quantitative easing is an unusual monetary maneuver—or at least it was until 2008. Since then, it has been repeated several times. It essentially serves to inject liquidity into the economic system by distributing it to companies in the financial sector. This can happen when cutting interest rates no longer works because they are close to zero or when there is no more liquidity in the system, as happened in October of 2008 when the repo market dried up.[96] In 2008, for the first time, the money of the quantitative easing was created electronically by simply pressing a few keys on the Treasury keyboard. Money literally materialized out of thin air. Once produced, the new supply of money was deposited in the United States in the balance sheets of the Federal Reserve and in Europe in those of the European Central Bank. It took a few seconds to complete this operation. The central banks used the money to buy bonds and securities from banks and financial institutions on the brink of bankruptcy, injecting liquidity into the system. The entire process was done digitally; no cash ever moved. And the rescue package was carried on for years by pinching numbers on keyboards. The vast majority of the securities that the Fed and the ECB bought were the product of financial engineering— MBSs and CDOs—and their price was way below their nominal value. But central banks decided to purchase them above market price. In many cases, they bought securities that nobody else was willing to buy, at an arbitrary price, high enough to save the banks that were selling them.

According to the double entry principle, the money created with quantitative easing corresponds to an identical increase in public debt, so quantitative easing is not free money. The theory states that as the money gets repaid—and indeed most of it has been returned to the Federal Reserve—it should be neutralized, i.e., destroyed, and the corresponding level of the debt lowered. But none of these actions have happened. Those trillions and trillions of dollars could not be and were not burned in gigantic bonfires or buried in landfills, because they never physically existed. They remained trapped in digital figures and moved around from one balance sheet to another, and the Fed used them to purchase treasury bonds, i.e., to fund the national debt. So the digitally produced money remained in the system and increased the money supply. Since the end of the convertibility of the dollar into gold in 1971, money creation has taken place through indebtedness of the Treasury, this explains the ballooning debt of industrialized nations in the last 50 years.

At first glance it seems absurd that for decades the engine of monetary growth has been the debt and not the wealth of nations. However, considering that traditional economic theory states that the debt must be repaid with taxes, one could argue that as long as people can afford to subsidize the debt through taxation, the size of a nation's debt can be seen as an indicator of economic growth. As we shall see in the next chapter, Modern Monetary Theory rejects this interpretation and claims that any state that has monetary sovereignty does not need to collect taxes to repay the debt. It can simply print what it needs.

What is relevant at this point is that quantitative easing ended up monetizing the massive debt that the private sector had created via excessive leverage. By bailing out the financial sector, the Federal Reserve and the European Central Bank gave a monetary value to the financial engineering that produced the toxic products that had flooded the market. The reckless behavior of the private sector became a source of money creation.

The surreal conclusion is that the end of the gold exchange standard, coupled with the deregulation of the 1980s, transformed debt of all kinds into the engine of monetary growth for the state through the Federal Reserve's purchases of treasury bonds to service the national debt, and for the private sector through the securitization of retail debt, especially bad debt. Quantitative easing monetized the toxic financial engineering products in the balance sheets of banks and financial institutions. Do people know that debt has made fiat money grow? Perhaps, but most of them do not care. Since 1971, fiat money is only an act of faith. The value of the dollar, of the euro, of the pound sterling, rests upon the trust that people have in the issuer, the state.

Against this scenario, it is worth asking if trusting software that produces bitcoins as a source of money creation is indeed so absurd.

CHAPTER SIX

Modern Monetary Theory

The double-digit inflation of the 1970s took place against the emergence of a totally fiduciary system where the engine of the money supply was the national debt and the legitimacy of the currency in circulation sprang from the monopoly of the state, the issuer. These events represent a massive watershed in monetary history. For the first time in modern history, money is not anchored to any commodity but freely circulates on trust. To understand the central role that trust plays in money as a means of exchange, let's use an anecdote from Warren Mosler, considered the father of Modern Monetary Theory.[97]

> Let's assume for a moment that we are in a house where a father lives with his children. One day, he announces that the children can earn bills he produces after doing various household chores. These banknotes have no value and therefore the children have no interest in working to accumulate what they consider just pieces of paper. But when the father tells them that to eat and to continue living in the house they have to pay, say, two hundred of those bills a month, those pieces of paper become valuable and the children start doing housework to earn them.
>
> The children trust their father. They do not even consider the possibility that he would not respect the commitment he has made with them, so they do their chores for a month until the father pays them. The children are also too young

to take care of themselves or to go and live in another house. They are dependent upon their father; in other words, they have no choice.[98]

How does the parent pay their wages? It's simple: he prints the banknotes. According to Modern Monetary Theory, the father (the state) who issues the banknotes can never fail to pay the salaries of the children (the creditors). Why? Because he prints the banknotes and therefore cannot ever run out of money. In essence, nations that possess monetary sovereignty can always issue paper money to make any payments due in their currency, which is exactly what has happened in the United States since 1971.

To pay the father every month, the children must receive the compensation from him. So, first of all, the parent prints the banknotes and then uses them to pay the children a salary. In turn, the children allocate part of it to pay the father for room and board. If we consider this latter payment a tax, and the banknotes the father prints to pay the salaries an expense, the amount of notes that the parent needs to print is equivalent to the debt that he owes towards the children.

The fiscal implications of this totally fiduciary monetary system are very relevant. If before collecting the banknotes that the children pay in taxes, the father has to print and distribute them, it is clear that the state that possesses monetary sovereignty, for example the United States or the United Kingdom, does not need to collect taxes to pay for what society needs, from wages to public works. As the issuer of the banknotes, the state can simply print as much as it needs.

So why do we pay taxes? Firstly, taxes legitimize the currency in circulation and help maintain the monopoly of money in the hands of the issuing state. If, to eat and live at home with their father, the children must pay taxes exclusively with the banknotes that he prints, it is irrelevant that these are made of wastepaper; the children must earn them. It is clear at this point why cryptocurrencies represent a threat for the state; their use inside its borders erodes the monopoly of the currency of the state.

Secondly, taxation is used to manage inflation and ensure a fair redistribution of income, not to fund the national debt. Against this background, Mrs. Thatcher's statement at the 1983 Conservative Party conference about state finances was incorrect: "Let us never forget this fundamental truth: the State has no source of money other than money which people earn themselves."[99] She implied that if the state wished to spend more, it could do so only by borrowing people's savings, i.e., selling bonds or raising taxation. The state as an entity has no money; the population owns it and gives it to the state by paying taxes. In fact, the opposite is true. Thatcher's mistake was to believe that the finances of the state are identical to the finances of its citizens.[100] To prove the point, let's go to Japan.

Japan's public debt has increased for three decades and today is more than double its GDP, 274 percent at the time of writing, the highest among industrialized countries. Still, Japan has not gone bankrupt, nor does it appear to be on the verge of bankruptcy. A Japanese family in the same condition, however, would have gone bankrupt decades ago.

Japan does not go bankrupt because it has monetary sovereignty; it can print all the yen it needs to service its debt. The Japanese family, on the other hand, is a user of that same currency; to live it must spend yen, and to obtain them it must earn them. If it earns less than it spends, the family goes bust.

Let's borrow another anecdote from Mosler during an interview with Alan Kohler to prove why a country that has monetary sovereignty cannot default on a debt denominated in its currency:

MOSLER: The largest one was in the early '90s where Italian bonds were paying 12 percent and you could borrow the Lira to pay for them at 10 percent. So you just buy the 12 percent bonds, you borrow the money at 10 and you make 2 percent for doing nothing, it's just pretty easy money, right? Except, if the bonds defaulted you're going to lose everything and if the currency went down it didn't matter, you still made 2 percent in Lira, you'd just have a little bit less profit than you thought. So it wasn't a currency risk but it was just the idea that it might default. The question became, if you can come up with reasons why they won't default, this is a good trade, this is maybe the best thing we've ever seen.

And so, the first thing I realized was that governments with their own currency, historically I didn't know of any of them that ever defaulted, I didn't think there ever was such a thing . . .

KOHLER: Well, a default is said to be when bond investors take a haircut.

MOSLER: Yeah, so that never happened with US bonds in Dollars or Spanish bonds Pesetas or Greek bonds in Drachma, it never happened, nobody ever took a haircut on bonds [denominated in their own currency]. . . . The reason given was, was because they could always print the money.[101]

Mosler was right; Italy did not default. It simply printed the money required to service the debt. And the company Mosler worked for made about $10 billion worth of Italian liras, without making any payment up front, as they borrowed all the liras needed to purchase the bonds.

In 2008, as described in the previous chapter, the United States created out of thin air trillions and trillions of dollars by tapping on the keyboard of the Treasury, and it used them to bail out the financial system without generating any inflation. Let's see how these funds were accounted for using the double entry scheme. For the state they were an expense which increased the public debt. However, because the Federal Reserve bought bonds and securities from financial institutions with the money, the trillions of dollars electronically printed showed up in the security accounts of the Federal Reserve as assets. In the budgets of banks and financial institutions on the verge of bankruptcy, those dollars were recorded as credits produced by the sale of bonds and securities; they were money, real money, that was spent to avoid bankruptcy. The higher deficit in the state finances became an asset in the private sector and, in the balance sheet of the Federal Reserve, it corresponded to an increase in the assets of the securities accounts.

Printing trillions of dollars not only avoided the collapse of the economic system, it also produced new wealth which was injected into the economy. All of this happened without inflation rising a single digit because the debt was denominated in dollars and people had faith in the issuer, the United States.

The public debt is like an accordion: it opens and closes depending upon the notes we want to play. When the economy grows too fast and prices start to increase, it is time to reduce it. There are various ways to shrink the public debt, for example, by raising taxes. Increasing taxes reduces the amount of money households and businesses have at their disposal. It forces them to spend less and in doing so it eases the pressure on prices. When the economy contracts, as in 2008, the opposite is needed and money is printed.

Since the days of President Bill Clinton, the United States has pursued this policy, although officially no president has ever admitted to it. Even Mario Draghi in 2011, when he was head of the European Central Bank, applied these principles, and the ECB electronically produced trillions of euros.[102] It distributed them within the eurozone to fight the contraction of the economy that the sovereign debt crisis was causing. This process was repeated in 2020 when, to fight the economic consequences of the pandemic, governments printed money which they distributed to employers and employees. This process is called monetization of the debt, that is, the transformation of debt into money. The monetization of the debt, i.e., the electronic production of money to meet societies' needs, is an example of the Present Future and it has been happening for a long time.

Over the last two decades, central banks, including the ECB, have bought bonds with money produced electronically out of thin air. Many of these bonds live in the central bank's balance sheets for decades; those not repaid by the issuer get renewed when they mature and slowly, year after year, the maturities lengthen; at a certain stage these bonds are moved to the bottom of the balance sheets, then they are reaggregated, renamed, until over time they disappear from the balance sheets. All this is possible because this money does not physically exist and has never existed.

Modern Monetary Theory is considered an unorthodox, revolutionary theory, and many economists regard it as a nonsense doctrine. However, it is not really a theory but the product of the observation of the policies and behaviors applied to the monetary system since the collapse of the gold exchange standard. And because of that, it amounts to a taste of the Present Future: a modern explanation of money creation based upon the analysis of key changes in society, changes which occurred with the emergence of fiduciary money and the digitization of monetary flows. In recent years technology, not politics or economics, has been the driving force of change in monetary policy. This explains why American senators who are considered progressive—Bernie Sanders, for example—have employed MMT supporters such as Stephanie Kelton to analyze and explain such change to Congress, even if never publicly admitting that they believe in MMT.[103]

For states in crisis like modern democracies, politically weak nations run by politicians who are losing the trust of the population, the admission of the immateriality of money intrinsic in modern monetary policy, and of the true role of taxation, appears extremely dangerous. It erodes the belief that behind each currency there is wealth, tangible wealth, and threatens the monetary monopoly of the state, both of which are regarded as pillars of the modern state. Against this background, the serious menace that cryptocurrencies, and in particular bitcoin, pose to the state is not the mystery surrounding Satoshi Nakamoto, nor the leap of faith to let software be in charge of money creation, nor the difficulty in taxing a globalized digital currency. It is the realization that cryptocurrencies offer an alternative to national currencies, allowing people to bypass and even cut off the state from society. This is not necessarily bad. There are times in which the speed and agility of movement of cryptocurrencies in cyberspace, away from the traditional state channels, is highly positive, as Alex Gladstein, chief strategy officer at the Human Rights Foundation, explained at the outbreak of the war in Ukraine: "In Ukraine right now, you can download a bitcoin wallet open source—totally unconnected from your ID—and you can generate an address via a QR code or an alphanumeric string. . . . You can paste that to me, I can send you $1,000, and it goes through in a few minutes."[104] In February 2022, within a few hours of the invasion of Ukraine the equivalent of $50 million in cryptocurrency reached Kiev. The government used the money to buy bulletproof vests, helmets, and other items to distribute to civilians. The traditional banking system could not have performed better.

However, the state executes many important tasks for society, and trust in the state as the issuer of money derives from the management of such tasks by its institutions, from the courts to the stock exchange, from schools to town halls. Just as the children know that the father will use the bills they pay in taxes to look after them, so the citizens believe that the state uses their taxes to manage public affairs, and they trust that the state knows better than anybody else how to carry out these tasks. But what happens when the state becomes the enemy of the people, as has happened in 2022 in Russia and in 1938 in Germany? Three-quarters of a century ago, German Jews had to leave behind their assets and depart with nothing. Today, Ukrainians and Russians fleeing the regime of Moscow can carry in their heads the passwords of their crypto wallets and access them once they have reached safety. Perhaps fearing an occupation, in February 2022 the Ukrainian parliament passed a law legalizing cryptocurrency. According to the blockchain research company Chainalysis, before the invasion, Ukraine ranked fourth in the world in terms of crypto adoption; being able to freely move cryptocurrencies away from the danger of an invading army became very useful.[105]

As discussed in previous chapters, the legitimacy of bitcoin rests on blockchains, the system of transparency and security shared by the community. Blockchain is a technology, not an authority, and, unlike the modern state, it does not guarantee law and order or national security. The lack of this type of authority makes cryptocurrencies, including those like bitcoin linked to blockchain technology, appear highly risky and potentially desta-bilizing. For example, people worry that no mechanism can stop their value from plummeting if a market panic occurs, as the stop-losses built into the stock market have done on numerous occasions.[106] In May 2022 people had a taste of the magnitude of losses that a crypto panic could unleash. As Gillian Tett wrote in the *Financial Times*, "Most notably, Terra and Luna, the two so-called 'algorithmic stable coins,' imploded, creating $50 billion of losses in three days."[107] What people do not realize is that as long as cryptocurrencies are traded as financial instruments by financial institutions and by individuals motivated by greed, they pose a risk to society exactly as the subprime mortgages did. The abuse and manipulation of any financial product through financial engineering becomes a risk when the leverage is excessive. The issue is not the cryptocurrency, the issue is the lack of controls and regulation of an extremely complex system.

In May 2022 the European Central Bank showed concern about these issues. "Investors have been able to handle the 1.3 trillion euro fall in the market capitalization of unbacked cryptoassets since November 2021 without any financial stability risks being incurred," the ECB said to the *Financial Times*. "However," they continued, "at this rate, a point will be reached where unbacked cryptoassets represent a risk to financial stability."[108] Just a few months later FTX, one of the biggest crypto exchanges, collapsed exactly because the crypto assets it had created, FTX tokens, were totally unbacked, nothing more than Disney dollars. It is worth spending a few words about it. In recent years, platforms like Binance and FTX, which offer a wide array of complex financial products, have been instrumental to the growth of the crypto market. According to data collected by The Block,[109] which reports news in major cryptocurrencies, in April 2022 the world's biggest crypto exchanges processed the equivalent of over $700 billion in spot trading and $1.1 trillion in bitcoins. The ECB said that at times trading in cryptoassets even surpassed the volume of exchanges in the New York Stock Exchange.[110] However, much more relevant information that crypto data does not show is who is trading in cryptoassets—individuals or financial institutions—and what companies like FTX do with them.

The spectacular collapse of FTX sheds some light on crypto frauds at a much higher level than OneCoin. The regulatory and accountancy gray area in which crypto exists makes it possible for people like Ruja Ignatova and Sam Bankman-Fried, the man who founded FTX, to fool people, projecting spectacular earnings. The latter charmed the media, the rich and famous, and the politicians with the speed with which he had produced immense wealth. The richest billionaire below thirty was even celebrated as the new Steve Jobs, a true innovator. It was only after Binance, his rival and investor, decided to liquidate its position that the house of cards came down.

FTX converted cash deposited by investors and clients into tokens issued by the company and used the cash to speculate on the crypto market using its hedge fund arm, Alameda. But business had not been good during the crypto winter of 2022, and losses had to be covered by issuing additional tokens, which were not backed by any assets. When Binance asked for its original investment back, it was not handed cash but $2 billion worth of tokens. At that point people became suspicious and started withdrawing funds from the platform until FTX had to admit that it did not have sufficient cash. At the time of writing the "disappeared cash" is believed to be in the tens of billions of dollars.

The Cypherpunks and Nakamoto dreamed of a world in which financial literacy was universal, where people could take charge of their wealth and manage it, a world with a stable currency, no longer plagued by financial storms. To exist, this world has to be without greed. It is highly unlikely that such a world will ever be possible. In its absence, regulation can protect people against crypto fraudsters. Until this happens, the crypto universe is highly risky. According to the European Central Bank, many international and eurozone banks offer services in crypto assets to institutional investors. For example, since 2021, German institutional investment funds are allowed to put up to one-fifth of their holdings in crypto assets.[III] On behalf of their clients, these banks trade and clear regulated crypto derivatives even if they do not hold crypto assets. Sound familiar? This is the crypto version of the credit default swaps.

On the positive side, crypto can be a unique, powerful instrument in the hands of ordinary people. As shown during the invasion of Ukraine, it is undeniable that where governments are in chaos, when countries are at war, it's difficult to rely on traditional banks, and there is fear of surveillance. In these circumstances, a relatively anonymous system where no government is involved becomes appealing. Gold and cash do not offer these advantages.

Can we glimpse a future where the physical banknote will no longer exist and where the monopoly of the community replaces the monopoly of the state? A democratic monetary system that arises from an act of faith towards the members of a society, the users of the currency? After all, this was the dream of the Cypherpunks. Are individuals in society sufficiently mature both to accept the immaterial nature of money and to handle the responsibility of its creators' replacing the authority of the nation state? The European Union is racing to finalize legislation, called markets in crypto assets, to prevent the latter scenario.[112] According to the ECB, however, it will not come into force until 2024. How will the crypto world react?

Whatever happens, the digitization of money is a phenomenon that is here to stay, and governments must tackle the fact that the degree of control they retain upon money created electronically is much less than the control they have exercised for centuries upon paper money. To understand this concept, let's find out what has happened to the trillions of dollars of the 2008 bailout.

CHAPTER SEVEN

The Rise of the Techtitans

In 2007, the Canadian-born high tech entrepreneur Garrett Camp sells his start-up StumbleUpon to eBay for over $75 million.[113] StumbleUpon is a discovery and advertisement engine that pushes web content recommendations to its users. In 2007, the company had relocated to the Bay Area, with Camp setting up new offices in SoMa, San Francisco. Without the pressure of ownership, Camp has time to relax, "enjoy his millions," and go clubbing. However, in the early hours of the morning, he finds it increasingly frustrating to get a cab. In 2008, the taxi system in San Francisco, as in most major US cities, is highly regulated, and supply and demand are often out of sync because the former is inelastic while the latter fluctuates due to the ups and downs of business and economic—and clubbing—cycles.

While Garrett Camp is confronted with the inefficiency of the private transportation system in San Francisco, in New York, Bear Stearns, one of Wall Street's financial giants, battles against the early signs of what will become the subprime crisis. The universe of high tech and the world of high finance could not be further apart. The reasons are many: the former is well insulated from the forthcoming financial meltdown, which has its epicenter in the real estate market, while the latter is deeply enmeshed in it. In addition, at the beginning of the new millennium, the tech industry experienced its own financial bust, the dot-com crisis: a hard lesson to digest, which has left the entire sector wiser and less risk prone. As a result, unlike the financial sector, tech companies are not highly leveraged.

Of course, Camp's problem is infinitely less serious than Bear Stearns's, and it is easier to solve. But in 2008, the two industries—tech and finance—which had been on parallel but divergent paths, are about to start to travel hand in hand.

One evening Camp has an idea: instead of taxi cabs, he'll try using black cars. Black cars are part of the rental car service industry, and, like the New York limousine or the UK minicab services, they are used by companies and corporations to transport their top management. Black car services are regulated by rental contracts between the parties, not by the strict municipal or national license systems that apply to taxis. Because of that, black car drivers cannot pick up passengers on the street and often sit idle behind the wheel waiting for their next scheduled customer. To earn extra money, some of them drive to train stations and airports and ask people if they need a ride. Potential passengers, however, tend not to use them—since they are unregulated, people are afraid of being overcharged or even robbed. Camp is not bothered by these issues, so he gathers the phone numbers of several black car drivers, and in the early hours of the morning, before leaving a club, he calls one number after the other until someone answers and agrees to give him a ride.

In 2008, Camp also spends time watching James Bond films. After the intense years spent building up StumbleUpon, he feels that he's earned the right to chill out, and why not? He is young and behaves accordingly. But, like many other successful entrepreneurs in the high tech industry, he has a serial start-up mentality, and with many millions of dollars at his disposal, he cannot stop thinking about what his next big project will be. One day, while watching *Casino Royale*, he is struck by a scene where 007 gets his car to self-drive to him using his smart phone. Bond is guiding the car on an app which shows its position and movements on a map in real time. Astonishingly, this is no longer just one of Bond's science fiction gadgets, and Camp knows this because he is very familiar with technological innovation, i.e., the 2008 iPhone with the 3G map application. The idea to run a digitized limo service that people can access on their smart phones begins to take shape in his mind.

What triggers this mental process? And what is Camp's true motivation? To develop a profitable new transportation system that will improve the transportation industry in San Francisco and, possibly, beyond, for the benefit of all? Or is the Canadian high tech millionaire solely motivated by the desire to build another start-up, similar to StumbleUpon, that will make him and his future sponsors even richer? The answer may not be what you think.

A few months later, in January 2009, Garrett Camp attends LeWeb, an annual tech conference in Paris, with a group of entrepreneur friends. Among them is Travis Kalanick. Unlike Camp, Kalanick experienced several serious setbacks before securing the sale of his second start-up, a peer-to-peer file sharing company called Red Swoosh, to Akamai Technologies for $19 million.[114] Kalanick and Camp spend most of their time in Paris discussing the idea of a fully digitalized cab company that people could access through their smart phones. As in San Francisco, searching for cabs in Paris in the early hours of the morning proves to be extremely frustrating. It is at this point that the two realize not only that there is a gap in the private transportation system everywhere, an imbalance between supply and demand, but that they can profit from removing it. If by applying their knowledge of technology they can create an app capable of making these structural discrepancies disappear, their idea could be replicated globally. Did they envision right away how the app would impact the transportation industry and the people, particularly drivers, working in it? Not really, at least not at first. At this early stage their focus was on making it work.

Back in San Francisco, Kalanick convinces Camp that the best model would be not to purchase cars and build a digitalized limo-sharing service but to rent vehicles from ordinary people.[115]

The formula of what will become UberCab begins to take shape, merging the new mobile app mapping technology with the newly born sharing economy.

Interestingly, raising money from investors proves easy, and in 2010, less than two years after the 2008 financial meltdown, Uber launches its first ride after First Round Capital, a venture capital firm that specializes in providing funding to technology companies, raises $1.25 million in seed money from other venture capitalists and entrepreneurs operating in the tech industry.[116]

Uber was not the only high tech company raising money in the aftermath of the financial crisis. In 2009, Yahoo veterans Jan Koum and Brian Acton created the encrypted messaging app WhatsApp. The idea behind it was to offer people a way to message each other quickly around the world. That same year, college friends Iqram Magdon-Ismail and Andrew Kortina launched the digital payment app Venmo to allow peers to exchange cash digitally, without transfer fees. In 2010, the engineers Kevin Systrom and Mike Krieger created Instagram, a form of social media centered around images and videos.[117]

After 2008, high tech start-ups could rely upon a wealth of investors and venture capitalists eager to invest in the new sector. In 2009, the venture capitalist Bill Maris founded GV (formerly Google Ventures), which functions as the venture capital arm of Alphabet Inc. GV invested in several start-ups, all launched during or directly after the 2008 crash, including Uber, Slack, and Cloudera. In 2009, the American venture capital firm Sequoia Capital, founded in 1972 and headquartered in Menlo Park, unveiled its "scout" program, a network that offers investors the opportunity to participate in promising early-stage start-ups in the tech industry.[118] In the following years, other venture capital firms replicated Sequoia's scout program.

Data from Crunchbase, a platform of business information about private and public companies, confirms that, after the 2008 crash, seed money for the tech industry was the least impacted of all early-stage rounds of financing in all sectors. While in other industries, investment dried up due to the financial crisis, in the tech industry, seed dollars grew year-on-year from then onward. The slowest growth came in 2009, the post-crash year, with a 29 percent increase. In 2010, 2011, and 2012, seed money for the tech industry registered more than a 50 percent year-on-year rate of growth.[119]

From the end of 2008 for several years, therefore, the tech business cycle moved in the opposite direction from the financial cycle and from the economy as a whole, to the point where high tech companies' share valuations climbed to the top of the stock indexes and led the stock market's astonishing recovery—in 2021, during the coronavirus pandemic, Apple, Facebook, Google (renamed Alphabet), Amazon, and Microsoft were among the top ten companies of the Standard and Poor's 500 index.

One could guess the main reason: major innovation in technology, such as the cloud upon which Amazon web services were built in 2006,[120] coupled with innovation in communication via mobile systems, e.g., the iPhone, which was launched in 2007. Tech innovation fostered novel business opportunities, which appealed to investors who at the time were deeply scared by the financial meltdown, investors in search of higher returns in the new era of near-zero interest rates. Thanks to quantitative easing, liquidity was not an impediment. The financial sector had sufficient funds coming from the bailout to go after new high-earning ventures, and the tech industry was one of the few that offered them. Good returns registered from the previous decade—all springing from technological changes, from wireless broadband to more versatile software development tools—further encouraged investment in the tech industry. Finally, the field of technological innovations was sufficiently wide—from machine learning and artificial intelligence to device miniaturization, from cryptocurrency to autonomous vehicles—for investors to pick and choose where to place their money.

Because of all these factors, after the collapse of Lehman Brothers, not only private investors and venture capitalists but also institutional investors such as pension fund managers, insurance companies, speculators, hedge funds, and even banks began buying shares of established tech companies, e.g., Google, Amazon, and Microsoft, and by the end of 2009 a large portion of the bailout funds, money that the US Treasury was printing electronically month after month, ostensibly to stave off bankruptcies for millions of American home-owners and small businesses, was steadily flowing towards Silicon Valley and Seattle.

From a pure balance sheet perspective, funding the high tech industry was a good move for high finance, one that allowed it a few years later to repay a big chunk of the money it had received from the bailout. In less than a decade, a niche industry, i.e., the high tech sector, became the most profitable industry in modern times. Companies like Apple and Microsoft expanded exponen-tially, becoming far richer and even more powerful than financial enterprises, enjoying revenues from what I estimate to be thirty to seventy times higher than those generated in any other sector or industry, and investors got huge returns as a result. In the case of the Uber IPO in 2019, just ten years after Camp and Kalanick met in Paris, Uber saw its share value jump by a factor of five thou-sand, which made Uber one of the best investments ever.

Ironically, it was the tech industry, the sector the Cypherpunks, the archenemies of the state, had helped to create, that benefitted the most from post-2008 monetary government incentives. And, paradoxically, it was this industry that generated money for the financial sector to repay the bailout and that kept the profits flowing on Wall Street. Which answers the question formulated at the end of the previous chapter: where have the trillions and trillions of dollars the Federal Reserve printed gone?

The bailout money, however, even if instrumental to the rise of the new tech industry, was not the only critical factor injecting technological innovation into our daily lives. The time gap between innovations the tech companies implement and the laws that would regulate them has also played a major role in the global growth of companies like Airbnb, Google, and Uber. It creates a gray area, unreachable by the law, where tech companies operate freely, redesigning labor protocols and privacy instruments and payment protocols to their own advantage. Uber's kill switch is a stellar example of this phenomenon. Here is how the *Guardian* investigation "the Uber files" describes it:

> . . . Uber developed sophisticated methods to thwart law enforcement. One was known internally at Uber as a "kill switch." When an Uber office was raided, executives at the company frantically sent out instructions to IT staff to cut off access to the company's main data systems, preventing authorities from gathering evidence.
>
> The leaked files suggest the technique, signed off by Uber's lawyers, was deployed at least 12 times during raids in France, the Netherlands, Belgium, India, Hungary, and Romania.[121]

Far from encouraging an equitable distribution of wealth, the tech industry compounded inequalities. And it did this intentionally, because to a certain degree, the greed that had characterized the financial sector leading into the financial crisis did not die; rather, it emerged, scarred, and produced a cross-pollination between Wall Street and Silicon Valley. High finance shaped the ethos of the new sector according to its paramount principle: greed. It groomed the tech industry by exporting and facilitating the migration of the "correct" human capital: professionals trained inside its deal rooms and favorite law firms and leading business schools to high tech companies.

High finance gave lip service to the mission of improving the world within a relaxing work environment—free yoga at lunch time and casual clothes—and gave high tech companies the wherewithal to attract young professionals by dangling checks and promising bonuses as fat as those offered by their Wall Street mentors. In 2017, the median base salary of a new graduate from Harvard Business School who worked in finance was $125,000 with a $50,000 signing bonus. In Silicon Valley, the same individual earned $120,000 and a $30,000 signing bonus.

In 2008, 20 percent of graduates were employed in finance and 12 percent in the tech industry. In 2018, 13 percent of MBAs were employed in finance and 17 percent in the tech sector.[122] In 2020, the median income of Google employees was $200,000.[123] In exchange for such high salaries, employees had to remain silent about their employer's unethical and unlawful business practices.

During a decade of astonishing growth, the tech industry was also able to replicate what Wall Street had done in the 1980s and 1990s, before the 2008 crash, i.e., to project a powerfully attractive and falsely positive image of itself. How can we forget films like *Working Girl*? In reality, working conditions in the tech sector were and still are as harsh as in finance, and discrimination and sexual harassment was and still is rampant, as proven by a 2022 investigative report in *Rolling Stone* on Tesla. The report unveiled Tesla's culture of sexual harassment of women and of racial discrimination in its factories. The article stressed an important factor in corporate America: corporate culture comes from the top and the ethos of the men—they are almost always men—who run the companies trickles down to the employees. "Elon Musk is Tesla and Tesla is Elon Musk," writes the author.[124]

Musk's love life is well known. His collection of lovers appears as female scalps that he wears proudly as the chief alpha male warrior of a high tech tribe. His womanizer employees, who worship Musk because he is Tesla and Tesla is him, mimic his behavior, knowing that no punishment will be forthcoming because for the alpha male chasing women is a must. Reading the accusations that women have made against Tesla workers —blue- and white-collar alike—one cannot avoid thinking that inside the factories the female body is perceived as prey and that each hunting victory needs to be added to someone's scalp belt.

Another myth that the high tech industry successfully sold to customers is the creation of the sharing economy, the economy of the people, which has been presented as an empowerment of people through the merging of producers and consumers—exactly how Uber has marketed its economic model. However, the flip side of the sharing economy is what is commonly known as the gig economy, i.e., "a labor market characterized by the prevalence of short-term contracts or freelance work as opposed to permanent jobs,"[125] without benefits or the protection of national contracts. Here's a definition provided by the UK government: "The gig economy involves the exchange of labor for money between individuals or companies via digital platforms that actively facilitate matching between providers and customers, on a short-term and payment by task basis."[126] Indeed, Uber presents itself as a digital broker, which allows for matching between providers and consumers; for this service, the company charges a fee. According to this structure, drivers are self-employed; they are not Uber's employees, and therefore the company does not have to provide them with benefits, paid vacations, overtime pay, sick leave, or health insurance. Using this argument, Uber avoided the usual obligations companies have to their employees. But as we shall see, Uber did at the same time treat drivers as its own employees.

In the aftermath of the greatest financial and economic crisis since the Great Depression, consumers bought into the myths and welcomed the gig economy model. And why not? It appeared to lower the costs of services, to simplify accessibility, and to increase people's earning potential. Nobody envisaged the negative consequences for the labor market, i.e., the return of sweat labor, a feature of the Victorian area when people worked hard and in poor conditions for low pay to make goods, for which they were often paid by the piece. In other words they earned less if they worked more slowly, and they earned nothing at all when they were too old or sick to work, a bonanza for employers. People did not anticipate the hardening of the rental market that Airbnb would bring about, either, nor did they foresee that big investors would corner the short-term rental market by purchasing apartment buildings and allocating them to recreational and holiday rentals.

But high tech investors, studying the hard data, did foresee the benefits that a significant drop in labor costs would produce for their return on investment. For them the high tech reformulation of the capitalist equation to the advantage of capital and to the detriment of labor was an opportunity not to be missed. In the smoke and mirrors business environment created by technological innovation, at first people were easily fooled and clamored to join the new industry, sometimes influenced by young, unconventional recruiters. Again, Uber's rise to power offers an example of this phenomenon.

Uber's strategy to penetrate a market has been to fly a small team, known as "launchers," and hire its first local employee whose job is to find drivers and recruit riders. In London, a young Scottish former banker, Richard Howard, became Uber's first UK employee. Howard's job was not an easy one. As Sam Knight reported for the *Guardian*, London "was already served by a formidable private transport market, with one of the world's most recognizable taxi fleets—the black cabs—and a fragmented scene of some three thousand licensed 'private hire' operators." To secure drivers Howard gave everybody incentives: an iPhone and a twenty-five British pounds-per-hour guaranteed rate on the Uber app, a security they did not have with the other companies. The plan was to have Uber working in time for the 2012 Olympics and to project an image of plenty, to have cars showing up at every corner on the Uber app.

By autumn 2011, London Uber had around one hundred drivers on the books and Howard was given a weekly "burnable allowance" of £50,000 to "recruit more drivers to the platform." The money went to offer free rides to customers and bonuses to drivers. Was Uber making money? No, but it had plenty of funds available to pursue its launch strategy. Why? Because Uber had plenty of investors who believed in its model. And their faith was cemented in the belief that the gig economy had created among consumers and providers, a sort of atmosphere of empowerment; people really liked the idea. Uber's algorithm offered the illusion to the parties involved that it was a good deal for all of them, for the drivers and the riders alike. But like any illusion, the real deal was not so sweet.

Six months after the Olympics, Knight explains, "Uber began to replace the guaranteed hourly rate with pay by commission, but the money for drivers held up." Then the company flooded the market with new drivers and began cornering the market.

By 2014, two years after launching UberX in London, the number of private hire vehicles had jumped sharply—up thirteen thousand or 25 percent. At that stage, in August of 2014, Uber began cutting prices. In December of the same year, the average hourly rate for drivers had plummeted to £7 per hour. To maintain their earnings, drivers had to perform more rides, but they also had to work in a more competitive market. "During the winter of 2012," Knight explains, "there were five thousand active riders in London," but three years later there were 1.7 million—"around half the number of people who take the Tube each day."

The Uber algorithm manages competition among drivers. Naturally, it has been designed to achieve the maximum efficiency which corresponds to the maximum profits—Uber's fees range from 20 to 25 percent of the fare paid by the customer. And here is how it works:

A typical taxi spends between one-third and half of its shift idle. Place that vehicle on a ride-hailing platform, though—in a buoyant, busy market with the smartest vehicle-dispatching algorithms known to man—and that dead time will rapidly diminish, meaning it can pick up more jobs.

In three years, Uber drivers in New York have seen their idle time on the platform almost halve: from 36 minutes per hour, to 20.[127]

The aim of the algorithm is to achieve what Uber defines as "perpetual trip," i.e., drivers in a perpetual chain of pickups and drop-offs. In 2016 in London, drivers had fifteen seconds to accept or reject a job. If they refused three rides in a row, the algorithm logged them out of the app for ten minutes. Drivers who canceled too many jobs from Heathrow Airport were logged out for four weeks from airport service. The Uber app punished the less efficient drivers even if technically they were self-employed individuals, free to decide how to allocate their time and to accept or reject a ride. The algorithm also ignores drivers' needs to rest, to eat, and to go to the bathroom during their shift because it is designed by a machine and is not sensible to basic human necessities. And Uber seems ok with that.

This is what a London Uber driver, Ruman Miah, says about Uber: "I guarantee you one thing . . . Uber don't see drivers as humans. I don't care what they tell you."[128] In 2021, the UK Supreme Court ruled that Uber drivers must be treated as workers rather than self-employed independent contractors, a victory springing from a court case launched in 2016 by a group of Uber drivers against the company.[129] It had taken a decade for the law to catch up with the technology. That same year at Google, employees formed a union following increasing demands for policy overhauls on pay, sexual harassment, and ethics.

Following in the footsteps of high finance, the Techtitans had long resisted any efforts to organize their largely white-collar workforce. They had fired those who had attempted to challenge this approach and used the high salaries they paid to discourage criticism.[130] As a result, fewer than 1 percent of Google employees joined the union, which made it a "minority union," which means that it did not have the power to force the company into collective bargaining over pay and benefits. Yet this limitation was irrelevant because salaries were already very generous. The wider scope of the union was to examine and expose Google's role in society and help reshape the company's culture, not to get better pay. In addition to sexual harassment and racism, many employees were concerned about issues such as selling technology to US border agents and the military and being involved in human rights violations. In an interview with NPR, Ross LaJeunesse, a former Google executive, shed some light on this last issue:

> Until 2019, LaJeunesse was the global head of the company's international relations. He says he was forced out of Google for raising objections[131] about working with the governments of China and Saudi Arabia, saying such business ventures would make the company "complicit in human rights violations."
>
> Google disputed his firing was retaliatory, claiming LaJeunesse lost his job due to company reorganization.[132]

Together with the ethos, high finance also influenced the market structure of the infant tech industry in its preferred shape: the oligopoly. This was made possible through acquisitions that allowed a handful of companies to gather all the new ideas to themselves and to block any competitors. This strategy proved extremely profitable, not only for the tech companies but for their investors, as shown by data on the top ten most expensive tech acquisitions collected by *Acquired*, a popular podcast on the tech industry.[133] In 2006, before the financial crisis, Google bought YouTube for $1.65 billion.[134] In 2019, You-Tube's market capitalization was estimated at $86.2 billion, fifty times the initial investment, which is equivalent to an absolute dollar return of $84.5 billion.[135] In 2012, Facebook acquired Instagram for $1 billion.[136] In 2019, Instagram's estimated market capitalization was $153 billion, which corresponds to an absolute dollar return of $152 billion.[137] One could say that these figures prove that the modern equivalent of the town square, our public space where we inform each other of the news of the day and feel a sense of community, has been sold off for some beads and a few pieces of silver.

The progressive digitization of the planet coupled with the fast pace of technological innovation inflated the cost of acquisitions but did not stop them. In 2016, buying WhatsApp required more than $19 billion, which Facebook paid without batting an eye.[138] Both investors and companies had plenty of money to spend thanks to the astonishing profits generated by the first rounds of acquisitions. And their bets paid off—but only for the richest few of the world's population, a tiny percentage, not for the rest of us, the people that actually use Facebook and WhatsApp; we are not the owners of the "free" apps, we are instead the owned, the product, whose eyeballs and time are what create value for the actual owners.

Acquisitions were and are still regarded as a must in an industry that depends upon extraordinarily fast-paced technological advances and inventions. To survive requires a company to always be ahead of the innovation curve, and acquisitions allow the established companies to maintain their strong oligopolistic position. Against this background, it is easy to understand why the emergence of the tech industry has produced a generation of serial entrepreneurs.

People like Garrett Camp with StumbleUpon, who managed to penetrate the industry but could not compete with the big corporations, are constantly eager to chase after and implement the next project. Like experienced surfers, riding the technological waves on the shores of progress, they do business while waiting for the big one, the wave that will push them up to the Olympus of the Techtitans, where people like Jeff Bezos, Larry Page, Elon Musk, and Mark Zuckerberg sit. In 2010, Camp and Kalanick managed to catch such a wave.

The picture that emerges is of a unique industry: while serial entrepreneurs produce a constant stream of new ideas, the big Techtitans are permanently on the lookout to buy the best ones, secondarily to improve their own businesses, but primarily to prevent any competition. An illuminating example of these two-pronged strategies comes from the construction of Google Maps.

In 2003, Bret Taylor, a young product manager at Google, was working on a new feature, which he named "Google by location." The idea was to enter searches into Google by location, but Google did not have a map system to support the feature, so his idea appeared useless. However, Google had been interested in location technology for a while. For example, it was aware that AOL had purchased MapQuest, at the time the leading internet mapping system, and that Yahoo! had Yahoo! Maps. These internet maps were static and could be used only on desktop computers, but Google management was convinced that it was only a question of time before a major technological breakthrough in spatial digitization would make them interactive and applicable to the web. Google needed to compete in this field.

It was at this point, in the spring of 2004, just a few months before the Google IPO, that Sequoia Capital, which had invested in Google but also in Yahoo!, introduced Google's cofounder Larry Page to the founders of Where 2 Technologies, an Australian start-up.[139] The timing could not have been worse, Google was busy preparing for the IPO and did not want to be involved in acquisitions. However, Page agreed to a meeting with the four engineers, Lars and Jens Eilstrup Rasmussen, Noel Gordon, and Stephen Ma.[140]

Where 2 Technologies had developed a new system of mapping by assembling or stitching together dynamic tiles, where each tile constituted a small section of the map. Whichever way one looked at it, the aggregate view of all the mini tiles made up the map. This sort of collage made it possible to move the map around, to zoom in as well as to move and see different tiles. Larry Page liked the concept, but he was not interested in a desktop map. He wanted a web map. The founders of Where 2 Technologies agreed to go back to the drawing board and in a few months came up with the answer: the spatial programming language which they had developed for the map, based on C++, could be applied to an interactive online mapping system.[141] In October 2004, two months after the Google IPO, Google bought Where 2 Technologies and financed the C++ application to the web, from which Google Maps would be born.

The true innovation of Where 2 Technologies' map rests on the fact that, by making it big, zoomable, and searchable, the map could become a platform for other revenue-generating services, e.g., searching for particular shops in a given area, which is exactly what has happened. Google had the money and the tools to transform this technological innovation into a group of very useful and manageable apps: in October of the same year, it had bought Keyhole, whose technology allowed it to view geospatial data.[142] Keyhole made a desktop software called Earth-Viewer, which would become Google Earth. That same year, Google also acquired ZipDash, a company that analyzed traffic in real time. Both were incorporated into Google Maps.[143]

Google also knew how to market its new product. The launch of Google Maps took place in February 2005. In September of the same year, immediately after the devastation caused by Hurricane Katrina, Google Maps offered an interactive map of the areas affected by flooding. It was a huge success that helped Google Maps become the world's most popular space navigation application.[144]

In November 2007, Google Maps for Mobile 2.0 was released and it was featured in the first iPhone.[145] In 2008, when Garrett Camp began conceptualizing Uber, James Bond was driving his Aston Martin remotely using the features of the 3G map application on the 2008 iPhone.

By 2007, Google Maps had literally cornered the global market and had become the leading provider of digital maps, but it was still dependent on mapping data from other providers and satellite companies. The two largest were Tele Atlas and Navteq. The latter was acquired by Nokia and the former by TomTom, a competitor of Google Maps. At this point, it became apparent to the management of Google that it needed to produce and rely upon its own data and that, because it lacked the expertise and infrastructure to achieve such a goal in-house, it was imperative to acquire them from someone else: VuTool.

When Google bought VuTool in 2007, it was an embryo of a start-up constituted mostly of PhD students at Stanford led by Professor Sebastian Thrun, director of the Stanford AI lab. VuTool was a spin-off of the research technology project for autonomous vehicles known as the DARPA Grand Challenge.[146] One of the components of the challenge was to drive around the streets of America with big cameras mounted on top of the cars which took pictures of everything. The data was going to be incredibly useful for the future of navigation for autonomous vehicles.

VuTool's founders began by driving around mapping the areas in and around Stanford, which explains why TechCrunch defined it as:

> . . . "Google Earth" from the ground level. It is being created the hard way—a battalion of cars are traveling around major US cities and taking pictures at ground level, with 6 degrees of rotation. The company calls the experience "street level immersive imagery." Images are captured from

every possible angle—the default view is as if you are in the driver's seat.[147]

Google bought VuTool and turbocharged the project, funding cars everywhere to map the whole country. The project became known as Google Street View and when it was completed Google did not need to buy Tele Atlas and Navteq data anymore. It had its own.

CHAPTER EIGHT

The End of the Nation State

In 2013, Google learned that both Facebook and Apple wanted to buy Waze, an Israeli digital map service, and decided to outbid them by offering a whopping $966 million. The price, well above what Facebook and Apple were prepared to pay, set a record for the Israeli computer industry, and the employees of Waze received an average of $1.2 million each.[148] Google offered such a large amount of money to make sure it would secure the deal. Why did Google want to buy Waze so badly that it was willing to overpay for the acquisition?

Waze is a complementary app to Google Maps: it offers drivers less busy routes in real time. It is also very similar to ZipDash, which Google bought in 2004. Together with Keyhole and Where 2 Technologies, they became the building blocks of Google Earth and Google Maps. However, Google did not need to purchase Waze to improve its digital map; it could have easily designed its own system, identical to or even better than Waze, using the technology it already owned. Google bought Waze because it did not want the Israeli company to fall into the hands of Facebook or Apple, who could have used it to compete with Google's mapping system. The purchase was strategic and monopolistic. But it was even more than that. Having a monopoly of digital space representation goes well beyond the stream of advertising revenues that the Google Maps app can produce. Cartography has always been intimately intertwined with political power.

Spatial awareness, navigation skills, spatial representation, and communication are regarded as some of the key human skills that set our species apart from other animals. Scientists believe that they have played an important role in our evolution. Mapmaking incorporates and enhances our skill set, and many believe that the ability to draw maps boosted our ancestors past the critical threshold that the other apes failed to cross.

In his book *Unweaving the Rainbow*, Professor Richard Dawkins, a British evolutionary biologist, argues that primitive mapping allowed hunters and gatherers to communicate their tracking plans long before the development of language. Spatial representation was the main communication tool among them.[149] Imagine a hunting party at dawn, ready to depart for what most likely is going to be the last day of the hunt. The group is excited and gathers around the tracker, who has spent days following the trail of the animal. He has studied the prey and come to an understanding of its psychology simply by observing its movements. The precious and complex information that the tracker has acquired is communicated to the group, not through a common language that is still too rudimentary, but by drawing on the ground a spatial and historical map of the movements of the animal. When the tracker completes the map, the leader of the hunting party picks up the stick and draws in the dust a scale model of the strategy to trap the animal. By simply observing the drawing of the map, the hunters understand what they need to do.

In prehistoric times, hunting was the core power of society, as proven by cave paintings, which primarily depict humans and animals on their daily rounds of survival. But cave painting is very different from the mapping of hunting parties. Its aim is not to trap the animal, it is to celebrate an event which has already taken place, and the representation of the space is purposely bent to this aim. This is possible because cave paintings are also works of art. In several of them, spatial differences, scale, proportions, and even the direction of the arrows, are not factual but imaginary; they have been altered to honor and even enhance the successful outcome of the hunting party.

Beyond the visualization of space and its artistic representation, cartography has always reflected the societal hierarchy, the political power structure, and even the propaganda of nations in a specific place and time in history. Maps, therefore, carry biases. In the Mercator projection of 1569,[150] the dimensions of continents and countries have been greatly altered. Europe is the same size as South America, which is actually twice as big; Greenland is as large as Africa, when Africa is in fact fourteen times the size of Greenland. Finally, Europe is placed at the epicenter of the map and the equator line is two-thirds of the way down. Through these biases, the Mercator projection depicts European colonial powers in a positive and powerful light, in sharp contrast with the regions of the world near the equator where, at the time, colonization was advancing. The map is essentially the celebration of European political supremacy as seen by a European cartographer.

Space may be common to all societies, but different societies have very distinct ideas of the world and how it should be represented— and, one should add, how it should be ruled. This is what Jerry Brotton, a professor of renaissance studies at Queen Mary University of London, argues in his book *A History of the World in Twelve Maps*. Because maps have always been powerful imaginary representations of the world, cartography has been instrumental in nation building, playing a formative role in creating, sustaining, and, at times, even contesting the existence and legitimacy of nation states.[151] This is as true today as it was at the dawn of our civilization. In 2019, the Canadian Broadcasting Corporation reported that Ukraine complained after Apple ". . . began referring to the Russian-annexed Crimean peninsula as part of Russia in its Maps and Weather apps for Russian users."[152] Until the internet revolution, the monopoly of spatial representation rested in the hands of state institutions, which used cartography to project their own vision of their place and role in the world. In the Hereford Mappa Mundi of 1300, when religion was the language of power, Jerusalem was placed at the epicenter of the map.[153]

Throughout history, technology has been applied to strengthen this kind of narrative. In 1765, James Rennell, a twenty-two-year-old British naval officer, drew a map of the entire Indian subcontinent. In 1765, James Rennell, a twenty-two-year-old British naval officer, drew a map of the entire Indian subcontinent. As explained by Evan Ratliff in an article for *WIRED*, Rennell "used the advanced technologies of the time: a compass and a distance-measuring wheel called a perambulator" to translate India's geography onto paper. His map goes well beyond the understanding of the landmass of the Indian subcontinent; it shows the potential advantages of territorial acquisitions to meet the colonial state's immediate needs.[154] And the British Empire used Rennell's map extensively for its nearly two hundred years of economic, political, and military domination of India. The article elaborates: "'Mapping has always been a tool of dominance,' says Michael Goodchild. 'There is no such thing as an objective map.' It's no coincidence, he says, that the last golden age of mapmaking was the colonial era, when cartographers were dispatched to catalogue western Europe's conquests around the world."[155] Sadly, as we are about to discover, in the digital era, mapping is still a tool of power, and those who control it exercise it freely and to their own advantage.

The digitization of space has not democratized geography, as the Cypherpunks wanted, nor has it empowered the individual. Instead, it has added an extra layer, the Techtitans, between the masses and geography. In 2003, before it was bought by Google, Keyhole signed a deal with In-Q-Tel, a governmental venture capital firm partly funded by the CIA. In-Q-Tel had become aware of EarthViewer, an application of Keyhole that allowed zooming in to satellite pictures, when US TV news networks had applied it to visualize battlefields during the war in Iraq. The investment gave access to the new technology to the National Geospatial-Intelligence Agency, the department that handles maps and satellite imagery for US military and intelligence units.[156]

Digital mapping may have stripped the state of the monopoly

of spatial representation, but it has not altered its grip on its use. According to the BBC, during the war in Iraq, Google was accused of censorship when it swapped in alternative imagery of Basra after the British government said insurgents were using Google Earth to target its soldiers. In 2014, *WIRED* published satellite pictures of a structure in the desert in southern Saudi Arabia.[157] The images came from Bing Maps, an application that Microsoft owns, and were rumored to illustrate that the CIA had built secret drone bases in the region.[158] The corresponding satellite images from Google Earth showed only desert sand.

The US government, military, and intelligence have been among Google Earth's largest customers since its launch.[159] One should add that they have also supplied valuable data: most of the early imagery shown in Google Earth was commercially available pictures from US military satellites. [160]

The digitization of space representation did not democratize geography. Instead, it became yet another example of how capitalism hijacked the technological revolution. Proof of that is the proliferation of intellectual property litigation among tech companies, including the lawsuit between ART+COM and Google about who invented the algorithm of Google Earth.

In 1994, TerraVision, a pioneering project launched by an unknown German company, ART+COM, became the first application to virtually reproduce the world through satellite images and architectural data, i.e., pictures of buildings, roads, railways, etc.[161] Almost a decade before Keyhole created EarthViewer, TerraVision allowed users to zoom in on satellite pictures. As with Google Earth, TerraVision offered users the opportunity to visit any corner of the planet. In 2014, ART+COM filed a suit against Google for patent infringement by the Google Earth program.[162] The legal battle became the topic of a fictionalized German miniseries, *The Billion Dollar Code*, shown on Netflix. Google eventually won the legal battle.

From the reconstruction of events, the viewer of the Netflix miniseries is confronted with the ethos and role that technological innovation was playing at the time in Silicon Valley and in Berlin. While more and more companies were becoming more and more powerful and skillful in consolidating their monopolies, in Berlin the collapse of the wall and the implosion of the Soviet Union a few years later kick-started the libertarian frenzy of the Techno-Germans. With their utopian futurism and their digital art, they reignited across the Atlantic the cultural revolution of the Cypherpunks. The Techno-Germans were young artists and hackers, like the founders of ART+COM,[163] who essentially shared the Cypherpunks' anarchic vision of the future. History has proven that they both were delusional and naïve.

By the time Europe and Germany embraced the internet revolution, in the US it had crystallized in a new industrial model. In Silicon Valley, a plethora of start-ups had blossomed and a swarm of venture capitalists, angel investors, and lawyers, many with Wall Street pedigrees, and all operating under the umbrella of capitalism, were busy shaping them using money and patents. Competition was rife and often ruthless, not only among Techtitans but among everybody. By the beginning of the last decade of the millennium in the United States, the magical egalitarian moment of the technological revolution had already passed. But across the Atlantic nobody was aware of this transition. American tech pioneers were still celebrated as revolutionary antiestablishment heroes, and the Techno-Germans dreamt of cooperating with them. Against this background, it was easy for the predatory Techtitans to swallow up European start-ups.

From the 1990s onwards, the technological revolution moved across the world like La Ola del Mundial in crowded stadiums: from the United States to Europe to Asia. It carried with it the same libertarian, antiestablishment, anarchistic hype of the Cypherpunks while generating admiration for American tech pioneers. It hit

Europe at the very end of the 1990s, and the following decade it was Asia's turn. By the time it reached countries like Vietnam and Thailand, the Techtitans had become so powerful they could block any competition either through acquisition or simply by copying new ideas without major consequences. They had the money, they had the technology, they had the lawyers, the bankers, the engineers. And they controlled the global market.

Far from democratizing the world, the technological revolution gave birth to a new, extremely profitable sector of capitalism in the form of a global oligopoly. During the pandemic, with a market capitalization of over $4 trillion, the five largest American tech companies (Google, Amazon, Facebook, Apple, and Microsoft) symbolically outperformed the GDP of Germany, the fourth largest economy in the world.[164] Against this scenario, a transfer of sovereignty from the old-fashioned nation states to tech companies was inevitable.

The modern world springs from the Treaty of Westphalia of 1648, which established the nation state as the sole sovereign entity to regulate territories that still exist today. Naturally, technological innovation and its application in warfare—e.g., the improvements in the shape and length of cannons—did contribute to the birth of nations. The production of weapons able to knock down the walls of feudal castles, in fact, made the political construction of feudalism untenable.

According to the new construction, the territorial identity of the nation state mirrors the national identity of the population that inhabits it. The nation state is, therefore, the political expression of people who speak a common language and share the same ethnicity and the same territory. In exchange for the recognition of a common ruler, people receive protection from the state. The monarch guarantees law and order and national security. Geographically, the territory defines the area in which the nation state performs its tasks. They include the management of a postal system to facilitate centralized governance, the printing of money, and the provision of public accounting to curb fraud. In the eyes of the citizens, all of these duties spring from the social contract negotiated with the monarch, an agreement upon which the legitimacy of the nation state rests, a social contract that our seventeenth-century ancestors symbolically signed.

As proved by the 2022 war in Ukraine, the essence of the nation state is still linked to its territory, and the state retains the power to limit liberties within its borders, including access to the internet, as happened in Russia during the invasions of Crimea and of mainland Ukraine. However, the digitization of space and the rise of the Techtitans have weakened the interdependency of territory, nation state, and population. National postal systems no longer exclusively deliver the mail which instead, travels through cyberspace from one corner of the world to another on the wings of apps such as WhatsApp, Instagram, or Gmail. Cartography has ceased to exist as a service provided by the state; today, companies like Google and Apple control the spatial representation and produce sophisticated topographical maps that are used by the public as well as by state institutions including the military. The state is no longer the sole issuer of money: its monetary sovereignty has been eroded by cryptocurrencies that are produced by software and circulate freely across the world. And territorial internet blockades can be circumvented using systems such as VPN.

By stripping the state of its spatial monopoly, the Techtitans have pulverized most of its geographical boundaries and pushed its citizens into cyberspace, where the old social contract has been replaced by digital contracts in which people, no longer regarded as citizens, agree to be treated simultaneously as commodities and consumers. Are we conscious that each time we click on "accept cookies," we are de facto being dehumanized? The most common answer is no. On the contrary, people welcome Google Maps' navigation instructions or Amazon's itinerary suggestions.

Overall, they feel that technology is empowering, not enslaving them. But they are wrong.

Cartography projected a biased vision of the world from the perspective of the state it represented. This propaganda was primarily directed at the citizens: for example, James Rennell's map cemented in many British generations a sense of pride in the Empire and reinforced their loyalty towards the crown. The state monopoly of cartography meant that, in the eyes of citizens, maps and what they represented were factual, and geography was a reassuring certainty in people's lives amid political turmoil.

With the digitization of space representation, maps have lost most of the old biases, but they have acquired new ones. Digital maps are constructed around the individual, the blue dot. As I zoom in, the environment which surrounds me becomes more personalized, and the map that emerges is not the same as any other. An algorithm that tracks every single aspect of each individual, almost from birth, customizes the map. If I like ice cream, my maps will always show the ice cream parlors in the vicinity, no matter where I am or what I am searching for. If I frequently eat junk food, I will be shown places where I can buy it. The certainty and universality of geography is lost because infinite versions of space exist, potentially one for each inhabitant of our planet, for each blue dot flashing on a smart phone screen. The spatial anarchy constructed around the individual as the epicenter of geography empties the essence of villages, town, cities, and entire nations. In *Invisible Cities*, Italo Calvino brilliantly summarizes this concept: "Memory's images, once they are fixed in words, are erased. . . . Perhaps I am afraid of losing Venice all at once, if I speak of it, or perhaps, speaking of other cities, I have already lost it, little by little."[165] Cities are living organisms and they have a life of their own; they are as much about their inhabitants as about monuments, geography, politics, economics, religion, and so on. What Calvino implies is that by trapping cities inside personal memories—and, one could add, inside personal taste and preferences that we transmit using words or images, such as digital maps—they become a projection of ourselves. They are not objective representations of cities and they do not represent a single truth. It follows that digital maps are as biased as old-fashioned paper maps.

Far from empowering us, the digitization of space has plunged us into geographical anarchy, where each of us is offered a personalized spatial representation of the world in which we live. Geographical anarchy weakens the nation state and promotes social disintegration, polarization, and extremism. It carries with it a strong dystopian force, the wind of intolerance. We are not aware of these changes because digital mapping has physically and existentially narrowed our space, shrinking it to our individual size. And this is the world I believe I inhabit. As my blue dot moves, I see a world constructed according to my taste and my desires, but also a world that is conditioned by my biases and cultural limitations. This space appears unchallenging, and because of that, many see it as comforting. In reality, such narrow space is like a battery of chickens, where people do not move, never see the sunlight, and are fed only in order to be processed daily as consumers.

Inside this spatial cage, the algorithm verifies in real time the accuracy of our data. If I suddenly start eating meat, such information is registered and processed: it is valuable data for the butcher shop near my home but also for many other companies, institutions, and, of course, for the state and the political parties. These are the main clients of the Techtitans.

The true power of the monopoly of the digital representation of space, therefore, goes well beyond the possibilities for Pizza Hut to sell its pizza to the blue dot that loves junk food and that is fast approaching one of its outlets, or for a casino to attract the blue dot of a gambler who is walking around the corner. The true

power of the digitization of life rests in the gathering and verifi-
cation of human data in real time and the conditioning that such
information allows companies that process it to pursue. This is the
magic wand of technology and this is also its darkest power.

Far more valuable than gold or oil, human data is now the most
desired raw material on earth, and private companies like Facebook, Google, or Apple are built to mine it in cyberspace. Against
this background, society and democracy, the essence of the
modern nation state, have been pushed out of sync with modernity. They have failed to understand the potential danger that the
continuous empowering of tech companies poses to their survival.
In the aftermath of 9/11, the US and UK militaries in Afghanistan
and Iraq employed a wealth of communication and marketing
companies, such as Cambridge Analytica's parent company, SCL
Group, that specialized in big data mining, to help carry out psychological warfare ("psyops") to convince people not to support
jihadist groups. New technology coupled with defense industry
intelligence empowered these companies further, making it possible in the following decade to apply the same surveillance and
persuasion techniques developed by the military to influence electoral results, as the Brexit referendum and the election of Donald
Trump have proven.

No effort has been made to strip the Techtitans of their global
data dominance. On the contrary, their business model of collecting and processing human data for profit and growth has only
grown. Facebook has been the most dynamic in experimenting
with ways to bring more people online—and thus to Facebook.
One of these was a project referred to as Apollo,[166] which produced good results in the Philippines. Facebook partnered with
mobile phone provider Globe, the smaller of the country's two
dominant mobile companies, and offered free access to Facebook
for mobile users who did not have a data plan contract. Within
fifteen months of its launch, Globe's user numbers surged and

overtook its rival and Facebook gathered millions of subscribers. In 2022, on the eve of the political elections in the Philippines, sixty-seven million people in the Philippines used Facebook.[167]

A study conducted by Rappler, a Filipino news website founded by Nobel Peace Prize winner Maria Ressa, along with a group of fellow Filipino journalists, exposed the use of Facebook by the Marcos family to win the 2022 elections: "The Marcos network painstakingly seeded disinformation and reshaped the narrative surrounding the Marcoses on Facebook over the years prior to build 'an entire fortress of Marcos supporters.'"[168] In 2014, Facebook tried to apply the Apollo project in India. No country except China held the kind of potential that India did, and Facebook was banned in China. At the time, Facebook had about one hundred million users in India, and the company projected its potential market to be several hundred million more. Based upon the literacy data, considered a good proxy for how many people could be online, Facebook looked at a potential market in India of about seven hundred to eight hundred million users.

With the government's approval, Mark Zuckerberg offered to bring India online with the project Internet.org. On paper the proposal looked fantastic, but a close scrutiny of Internet.org showed its true nature. A *Guardian* interview of Osama Manzar of the Digital Empowerment Foundation, a Delhi-based not-for-profit organization whose task is to bridge the digital divide in India, explains why. Manzar's company had first "thrown its weight" behind Internet.org, but quickly he changed his mind, realizing, as the *Guardian* puts it, ". . . what Internet.org actually looked like: a threadbare platform that only allowed access to 36 bookmarked sites and Facebook, which was naturally the only social network available. There was one weather app, three sites for women's issues, and the search engine Bing."[169] Far from offering internet for all, Internet.org aimed at transforming Facebook into the gatekeeper of the web for the hundreds of millions of Indians who were unfamiliar with what the internet was or what services it could provide. If implemented, Facebook would have controlled the internet in the entire country. Any tech company in such a strong monopolistic position would have been able to influence the future of the country and even dictate its own conditions to the government. Fortunately, this did not happen. Facebook stumbled into a dispute centering upon mobile phone net neutrality, i.e., the principle that phone companies and internet providers should not be allowed to prioritize certain sites and services, because such power could alter competition within the internet. As a result, Facebook was denied a license to operate internet services in India.

The Indian fiasco did not change the long-term strategy of Facebook, which still looks at Asia as a key market for growth. In recent years, it has become apparent that social media have reached a plateau in Western countries. From 2015 to 2020 in North America, the number of Facebook users increased by 17 percent, to 259 million; in the Asia-Pacific region it doubled to 1.3 billion. In the second quarter of 2021, Facebook lost two million subscribers in Europe alone and registered no growth in Canada. In 2020, the Asia-Pacific region experienced a 28.8 percent year-over-year jump in profits, while North America had a 19.3 percent jump and Europe a 20.9 percent one.[170]

The extraordinary speed with which technological innovation in the information technology sector has revolutionized all aspects of our life, including spatial representation, is one of the reasons why neither the state nor its institutions have stood in the way of the Techtitans. Today, attempts to restructure the industry through the breakup of mega-businesses like Amazon or Facebook are not very successful. The excessive power of these companies on the global market means that no government is capable of dismembering them. In this respect, the Techtitans are above the nation state and have more power than parliaments. And this is very dangerous.

CHAPTER NINE

The Video Game of Finance

In June 2020, Alexander Kearns, a twenty-year-old University of Nebraska student, committed suicide. He threw himself under a train in his hometown of Naperville, Illinois. A few hours earlier he had received a message on his Robinhood app, the financial online trading platform. The message said that his account had been temporarily suspended due to a negative cash balance of $730,165.

After reading the message, Kearns panicked. He called the Robinhood phone line, but no one answered. It was the middle of the night; however, even in broad daylight, no one ever picks up the phone. As with many companies that operate online, Robinhood only communicates electronically with customers. Frustrated and scared, Kearns sent an email asking for an explanation. The answer arrived a little later; it was a robo-response and confirmed the $730,165 imbalance in his account. The email reminded him that he had a few days to cover the losses.

When Alexander Kearns took his own life, he was convinced that he had lost all that money. He did not know that such a frightening figure was not real, that it was not the sum of all the financial transactions he had conducted, including the risk coverage options he had bought a few hours before. The $730,165 imbalance was the result of a partial calculation; Robinhood's electronic system had not yet fully updated his account. By the time his body was found, Kearns's account was back in the black.

Before committing suicide, the young man wrote the following note to his parents: "If you are reading this, then I am dead. . . . How was a twenty-year-old with no income able to get assigned almost a million dollars' worth of leverage?" And then he concludes: "The amount of guilt I feel as I commit this is unbearable—I did not want to die." Kearns's painful words sum up the extraordinary challenges of the often unmanageable responsibilities and conditioning that the acceleration of time and advancement of technology place on our shoulders.

Alexander Kearns belonged to the generation that grew up playing video games and who, in recent years, have started online financial trading. Taking such a step is quick and easy. Online financial apps are designed with the same graphics as video games; they are interactive and have similar functionality so that they appear familiar to the gamers. The targets are young people, primarily the tail-end of the millennials and Generation Z, the first generations fascinated with finance, who grew up in a zero-interest-rate economy and who never experienced a war.

Beyond the identical digital choreography, equipment, and functionality, playing the market using online financial platforms presents many other similarities with playing video games for a simple reason: the latter have been constructed to mimic real life, including the real life of the stock market. In 2013, the newest chapter of the *Grand Theft Auto* series came with a stock market system identical to the real one, i.e., it had multiple exchanges, gamers could buy and sell shares of individual companies, and stock prices fluctuated exactly as in the real stock market. The release was so successful that it generated $1 billion in sales in the first three days.

It is unquestionable that all the above factors facilitate the transition from video games to online trading. However, these elements are insufficient to explain the surge in online trading activity since 2019 and the extraordinary events that took place in 2021 on the Robinhood online trading platform, which will be discussed in the next chapter. The strong pull that finance exercises upon millennials and Generation Z seems to match in intensity the appeal that video games have held since their childhood. Because of that, it cannot be attributed to making money. More likely, playing video games and playing the stock market are experienced as rewarding and fulfilling activities that push the individual into a specific state of mind, a mindset that scientists define as "flow."

Professor Mihály Csíkszentmihályi, who discovered and studied this phenomenon, offers this definition: "a state in which people are so involved in an activity that nothing else seems to matter; the experience is so enjoyable that people will continue to do it even at great cost, for the sheer sake of doing it."[171] Flow is a mental immersion that occurs when the challenge of a task is balanced by one's skills and ability, while performing an enjoyable activity. Both the challenge and the skill level must be high. Mowing the grass in the yard, for example, does not qualify. Csíkszentmihályi developed the definition of flow while studying professional athletes, music composers, chess players, dancers, and mountain climbers who achieved it while performing these activities. However, you do not need to be a professional athlete or a concert pianist to find flow: avid skiers feel it regularly on the mountain slopes; other people feel it by practicing yoga, by riding their bikes, or by going for a run. As long as a person's body or mind is stretched to its limits in a voluntary effort to accomplish something difficult, worthwhile, and enjoyable, writes Csíkszentmihályi in his book *Flow: The Psychology of Optimal Experience*, everybody can experience flow.

Flow is different from being in the zone. Why? Because it is much more than that. People who experience flow are focused on the task rather than on themselves, and when they enter flow they feel as if their actions and their awareness have merged. Scientists describe this state of mind as an "autotelic" experience: a deeply rewarding moment in which the self and the task performed become one. Here is an example. Having chosen the line to follow to come down a difficult black run, a skier begins descending, making all the right turns, and suddenly they are in flow. Each new turn seems effortless, both mentally and physically, and the skier wants this state of mind never to end, to go on and on. People say that the intensity of the reward in flow is so powerful, so fulfilling, that they believe they have been born to perform that specific task. Unsurprisingly, for Csíkszentmihályi flow is the secret of happiness.

Flow is a product of modernity and of the complexity that accompanies it. Ancestral positive feeling—pleasure, for example—does not trigger it; enjoyment, a much more sophisticated feeling, does. Here Csíkszentmihályi describes the difference between pleasure and enjoyment:

> ... pleasure is a good feeling programmed in our genes to make us do things that in the past, well before we were born, were good for the evolution of the human species. We feel pleasure when we eat to make sure that our body gets enough nutrition, we feel good about having sex because in this way our body is sure to reproduce itself. Pleasure is automatic, everybody can experience it and it needs no skills. The downside of pleasure is that it is necessary for survival but it does not make us grow. We can eat all we want and have as much sex as we can get, yet we would remain exactly what we were, without gathering new experiences or new skills. Pleasure can be dangerous because if we do not learn how to control it, we can become addicted to it and end up spending our life overeating or being trapped in routine sexuality, doing all the things the genes have programmed us to do because it feels good and, in this process, miss all the other exciting things that life has to offer.
>
> Enjoyment does not come merely from the satisfaction of our instincts. The enjoyment of flow is the result of recognizing new challenges and of developing skills we did not

have before, and for these reasons flow leads to growth, to higher levels of complexity.[172]

For Csíkszentmihályi, "games are obvious flow activities, and play is flow experience par excellence." The most popular video games are specifically constructed to generate flow: they produce enjoyment, not pleasure. In 2007, the video game *flOw*, created by applying Csíkszentmihályi's theory of flow, was incorporated into PlayStation 3 by its developer, thatgamecompany. As the players swim around, gobbling up beautiful, abstract creatures, *flOw* makes it possible for them to constantly balance their own skill with the challenge of the game. And so they keep playing.

Though flow is a positive experience for the individual, its monetization at the hands of developers and video game apps can be highly damaging. For example, it can generate addiction and alter people's perception of reality. Video game scholar Braxton Soderman argues that the deeply individual state of mind of flow "pushes away the external world and pitches the idea that happiness can only occur when you're engaged in a particular task. . . . The worry is that pursuing flow pushes out concerns of real life and disconnects people instead of connecting them."[173] The dark side of experiencing a state of flow while playing video games is, therefore, addiction and the isolation it creates. Flow streaming from playing video games needs to be kept under as much control as the quest for the pleasure of eating or having sex. But while nature, i.e., our genes, pushes us to seek pleasure in these latter activities, the addiction to video games springs from our desire to relive the enjoyment of flow and from the peer pressure of everybody else experiencing the same addiction. Successful online trading platforms are aware of this and have constructed their apps to maximize the personal and peer pull of flow: young influencers, who are the same age as potential customers, conduct the marketing, which takes place primarily on social media.

TikTok has been by far the most successful social media platform in the financial field because it fits the influencers' marketing format; someone has even renamed it "StockTok." Hundreds of thousands of young men and women between the ages of sixteen and thirty digitally interact daily with their peers, explaining network investment strategies, offering clarification on financial products, and commenting on market trends. This information is cleverly packaged in video clips assembled with the right music and enhanced with funny memes to entertain viewers. Finance is fun, say the influencers, finance is a game, a new video game where real money is earned. The mantra is reassuring: I earn a lot of money; come and trade on the digital platform I use; you will enjoy it and you can make money too. Or, if you prefer, I can teach you how to make money by attending my finance classes.

For the followers, financial influencers are cool! They are peers and at the same time they are smart cookies, which generates admiration. Their videos are so entertaining, and at the same time so personal and helpful, that it is easy to forget that they are just advertising and that the influencers are paid to produce them. For every new client they bring to online trading platforms, influencers receive a cut. Their social media accounts have links to financial online platforms and viewers are told to click on them to start their journey into finance. Depending on how many new customers they bring to the platforms, influencers can earn anywhere from a few hundred dollars to several million.

To lure new customers, influencers offer followers a free trade of a small amount of money on select digital trading platforms. For example, from the TikTok account of Elijah Brasley, whose picture in 2021 showed a boy apparently no more than twenty years old, users can go to a Linktree page, from which they can access his YouTube account or various trading platforms including Robinhood, Webull, and Acorns. There they can redeem through a promotion code a small amount of money to invest. In 2021,

Brasley, who described himself as a student, had over 16 million followers.

Older TikTokers like Angela Zhang (Zhangsta) who, in her profile, says that she has completed a bachelor's and a master's in electrical engineering, apply similar monetization models. In 2021, from Zhangsta's account page, followers were able to access her personalized explore page, a website just like Linktree. From there, they could click on her other social accounts as well as use her promotion code to gain free stocks on select online trading platforms and, in doing so, generate bonus rewards for her.

Not all influencers are happy to act exclusively as traffic lights for online trading platforms. Some have a more entrepreneurial approach. Take thirty-year-old Danny Devan, who, in 2021, had just over half a million followers. In his profile, Devan says that he started his own business after turning eighteen and deciding not to go to college but to begin investing instead. In his videos, he talks about stocks and financial markets and teaches viewers about trading and finance in general. Several of his tutorial videos specifically target youngsters wanting to start managing their own money. His monetization model differs from those of Brasley and Zhang. Instead of offering a promotion code to gain free stocks on online trading platforms, Devan encourages his viewers to join his online trading group and "investing classroom." From his page, followers click on a link to sign up for a free online newsletter or join his "Trading Classroom" with a one-time payment of $119.

The digital revolution has opened new fields in which to get into flow. Metaverse, the 3D network of virtual worlds, is the next frontier where people will seek the type of enjoyment that leads to flow. All these new and relatively new activities, if properly monetized, can be extremely profitable for those who package them well—as proven by the interest of venture capitalists, angel investors, and the giants of finance in online trading platforms.

Robinhood, by far the most famous online trading platform, belongs to the second generation of high tech start-ups that arrived after Google, Apple, and Facebook. These companies spotted a niche in the market and developed it. How? By repackaging the stock market into a reality video game, a business equally addictive as the games, and by offering it to young people, often illiterate in finance. In 2015, the average Robinhood customer's age was 26.[174] Financially, this second generation of high tech start-ups benefitted from the large profits that tech and Techtitans realized from quantitative easing. Robinhood, which was launched in 2013, received initial funds from Google Ventures and Index Ventures, which were joined by Andreessen Horowitz, Rothenberg Ventures, and angel investors such as Tim Draper and Howard Lindzon. The second generation of high tech start-ups also took advantage of the economy of scale of Silicon Valley, which, after the 2008 crisis, had grown exponentially. Robinhood, in fact, was founded by two Stanford graduates, Vlad Tenev and Baiju Bhatt, and headquartered in Menlo Park, California.

Following in the footsteps of the Techtitans, Robinhood purposely projected an antiestablishment image to maximize the appeal that the motto "finance for all" exercised on young people, its core customers. The choice of the name Robinhood, evocative of the noble thief who robbed the rich to give to the poor, the abolition of users' commissions, and the immediate free access to the market were aimed at strengthening the revolutionary narrative, which represented the essence of Tenev and Bhatt's marketing strategy. Robinhood was intended to democratize finance by putting the financial investment tools that the rich have always used into the hands of nonprofessionals; this is the message that the marketing spread. And while doing that, it was believed it would reduce inequality. Robinhood's marketing mantra, cleverly manufactured and delivered, was carried by high school and university students, young professionals, almost anybody who was young and computer literate.

Tenev and Bhatt's marketing campaign is a rare example of anticipation of this. Both sensed that their product would be liked by young people when no one else in finance believed that such a thing was possible. On the contrary, finance was perceived as an unappealing sector for youth. The concept of making finance accessible to all in order to rebalance society also went against the current culture; finance, it was believed, is by definition undemocratic. But it worked—it worked extremely well. Young people perceived Robinhood as a weapon against Wall Street and, as we shall see in the following chapter, eventually used it themselves to punish high finance for what happened in 2008. Naturally, as with most marketing campaigns, the advertised goal of Robinhood—the democratization of finance—was never achieved because it was just a clever marketing illusion. However, Tenev and Bhatt did achieve their goal of becoming billionaires. When, in 2021, Robinhood went public, the two gained one of the most generous stakes in the history of Wall Street: Bhatt's stake was valued at $3.2 billion whilst Tenev raked in $2.2 billion.[175]

To understand how, simultaneously riding a technological and financial wave, two geeks from Stanford made it big through a digital mass uprising never before seen in history, we must first of all take a step back in history and revisit the financial deregulation of the 1990s.

CHAPTER TEN

Assault on Wall Street

In December 2000, only weeks before leaving the White House, Bill Clinton signed the Commodity Futures Modernization Act which marked the beginning of the age of financialization.[176] In the same way that departing presidents give pardons to criminals, Clinton gave this giant sop to the big Wall Street firms on his way out the door. Thanks to the new legislation, finance began exercising an increasingly strong influence on the overall economy and, as a result, large sectors of the economy moved out of real sectors, e.g., industry, and focused on making money with money in finance. Financial engineering, with its exotic instruments from mortgage-backed securities to credit default swaps, offered great opportunities to earn mega-profits, and this explains why the deregulation of the 1990s unleashed the forces of market speculation. Year after year, Wall Street morphed more and more into a stock market casino. Progressively detached from the real economy and highly computerized, finance began resembling a web of highly sophisticated video games. To illustrate this concept let's look at high-speed trading, i.e., trading by machines, also known as high frequency trading, or HFT.

According to various estimates, computer trading may already represent the vast majority of all trades. NASDAQ, the American stock exchange, however, prefers a somewhat more conservative estimate: its website mentions that "computer-backed high frequency trading" accounts for 50 percent of all trades on NASDAQ.[177] High frequency traders rely on networks of computers, directly connected to the stock exchanges, which generate automated, high-speed trades. Naturally these operations are governed by algorithms, known as "algos," whose main characteristic is high-speed performance; they trade so fast that their reaction time is measured in milliseconds. Speed is money because it allows the trader to obtain small discounts on the value of each trade.[178] These are not small margins—when added up, all trades of HFT amount to a high volume of very profitable transactions, which explains why, in order to send their orders to the market faster than their competitors, financial institutions even pay to place their servers inside the same building used by the stock exchange. This move is known as co-location; basically the algos are the housemates of the exchanges.

In a not so distant era, speed was not the main issue in trading. The financial game was played by people who primarily tried to gain an edge over their competitors by outsmarting them; for example, professional investors were trying to outsmart retail traders and hedge fund managers were trying to outsmart fund managers. Psychology played an important role—but not anymore. In the Present Future of finance, human beings hopelessly go into battle daily against automated sharks, the algos, exactly as happens in a video game. This is how a trader describes the interaction with the algos:

> Sometimes, the "algo" tries to outsmart the emotions of human beings with its unbiased and rational behavior. But in most cases, it beats its human opponent just relying on its sheer higher speed. By the time a human trader has placed a single trade, its algo opponent may have traded several thousand times, across multiple markets, in different financial instruments.[179]

In the 1990s and early 2000s, self-regulation failed to monitor the market, and financial products were not only traded privately, without any controls, but they were also manufactured to meet the pure speculative demand of players, without any connection to assets in the real economy. Using exchange traded funds or derivatives, the most popular products of financial engineering, investors can conduct trades in the fluctuation in commodity prices, inflation, or exchange rates without owning any commodity or currency, and therefore without having any exposure to these assets.[180] A private individual can amass copper or uranium they do not own, and a bank can get credit exposure to entities they never even meet. If ownership of assets is not required, the risk built into synthetic financial instruments is still very real, as proven by the 2008 subprime crisis.

Financial engineering risks turning any asset of global finance into the accessory of a dangerous video game. No financial product and no currency, including cryptocurrencies, seem able to escape such a destiny. In a recent *Financial Times* article, Martin Arnold writes that the European Central Bank denounced the risks of

> decentralized finance, or DeFi, in which cryptocurrency-based software programs offer financial services without the use of intermediaries such as banks. "Crypto credit on DeFi platforms grew by a factor of 14 in 2021, while the total value locked was hovering at around €70bn until very recently, on a par with small domestic peripheral European banks," it said. Rehypothecation, in which collateral for a loan can be repledged against another loan, increased the chances of leverage limits being breached.[181]

As in the past, those who suffer the consequences of the crash are always common people. Finance is a main pillar of society; its task is not to enrich those who play the stock market, but to provide liquidity to the system. When finance cracks, society suffers. One more reason why it must always be properly regulated. The bailout of 2008–2009 saved financial institutions and banks, but not the millions of people who lost their jobs, their homes, and their savings.

Against this backdrop, in 2011, the Occupy Wall Street movement erupted. Its purpose was to protest against bankers and financial institutions, to make sure they did not get away with gambling with other people's money. However, within a year, the movement disappeared and the focus of people's anger shifted to personal differences, i.e., income inequalities. People seemed to have forgotten about the dark side of finance, and financial institutions and banks carried on investing in the high tech industry, undisturbed.

Fast forward to 2020. When the pandemic hit, people noticed that the virus was financially squeezing small businesses and private individuals, but Techtitans like Amazon or giant corporations like Walmart were making even more money than before, and the financial market was booming because stocks kept climbing. The financialized economy had struck yet another blow against ordinary people: the rich were getting richer while the middle class was getting poorer. The desire to undo this unjust system resurfaced. This time, the wind of revolution started to blow across the internet, through online forums like Reddit, where an army of young people in lockdown, known as Redditors, spent most of their time staring at their computer screens while exchanging ideas and financial strategies with each other. One of the most popular forums for "pajama traders" was WallStreetBets.

Created in 2012, WallStreetBets is a subgroup of Reddit, known for its motto "make money and have fun at the same time."[182] Until 2019, WallStreetBets had a few thousand subscribers. Then, when a few big brokerage firms eliminated commissions from their apps, making online trading free and accessible to everybody, the forum exploded. Within a few days, the number of subscribers reached half a million. People were eager to invest, but they were even more eager to have fun talking about it at the same time. By spring 2020, when the first lockdown got underway, the number of participants in WallStreetBets had risen to one million and exchanges on the forum began taking a dangerous turn. Vulgarities and violent rants, mixed with funny and outrageous memes, threatened its integrity. Here is how a *Washington Post* article described the atmosphere on the digital platform:

> . . . anonymous posters using monikers like "chainsaw vasectomy" traded stock tips in a blend of casual profanity, mutual cheerleading and savvy analysis. . . . Users celebrated their "tendies," a shorthand for chicken tenders that meant profits. They referred to each other with the self-deprecating, if offensive, term "retards." Investors with "diamond hands" had the nerves to hold an investment position until, like the rocket ship icon that decorated many posts, it headed to the stars.[183]

But in April 2020, the moderators kicked WallStreetBets' founder, Jaime Rogozinski, out of the forum for "attempting to monetize" the subreddit community. WallStreetBets had developed a life of its own.

Among the participants in the forum was Keith Gill, known by the Reddit username "DeepFuckingValue," and the YouTube and Twitter alias "Roaring Kitty."[184] Gill, who was a professional financial analyst from Massachusetts, had been tracking GameStop shares since 2019. GameStop is a 1984 store chain that sells video games and gaming equipment from real shops mostly located in strip malls and shopping centers. In his YouTube channel, Gill had been posting his analysis, which can be summarized as follows: GameStop shares are undervalued and therefore people should buy them.

Around the same time, well-known investor Michael Burry of Scion Asset Management—who had been the first to anticipate the bursting of the subprime bubble, making a fortune shorting the housing market, as featured in the film *The Big Short*—acquired a 3.3 percent stake in GameStop. He shared Gill's view and even wrote to the company's board of directors urging them to buy back the company's shares. With stocks at an all-time low, he argued in the letter, the company could buy back all the shares using the $480 million it had in cash. Michael Burry's analysis not only failed to convince GameStop's board, but it also never appeared on the online forum. Keith Gill's postings did.

Gill's analysis attracted growing interest. Millennials were familiar with GameStop. During their childhood and adolescence, they had often spent time in these outlets buying or exchanging video games and socializing. For them, GameStop was a quintessential American product, the equivalent of an electronic-age apple pie.

The online distribution of video games had weakened the GameStop business model; kids could now download video games from their computer, and such technological innovation had been reflected in the value of the store's shares, which had declined by 70 percent. GameStop lost most of its appeal and the video game chain began closing down outlets across the US. Gill argued, however, that the company was still solid. It was cash rich and had very little debt, and with good management could recover, which is what Michael Burry also believed.

Gill was convinced that the online distribution of games would take place at a slower pace than the market was anticipating; big games for consoles, for example, were still coming to the retail market and selling well. Acting as a professional financial influencer, Keith Gill presented his case for buying GameStop on his YouTube channel, showing data, blogs, comments, and interviews to back up his analysis. His advice was to buy GameStop's stock at current prices and hold on to them for the next two years, when he believed it would be possible to resell them at a higher price. To prove his point, he invested $53,000 of his own money in GameStop.

At the end of 2020, stimulated by this analysis, some Redditors noticed that 84 percent of GameStop shares were held as short positions by a group of hedge funds, among them Melvin Capital.[185] Short positioning is when one trader borrows stocks from another and sells them in the hope of rebuying them in the future at a lower price—pocketing the difference. GameStop's weakness had drawn the attention of people specializing in shorting the market, speculators who bet against the stock of weak companies. These "short sellers" are very unpopular because their profits originate from the misfortune of others. By late 2019, short sellers accounted for nearly two-thirds of the GameStop shares in circulation: an indication that the hedge funds were betting the company would go bankrupt.

To the Redditors, it seemed that the hedge funds had colluded to achieve such a goal. Instead of liquidating their position when the stock was worth a few dollars, they were holding on, pushing the company into bankruptcy. If that happened, they would not have to pay any money for the stocks to be returned, because they would be worth zero. They were greedy, too greedy.

By holding the stock until it was worth nothing, the hedge funds became vulnerable to the assault of the Redditors, who plotted not only a popular digital financial uprising but one of the most spectacular short squeezes in the history of Wall Street. A short squeeze happens when investors push the prices of a stock up, in opposition to short sellers. As stocks climb, the profits of the short sellers get squeezed, eventually turning into losses. Here is how the Redditors orchestrated the short squeeze of 2021.

In January 2021, within hours of launching, the mantra "buy GameStop to squeeze the hedge funds" went viral. Young Redditors in lockdown, bored out of their minds, living in their pajamas, enthusiastically embraced the call to action. They opened their Robinhood app and began emptying their bank accounts to buy shares. Money from the stimulus packages that the US government had handed them went straight into purchasing GameStop's shares. The Robinhood platform jammed and had to be reloaded many times to handle the volume of trade.

Many Redditors remembered the catastrophe of the 2008 crash, how it had impacted their parents' lives, and they wanted to get back at those who had caused it. Others had personally experienced the negative consequences of the financial meltdown and wanted to punish the perpetrators, as summarized in a quote from a Redditor published by the *Washington Post*:

> "I bought a house in 2008 at the ripe age of 21 just months before the crash. I was lucky to be making decent money so young but the truth is I could just barely afford it with a roommate. Then the bottom fell out. These a--holes f---ed me. When I sold that home 5 years later, I was still down 15%," wrote solidtwerks. "These f---ers owe me. I'm taking what's mine."[186]

Buying GameStop shares suddenly made possible what Occupy Wall Street had failed to achieve, i.e., to punish Wall Street. Many Redditors understood what squeezing the hedge funds meant since they were familiar with online trading, having already used their part of the stimulus money to play the market, as suggested by influencers. In one of his videos, for example, Elijah Brasley had mentioned that he had spent the $600 stimulus to buy Tesla stock instead of buying clothes and shoes, or putting it in a savings account.[187] But many other Redditors were new to the game of finance. They had recently joined the online community of WallStreetBets, and enjoyed its irreverent atmosphere, the chats interspersed with the inevitable memes, the vulgarities and swear words. They decided to follow what the others were doing and bought GameStop without understating what the next move would be. They were following the flow.

The GameStop financial battle invigorated the Redditors and

energized the influencers. Messages of solidarity for GameStop flooded the online financial forums, and new subscribers flocked to join them. WallStreetBets subscribers surpassed five million. The same phenomenon took place on the Robinhood platform, where business became more and more hectic. On January 22, 2021, nearly 22 million shares were exchanged on Robinhood, up from 5 million on a typical day earlier in the month. As the price of the stock began to rise, the forum's encouraging messages to hold on, not to sell, to make the price rise further, multiplied. The phrase "apes together strong," from the movie *Rise of the Planet of the Apes*, became the most popular stock trading slang. And just as in the movie it symbolized the strong solidarity among the apes, in real life it encapsulated the bond among WallStreetBets members, the unity of the Redditors versus the greed of the hedge funds.

The GameStop revolt kept gaining momentum. On the wings of demand, shares recovered, surpassing the level at which most of the short sellers had bought them. Soon, the condition for the short squeeze that the Redditors had planned materialized. Stock prices and volumes reached a level at which, to limit their losses, hedge funds had to rush to the market and buy the stock of GameStop from the Redditors, who by now held a big chunk of it. This move, in turn, pushed prices even higher, further squeezing the short sellers. Because several of them had used borrowed money, a technique that amplifies gains as prices fall and multiplies losses as prices rise, the hedge funds were in for massive losses.

The Redditors' uprising attracted the interest of the media, which began describing the dichotomy of us-against-them as the revenge of the commoners, as an uprising of young people in their pajamas against the arrogant financial elite. But this characterization was not correct. As GameStop shares kept rising, the big firms in Wall Street like BlackRock and Fidelity Investments grabbed the opportunity to make money themselves; they joined the Redditors' camp, buying the stock and squeezing their competitors. They put their phenomenal knowledge and resources behind the scheme, helping GameStop shares, which initially were worth just a few dollars, reach a peak of almost $500 per share. The company, which at the beginning of 2020 was worth $200 million, was now worth $28 billion. And a handful of Wall Street giants were making big money while weakening their hedge fund competitors, a win-win situation.

For Redditors, the assault on Wall Street had become something more than trading stocks or playing a video game. It was a justice crusade, a battle to prove right from wrong. Supporting each other, encouraging each other not to sell, using the expression "diamond hands" as if they were all on a team playing a video game, they entered flow. For each click to buy shares, they watched the price of the stock rise, which generated euphoria and motivated them to keep on clicking, to keep on buying. Trading became natural; the task and the self merged into one single, magical action. Many Redditors described their feeling as "ecstatic." By January 28, 2022, the short sellers had lost $27 billion and five thousand American financial firms had been affected. The Redditors were winning.

It was at this point that the Redditors began expanding, targeting the stocks of other companies considered undervalued, such as AMC Theatres and Nokia, a move that alerted state institutions. The assault on Wall Street had become too big for the White House, the Treasury, and the Federal Reserve to ignore. Top hedge funds, such as Melvin Capital, caught in a short squeeze, had to be bailed out, and billions of dollars started to move towards them from different investors. Money did not come cheap, but it came. And with money came something else: the financial establishment fought back using the weapon of regulation.

Blaming hate speech, Discord, the instant messaging platform, banned communication among users of the WallStreetBets Discord server.[188] This move only increased the popularity of the Reddit forum, which jumped to eight million subscribers. Facebook also banned a Robinhood trading discussion group from its site. But the mortal blow came from Robinhood, when it banned the purchase of the stocks targeted by the Redditors, allowing only their sale. Naturally shares of GameStop and of the other stocks began declining. This generated an uproar. Many class-action lawsuits were launched, and Redditors voiced their outrage online. They accused Robinhood of market manipulation, of taking the side of the short sellers and Wall Street giants, some of which, like Citadel, were clients of the online platform.

Far from being a paladin of the people, Robinhood was very much part of the financial system. Its business model rested on selling data to the high frequency trading firms that processed them. Redditors did not know that Robinhood was able to waive the cost of transactions by diverting customer orders to these firms, which in turn used their algos to obtain small discounts, money they pocketed, to process them.[189] The highest earnings for high frequency trading firms come from simple transactions, exactly those that the pajama traders were conducting on online platforms. In exchange for the flow of orders they receive, high frequency trading firms pay Robinhood a percentage of each transaction. These earnings are minimal, sometimes a few cents per transaction, but multiplied by millions of trades they become relevant. In the year following the Redditors' uprising, Robinhood pocketed $700 million from HFT.[190]

In an interview with Elon Musk, Vlad Tenev, one of the founders of Robinhood, justified the decision to halt the purchase of GameStop on its platform to comply with financial regulations. Due to the increased volume of activity, the National Securities Clearing Corporation (NSCC) had asked Robinhood to increase its security deposit by $3 billion, literally overnight.[191] Robinhood had to obey and raise the funds among its investors. This was Tenev's explanation and it was correct. Redditors were victims of the marketing illusion projected by Robinhood through slogans such as "finance for all." The truth is that Robinhood was every bit as much a part of the system as the short sellers and the hedge funds. The Redditors had been sucked into the same structure without realizing it.

Though the price of GameStop stock kept falling, Redditors held on, hoping that short sellers would eventually have to buy their stocks. But the short squeeze had been crippled. The big short sellers had liquidated their positions, and some had been bailed out by other big players in the market. When activity on the Robinhood platform fully resumed, there were as many victims as winners on the battlefield. Few Redditors had sold their shares at peak value, and many ended up with bundles of stocks that were now worth much less than when they had bought them. Overall, however, Redditors were satisfied with their uprising. Even those who had not used the stimulus checks and had lost their own savings admitted to having enjoyed squeezing the hedge funds. Everyone had fun; for them the assault on Wall Street had been part of a very enjoyable video game.

The Redditors' assault on Wall Street unveiled a thick web of interdependencies inside the world of financial and regulatory institutions. Whatever the true reason of Robinhood's ban on buying GameStop, it happened because the system is structured in a way that some companies are deemed too big to fail—as was apparent in 2008. Very little has changed since the big crash. As is routine for paper money circulation, almost 23 percent of all US dollars in existence were printed in 2021, but only a tiny percentage reached regular people and an even smaller amount was used by the Redditors to bring justice to Wall Street. When the big hedge funds needed to be bailed out, however, there was no shortage of cash. Equally, the NSCC's request to raise Robinhood deposits by $3 billion almost overnight was met without any problem.[192] There is always plenty of cash for the system to stay afloat, providing you respect the rules of the game, but not for millennials and Generation Z to pay off student loans, or to buy a home and raise a family. And they are the future.

Very little has changed since 2008 also because the internet is not as free and democratic as the Cypherpunks had hoped it would be. The online network of the Redditors needed a means of communication they did not control, and so it was possible to shut down their voice by simply banning them from accessing the apps, the gateways to online communication.

The democratization of finance may still be a long way away. Perhaps we need to wait until the people take control of the internet; however, the Redditors' short squeeze proves that the merging of social media and online trading can be a potent formula to wipe away some of the injustice the present system perpetrates. In May 2022, Melvin Capital sent a message to its clients saying that it was winding down its fund, possibly because of the billions of dollars of losses caused by the Redditors' short squeeze.[193]

Perhaps, as in the past, what is needed to change the system is a total collapse, a catastrophe like the world wars of the last century or the Great Depression. Could the conflict in Ukraine be the spark that ignites a new world war or an economic meltdown triggered by the energy crisis that the war has caused? Nobody wants this to happen. Neither do people wish for the reinvention of our world from other, very powerful forces that threaten us, namely the climate change we are all witnessing. Sadly, this is a catastrophe that too many have chosen to ignore, despite the fact that it is imperative that we prevent it now, without further delay.

CHAPTER ELEVEN

The Mythology of Carbon Credits

In October 2020, Total, the French energy company, announced in a press release its first shipment of zero-emission Australian liquefied natural or fossil gas (LNG), predominantly liquid methane, to the China National Offshore Oil Corporation (CNOOC). Here is the definition of LNG according to the nonprofit Global Witness:

> Liquefied fossil gas is formed when fossil gas is supercooled into its liquid state at about -260 degrees Fahrenheit (-160°C), a process known as liquefaction. It is then loaded onto huge tanker ships or trucks and exported abroad, where it is returned to its gaseous state in the process of regasification. It can then be transported as fossil gas through pipelines and burned in power stations, home boilers, or used in industry.[194]

Although liquid methane is currently considered one of the least polluting fossil fuels, so much so that its use is being promoted within the European Union's ecological transition program, the extraction, liquefaction, shipping, and re-gasification of LNG emits considerable quantities of CO_2. LNG also leaks methane into the atmosphere at almost every step of the supply chain. Eighty times more potent than carbon dioxide, methane is a greenhouse gas responsible for more than a quarter of global warming to date.[195]

In a footnote to the press release, Total boasted that all the carbon emissions of the shipment to CNOOC had been "offset." However, it did not specify how this was achieved: for example, by recapturing the CO_2 emitted? Total's press release cleverly avoided explaining how the company had neutralized the carbon dioxide produced during the gas extraction in northern Australia, the cooling, the liquefaction, the shipping, the delivery, and the re-gasification. CNOOC was equally ambiguous. Though proudly declaring that the shipment was carbon-free, the company did not explain how it had neutralized the emissions triggered by the delivery of the gas within China. How much CO_2 are we talking about? According to both companies' estimates, the deal released about two hundred forty thousand tons, the same amount that thirty thousand US households produce in a year, which is a considerable quantity.

The words "zero emission" suggest that all carbon dioxide has been removed according to specific procedures and under the supervision of international institutions. But this is not the case. Neither legislation nor an organization that grants such a label and that is accepted by the international community exists. Though in Europe and in California heavy-emitting industries like steel are allocated allowances to release certain quantities of carbon, which can be bought and sold, "zero emission" is a self-certification and the issuer is not required to explain how or how much CO_2 has been neutralized, recaptured, compensated, or more generically offset. None of these definitions, in fact, have any real meaning.

Total and CNOOC issued the "zero emission" label after purchasing carbon credits through a specialized broker, a common procedure in the energy sector. The broker offered them a range of green investments which generated carbon credits; the two they selected were the Hebei Guyuan wind farm in northern China and the Kariba REDD+ forest protection plan in Zimbabwe.[196] The cost was $600,000, a fraction of the $17 million cost of the shipment of liquefied natural gas.[197]

At first glance, carbon credits appear to be an integral part of the ecological transition, green investments which benefit all the parties involved. CNOOC declared that it was importing zero-emission gas in line with China's program aiming to achieve carbon neutrality by 2060; the Hebei Guyuan plant increased the number of wind turbines, which will generate more clean electricity in the region; Total got involved in one of Zimbabwe's poor communities: the Kariba REDD+ forest protection plan received funds to clear dead branches and trees from the dense forest along the Mozambique border, essential for building fire breaks. Fire breaks prevent CO_2-producing forest fires from leaping into Mozambique's territory. However, none of these investments and projects has removed the 240,000 tons of CO_2 released into the atmosphere by the sale. In fact, all that carbon is still in the atmosphere. How is this possible?

The carbon credits that Total and CNOOC purchased have nothing to do with recapturing the carbon both companies have released into the atmosphere. The credits are not attached to negative carbon activities. Instead, they refer to "preventive" measures that will reduce CO_2 emissions in the future. The purpose of the fire breaks in the Kariba Forest in Zimbabwe is to block the next forest fire in Mozambique from jumping across the border. The new wind turbines in China aim to reduce the use of electricity produced by the Hebei coal plant. Not only does neither investment capture the amount of carbon released into the atmosphere by the deal, but some of the carbon credit benefits purchased may also never be realized: for example, if no forest fires from Mozambique jump the border to the Kariba Forest.

What the carbon credit broker sold to Total and CNOOC is a well-known agreement in the voluntary carbon credit market, in which the polluter spends a little money on green projects, aimed at reducing greenhouse gases that do not yet exist and which will only occur in specific circumstances and, in exchange, self-certifies that the carbon it has already released into the atmosphere has been neutralized. The former Bank of England governor Mark Carney, now a United Nations special envoy for climate, argues that carbon credits are ambiguous.[198] It is easy to see how they can be used as a sort of license to pollute.

Ambiguity and opacity well describe most aspects of the "official" transition to cleaner energy. Let's take into consideration electric cars, for example, which are promoted as an ecological means of transport, as if their carbon footprint were nonexistent. In reality, it is considerable—as shown by the journey around the world required for one of the key components of the batteries, cobalt, before it can be put to use.

The largest producer of cobalt in the world is the Democratic Republic of the Congo, where children often mine the mineral by hand in old mines, a dangerous process of extraction performed without the use of modern technology.[199] From the Democratic Republic of the Congo, the cobalt sails to Finland, home to the largest refinery in Europe. From Finland, it travels to China, where most of the battery's cathodes are produced. From China, the cathodes travel to the United States, to Nevada, for example, where Tesla car batteries are manufactured and assembled. Once ready, the batteries make the final journey to an electric automobile assembly line, in California or elsewhere.

Before a buyer puts the zero-emission sticker on the bumper of his electric car, the cobalt inside has traveled more than twenty thousand miles, leaving behind a dense trail of carbon. Lithium, nickel, manganese, and other elements of the electric car also pollute the environment—the extraction of one ton of lithium emits five to fifteen tons of CO_2, equivalent to the carbon released in a year by one or two American families—and travel around the world. A Chinese study published by the *Financial Times* in 2021[200] shows that the production of an electric car emits 60 percent more CO_2 than the manufacture of a traditional car, mainly due to the carbon footprint of the batteries. Indeed, it is estimated that more than a third of the CO_2 released to manufacture an electric car is attributable to the production of batteries. Charging the electric car in a country that uses renewable energy sources does not pollute, but in a country where fossil fuels are still used, it generates CO_2. Therefore, where fossil fuels are still used to generate electricity, the carbon footprint of an electric car could be as bad as the carbon footprint of a vehicle run on fossil fuel.

Why are we not aware of these facts? Because society has built a complex and reassuring mythology around the looming catastrophe of climate change. Carbon credits and electric cars are among its characters. The motives are self-evident: the climate chaos already upon us is too big a challenge to be properly addressed without reinventing the way we live and the way we have conducted politics for millennia. Therefore, politicians, the media, and people in general have embraced the illusion that the process of the destruction of the planet at our hands can slow down and eventually even be blocked by showing good intentions, e.g., carbon credits, without having to take immediate radical action. On the surface, carbon credits are green investments which confirm our commitment to go green, but in reality they prolong our dependency on fossil fuels. Carbon credits are indeed a license to pollute.

Thanks to the mythology of carbon credits, society continues to be delusional, living in an imagined reality, refusing to reinvent itself to stop the fundamental changes we are observing in nature. The way the war in Ukraine has been conducted and supported and the use of an ambivalent energy embargo on Russian oil as an economic weapon against the invading power are good examples of how much out of sync with nature our society is. Both events are big polluters; war always is, but because of modern technology, its environmental impact is much larger than in the past. A report released by Brown University's Watson Institute for International and Public Affairs in 2019, for example, showed that the Global War on Terror that began in 2001 has released 1.2 million metric tons of greenhouse gases, equivalent to the emissions of 257 million cars per year, more than twice the number of vehicles on the road in the United States.[201] Although it is still impossible to estimate the environmental impact of the war in Ukraine, it is likely to set us back by years in terms of the containment of greenhouse gas emissions in Europe.

As for the sanctions on Russian energy, we know that the substitution of natural gas supplied and delivered through pipelines with shipments of LNG significantly increases carbon emissions.[202] A study conducted by Sphera, which aims to help companies achieve their sustainability goals, published in October 2021, showed that LNG imports generate between 61 percent and 176 percent more greenhouse gas emissions than the supply from Russia via the Turk-Stream pipeline. TurkStream is a newly developed pipeline system with a capacity to bring 31.5 billion cubic meters of gas from Russia to Turkey and countries in southeast Europe. The higher emissions are a result of energy-intensive liquefaction (including purification) and LNG carrier transport.[203]

The environmental impact of the sanctions, however, goes well beyond the higher polluting effect of LNG versus the preexisting gas pipelines because the sudden demand from Europe has led to the reopening of carbon-emitting plants and has further boosted the US shale industry producing LNG. It is worth explaining how.

Until a decade ago, gas was mostly transported through a network of pipelines because the cost of producing and shipping LNG itself was prohibitive. However, in the last decade, fracking, the technique used to free gas trapped inside rock formations deep below the earth's surface, has boosted its production and lowered the costs of extraction to a point where the export of liquified fossil gas has become economically feasible, which in turn further increases production. LNG is now shipped everywhere. Since 2015, the United States, which possesses the largest fields of cheap shale gas in the world,[204] has invested heavily not only in the extraction but also in the export of liquefied fossil gas, building many terminals for shipping along the Gulf Coast. Such a large and time-consuming investment—it takes between three and five years to build a new LNG terminal—has been driven by the anticipation of the growth of demand from various countries in Asia. When the invasion of Ukraine started in February 2022, triggering a series of sanctions on Russian energy exports, it was serendipitous for the American gas industry. Producers of liquefied natural gas exported their increased capacity to satisfy the sudden surge in demand from European countries no longer able to rely on Russian pipelines.

The sharp increase in European demand has come just as the US has stepped into a new role as the world's largest LNG producer, overtaking Australia and Qatar in 2021. It has been an incredibly rapid change since 2016, when the US first began exporting in earnest. Over the last three years, production has tripled. There are reasons to believe that the American trend to increase production and shipments of LNG will continue to satisfy the European demand for natural gas for years to come. Of course, such a trend goes against the Paris Agreement's goal, which states that to contain the warming of the atmosphere to below 1.5 degrees Celsius within the next decade, a 40 percent drop in gas production and consumption must be achieved.[205]

The embargo on Russian energy supplies is clearly a political decision, as was the decision of Moscow to close indefinitely the Nord Stream pipeline, and because of that its environmental consequences have been purposely ignored. Indeed, Washington has enthusiastically embraced the role of long-term energy provider for Europe, increasing LNG exports during the first quarter of 2022 by two-thirds over the previous year. President Biden has even promised to boost production to reach a yearly output of at least fifty billion cubic meters by 2030.[206] Apart from making the powerful US energy lobby very happy, being the guarantor of European energy security has reinstated the United States into a dominant position among the NATO allies.

Climate change is not affecting world politics, just as the War on Terror ignored the negative consequences it would have upon global pollution. The possibility of purchasing carbon credits for self-certification of carbon neutrality is the fig leaf that hides this shocking truth: that carbon credits have become an incentive to pump more natural gas and to sell it, projecting the false image that the business is clean.

As more and more LNG ships cross the Atlantic, many will travel with self-declared carbon-neutral certifications, thanks to the carbon credits acquired. Originally seen as an unavoidable part of the energy transition, carbon credits have become an instrument with which to resist change and to maintain the existing dependency on fossil fuels. Politically, they offer a fake environmental clean bill of health. In addition, buying them diverts money from investment in technologies capable of actually capturing emissions. Only by capturing emissions, in fact, is the carbon we produce really neutralized. To do that, however, you have to remove it from its source and, therefore, you need to have the capturing facility near the place where the emission originates.

In 2021, about forty million tons of CO_2 were neutralized using carbon capture projects. The figure is very small: to achieve a zero-emission planet we will need to capture 1.7 billion tons annually by 2030.[207] Recapturing this amount of CO_2 must be economically viable, i.e., it has to be profitable. To achieve such a goal a joint venture between the private sector and state institutions is needed. As we shall see in the following chapters, this approach has opened for business the low Earth orbit.

At the moment, most of the recaptured carbon is stored or buried underground, and so it is useless. Of this program, *Finan-*

cial Times correspondent Richard Milne explains in an FT video: "Norway started with this already in the 1990s. They've got a North Sea oil and gas platform where they've been pumping CO_2 into the seabed since 1996." Grete Tveit, the Senior VP for Low Carbon Solutions at Equinor, continues, "For the Sleipner field and Snøhvit together, we have avoided CO_2 emissions for 25 years of 1 to 2 million [metric tons] per year.[208] The idea of reusing the carbon captured is part of the "circular economy," which centers upon the necessity of recycling everything. Many companies, including some of the largest enterprises in the world, have embraced it. Apple, for example, is using recycled materials to manufacture its products,[209] and Ford is building 3D-printed auto parts with so-called waste dust from its factories.[210] Several start-ups are experimenting with new technologies to recapture the carbon already present in the atmosphere; some are even attempting to convert it directly into products, a process called carbon transformation. These are already considered carbon emission-negative companies. Among them is an American chemical company called Twelve.

Twelve brings carbon dioxide back into the supply chain by transforming it into the building blocks of a huge range of products, from shoes to luxury cars.[211] Let's not forget that various industrial processes, from vacuum-packing foods to refrigeration to carbonating drinks to making fertilizers, already use carbon dioxide.

Twelve has developed a catalyst that breaks down carbon dioxide molecules into their chemical components and rearranges them into new compounds using electricity and hydrogen extracted from water. The process mimics what we find in nature: a tree sucks carbon dioxide from the air and water from the ground, and uses sunlight as a source of energy to transform the carbon into sugar. The new technology captures the carbon, breaks it down, and then recomposes it into various products using hydrogen and oxygen from water, as well as electricity as an energy source from renewable sources for transformation.

Technology can also help regulate the carbon offset market. Sylvera Ltd., a London-based company, provides ratings for carbon offsets similar to credit scores. Utilizing satellite images, 3D laser scans, and other data, it estimates how much carbon is stored in trees. Ed Ballard of the Wall Street Journal explains: "It crunches that information using machine-learning technology to grade the likely effectiveness of offset projects that plant or protect forests. The company has signed up clients including Delta Air Lines Inc., grain trader Cargill Inc., and consulting firm Bain & Co. since it launched in 2020."[212]

Carbon is an essential element of our planet, so using it in correct ways—for example, to enrich soil depleted by a prolonged use of chemical fertilizers—can be beneficial. Carbo Culture, a Helsinki start-up, has developed a technology that removes CO_2 and reuses biomass that would otherwise be burned. The process creates from the biomass "biochar," a potent natural fertilizer that can restore the planet's precarious soil health.[213] Carbo Culture is part of a holistic approach to climate change, one that takes into consideration the difficulties of staging an efficient energy transition within the parameters of infinite growth. The insurmountable challenge of climate change, in fact, is not the change in the climate itself but the infinite growth model upon which our species has constructed the human supremacy that led to the age of the Anthropocene. And this explains why the commercialization and industrialization of the low Earth orbit has benefitted from a wealth of joint ventures between private enterprises and state institutions such as NASA, while business initiatives to mitigate climate change have not enjoyed the same treatment. And, as discussed in the following chapters, the zero-carbon revolution through space-based solar power has not come about because, so far, such technology has been put at the service of the military and its industries.[214]

Containing and reversing climate change will demand a new political and economic paradigm. It cannot be based on unlimited quantitative growth—the model of infinite economic growth discussed in the following chapter—but on qualitative containment of growth—and demilitarization.

CHAPTER TWELVE

The Model of Infinite Economic Growth

On Valentine's Day 1945, President Franklin D. Roosevelt secretly met with Abdul Aziz Ibn Saud, the king of Saudi Arabia. The meeting took place on the American cruiser *Quincy*, in the Suez Canal. Roosevelt was on his journey back from Yalta, where with Winston Churchill and Joseph Stalin he had drawn the borders of the post-war world order. However, neither Churchill nor Stalin had been briefed about this meeting. The US administration had purposely kept them in the dark because Roosevelt's intention was to strike a secret deal with Ibn Saud. Theirs was an unusual partnership, aimed at securing exclusive US access to the Saudi oil fields, and in the years to come it was going to shape a different map of the world: the map of American economic supremacy.[215]

Throughout World War II, the United States, at the time the largest producer and exporter of oil in the world, had supplied energy to the Allies' war machine. However, by 1945 it had become apparent that the US would soon lose its position of primacy in the energy sector because of the depletion of its natural oil and gas reserves.[216] Roosevelt was very concerned about it; he believed that whoever controlled the oil supply would control the world. If the US was to continue to be the largest economy in the world and become the strongest post-war superpower, it needed easy access to plentiful oil. For the US administration, Washington's partnership with Saudi Arabia was the most effective strategy to maintain a firm grip on the world oil supply. Against this background, the two leaders signed a historic agreement on the USS *Quincy*:

although it was not made explicit in the agreement, in exchange for access to the vast Saudi oil reserves, the United States agreed to guarantee Saudi Arabia's national security. Almost seventy-five years later, the deal is still in place.

In the 1950s, the energy alliance between Riyadh and Washington, at the time still the largest oil producer in the world,[217] boosted the US economic model of infinite growth, an economic system that had proved so successful during the war. Resting upon a plentiful and easily accessible supply of oil for the economy, the model had been incorporated into the American dream: American families were encouraged to buy homes in the suburbs and to drive cars to work in the cities. To promote this unique lifestyle, in the post-war era, the federal government invested heavily in building a network of interstate highways. In 1956, President Dwight D. Eisenhower signed the National Interstate and Defense Highways Act, which allocated $25 billion to the construction of 41,000 miles of the Interstate Highway System, at the time the largest public works project in American history.[218] Like a gigantic spider's web of asphalt, the Interstate Highway System made it possible for vehicles to reach every corner of the country.

The economic model of infinite growth was also incorporated into the Marshall Plan, the blueprint for the reconstruction of war-torn western European countries. The plan promoted and encouraged the growth of oil-dependent industries, from automobile to construction, from mining to textiles.[219] During the economic boom of the 1950s and 1960s, fossil fuel products became the building blocks of the European reconstruction. So did their derivatives, such as plastic, which became one of the main components of consumer goods. Most of these products were made in America. Thanks to the funds allocated by the Marshall Plan, the European market was able to absorb the enhanced production capacity that the US had developed during World War II, which otherwise would have remained unused, undermining the economic model of infinite growth.

Within this economic construction, the most relevant indicator of growth was the gross domestic product (GDP). Developed as a measure of wealth by American economists during the war, the "mighty GDP" became the global barometer of progress and a proxy for the economic recovery of Europe. Because GDP valued quantity over quality,[220] consumption over savings or the conservation of goods, the more a society produced and consumed, the more prosperous it was perceived to be. If in the late 1940s, among the ruins of a continent ravaged by war, this mantra sounded like a sweet melody, today its echoes are the funeral march of our planet.

The promise of infinite growth, which requires an equally infinite supply of fossil fuels for factories, cars, homes, transport, etc., has become the primary source of a perpetual cycle of pollution, environmental degradation, and climate change that is killing us and the planet. Earth's resources are, in fact, consumed at an astonishingly fast rate, as if they were unlimited and with shockingly serious consequences for the planet and for us. Think of the Amazon Rainforest being burned to clear land to plant crops which are in high demand. In the Italian newspaper *il Fatto Quotidiano*, Giorgia Colucci explains: "In 2021, the world lost 11.1 million hectares of tropical forests. This is an area equivalent to that which covers all the woods in Italy. . . . the disappeared forests stored 2.5 Gt of carbon from the atmosphere, an amount equal to that produced every year by India."[221] Though we are reminded daily of the catastrophic consequences of the economic model of infinite growth, we seem unable or unwilling to abandon it. Instead, we keep developing strategies to prolong its life span, including the system of carbon credits. Fossil fuel is the junk energy we consume; we cannot stop binging on it. Think of the reactivation of coal plants following the embargo on Russian energy exports: Are we blinded? Are we delusional? Or are we simply fossil fuel addicts?

None of these definitions seems correct. We are an intelligent species, highly adaptable, so we possess the skills to conceptualize an alternative economic system: the circular economy, for example, in which everything is recycled. We also have the technology to make that happen. Take electric car batteries: why not use recycled materials to produce them? That is what one of Tesla's cofounders, J.B. Straubel, has been trying to do with the start-up Redwood Materials. Redwood Materials recycles everything, from old iPhone batteries to those of scooters and electric bicycles, and even those used in electric toothbrushes. In 2021, about half the company's products originated from old batteries.[222]

We all know that batteries cannot be disposed of easily. Throwing them in the bin or burying them in a landfill contaminates the environment. And such a hazard is only going to increase in the future, as electric vehicles replace fossil fuel cars. This is what the International Energy Agency says about it: "A predicted 23 million EV cars sold globally in 2030 could lead to 5,750,000 tonnes of retired batteries by 2040, assuming a battery lifetime of 10 years and 250 kg per battery pack."[223] A good way to dispose of batteries is to dissolve them using a special solution, which has a cost.[224] Better would be to recycle them, but that too has a cost. Calculating the costs is complicated. For example, recycling batteries recuperates valuable metals, e.g., cobalt and nickel, and, when done on a large scale, it can lower the demand for expensive raw materials and secure an alternative supply chain. It can also reduce the price of electric cars. According to the International Energy Agency, in 2021 the average price of a metric ton of battery-grade lithium carbonate was $17,000, while that of lead was $2,425 in the North American market. One of the key ingredients for electric cars is battery-grade lithium, whose price quintupled in 2021 to reach a record $34,000 per metric ton.[225] These high costs account for more than a third of the final cost of an electric car.[226]

Several companies are already working in partnership with battery producers and users to create a healthy loop within the circular economy and in doing so curb the price of electric vehicles. For example, the rechargeable lithium-ion battery recycling specialist Li-Cycle, a company headquartered in Canada that operates globally, has partnered with Glencore, which supplies battery metals for electric vehicles, to recycle old batteries into new ones. Li-Cycle recovers and processes 95 percent of the components of batteries, including lithium, manganese, cobalt, and nickel.[227]

According to a recent study[228] about the costs and profitability of recycling batteries, without policy interventions in the form of government subsidies and other financial incentives—for example a partnership between the above Li-Cycle and the Department of Energy—recycling batteries is not always profitable. The major obstacles are high fixed labor and transportation costs, the absence of economies of scale, and the high investments required to implement the process and technology used to disassemble battery packs. This is the main reason why the business of recycling has not been developed in parallel with the production of electric cars. To foster the industrial reconversion under the banner of sustainability, the state, as the representative of society, has to get involved through subsidies or partnerships with the private sector. This approach is not only economically feasible but can be very profitable; so far, recycling batteries has made commercial sense when it is highly decentralized, done in large volumes and with the best possible technology.

Our reluctance to abandon the model of infinite economic growth and embrace an alternative system that focuses on quality of life, e.g., the circular economy, may also spring from our biological make-up. I am referring to human biology and to our desire to survive as long as possible. More than the nature of the capitalist system, what influences us may well be the quest for longevity and our primordial instincts, what Darwin defines as "the indelible stamp" of our ancestors.[229] We may be programmed to accumulate; our ancestral fear of starvation may well be one of the reasons we have instinctively embraced the model of infinite growth. This is, indeed, a very controversial issue and for many it may sound like a shocking statement.

In his highly criticized book *The Social Conquest of Earth*, Professor Edward O. Wilson isolates the secrets of the success of our species. Without ignoring the role that luck has played, he mentions the ability of every human to reproduce and the formation of groups, implying the extended family and the tribe. Even if many will disagree with this classification, it is unquestionable that increased longevity has contributed to demographic growth and that our social skills have facilitated our territorial conquest of the planet. All these traits spring from our biology. Professor Wilson believes that biology is paramount in our journey as a species, not economics or politics. If so, biology has written not only the stories of the creation and of evolution, but also of the key passages of the history of humanity. As Professor Wilson puts it, "History makes no sense without prehistory, . . . and prehistory makes no sense without biology."[230] Both biologically through procreation and socially through the formation of the family and the tribe, humans are programmed to survive, to seek longevity, and, therefore, to grow numerically. According to Professor Wilson, the family and the tribe are the products of an evolutionary jump our prehistoric humanoid ancestors experienced around two million years ago. It happened when they began cooking their food and living in campsites as a group. This move gave birth to "a society based in part on a division of labor, in which individuals act altruistically, that cover two or more generations, and that care for the young cooperatively."[231] Biologically, this construction may well be the product of a simple change in a single gene.[232] Such a tiny alteration could have been sufficient to revolutionize the way our species dealt with its offspring. How did that happen? The process of the maturing of the young slowed down, impacting, among other things, the trait of separation to carry on their own independent reproduction. This allowed humans to form the family, the extended family, and the tribe. Through these processes the individual yielded some of his or her own self-interest to the interest of the group, a sacrifice that led to the construction of "nests," the camps, similar to those of other primates, primarily to protect the young. As several generations at once took it upon themselves to defend the camp in which they and their offspring were born, the tribe emerged. The tribe also offered the individual much better food security, a key factor in the decision of individuals to be part of the group.

Within the tribe, humans developed new social skills. We enjoyed being part of groups and learned how to read people's behavior, a skill that Professor Wilson says was enhanced by our fascination for gossip. Another characteristic that developed at this time was the constant negotiation whereby we reconcile our individualistic instincts with the social needs of the group. As explained by the American writer Stewart Brand, quoting Professor Wilson, "In our eusocial species, that mix of traits makes us 'permanently unstable, permanently conflicted' between selfish impulses and cooperative impulses."²³³ He believes that from the endless effort to reconcile these conflicts springs our vibrant culture.

Our social skills made it possible to engage in collaborative warfare. Because food was the primary resource, hunters and gatherers were involved in territorial warfare to gain control of food supplies. Access to food remained the main limiting factor to population growth until the Neolithic revolution, when agriculture was invented. Cultivating crops and raising livestock boosted food production. Interestingly, in the transition health declined, possibly because of the change in diet, lifestyle, and proximity to animals.

The spectacular innovation of agriculture did not alter people's instincts: the pressure to grow numerically remained unchanged as did the pressure to accumulate food stocks when available. As food supplies rose, so did the population until, eventually, in a Malthusian loop, food became scarce once again. To regain food security, people reverted to wars of territorial conquest, as their Paleolithic ancestors had done.

Fast forward to the present day and we find along the Nile a similar pattern of behavior to secure the most important resource: water. Modern irrigation has improved food production, which in turn has boosted economic growth, increasing the demographic pressure in the countries that the Nile crosses. Food is once again scarce. In response to overpopulation along the shores of the Nile, nations have built dams to divert the water to their own land to the detriment of others.

The struggle to control vital resources has never ended. What has changed are the instruments we use. Such tension is deeply rooted in the ancestral certainty that to survive as a species we must never stop growing demographically. This is what Darwin meant by "the indelible stamp" of our ancestors. In 1945, President Roosevelt acted as his Paleolithic and Neolithic progenitors would have: he secured for his tribe, and his tribe alone, access to the most vital resource of the day—oil. And he did it to maintain the United States' economic supremacy, the modern-day equivalent of a prehistoric tribe's food security.

Throughout the history of our species, nature has been the sole arbiter of our constant push to survive. As Thomas Malthus has observed, overproduction in agriculture led to overpopulation, which in turn opened the doors to famine, until the cycle started all over again. Wars of territorial conquest, wars of independence, and even genocides, have often rebalanced the equation between demographic growth and food production, i.e., nature. However, none of these factors altered the belief that to survive we need to keep growing numerically.

The Industrial Revolution ended the Malthusian cycle. Technological innovation triggered astonishing improvements in living conditions in Western countries; people went to work in factories and earned enough money to regularly feed and take care of themselves. Together with better sanitation, these improvements made people healthier and boosted longevity and demographic growth.

The Industrial Revolution also marks the beginning of the age of the Anthropocene, when nature no longer drives change but humanity and its own creation, artificial intelligence, do. Such conquest, however, came at a high price: it speeded up the exploitation of resources and kick-started environmental degradation as well as climate change, tilting for the first time the delicate balance between us and nature.

However, it would be a mistake to believe that, until the Industrial Revolution, human progress had never dramatically or permanently altered the natural environment. Our ancestors hunted and killed off all very large animals by developing better weapons and hunting strategies. Our species has caused the extinction of many others,[234] and although throughout history it mostly happened out of necessity, i.e., to secure our survival, we still have deprived nature of many of its creations. What is unprecedented today is the scale of our impact on the planet.

Should we feel guilty or congratulate ourselves for winning over the world? A mix of both feelings seems appropriate.

The Industrial Revolution prompted the birth of modern capitalism. Every single component of this economic model satisfies our instinct for quantitative growth: profits, production, accumulation, markets, supply and demand, consumption, stock market indexes. These are indicators that must grow constantly. Even the exploitation of resources and of labor, two means of production, must have an infinitely growing trajectory for the sake of productivity and profitability. Capitalism carries the indelible stamp of our ancestors because we humans created it.

So do economics and technology. In the age of the Anthropocene, however, the pressure to grow is no longer a powerful tool for avoiding extinction. On the contrary, it is a threat to our survival. How did that happen?

When applied to modernity, the economic model of infinite growth generated consumerism, what Thorstein Veblen defined as conspicuous consumption, the consumer habit of buying goods in greater quantity than required by necessity. This behavior is not conducive to survival but to waste—and in particular waste of resources, with a consequent negative impact on the environment and, eventually, on our own survival. This scenario does not scare us, not because it never happened before, but because we consider it inconceivable. The idea that in the age of the Anthropocene we could become the cause of our own extinction by behaving as our ancestors did is regarded as folly. Biologically our brain is wired as it was in the Paleolithic age: accumulation of resources is still regarded as the key to survival.

Recently, it has become apparent that we are less afraid of the consequences of environmental degradation than of pandemics, but in a not-too-distant future, the likely end of our permanence on Earth may very well spring not from our species' spectacular success in surviving, growing, and conquering the planet but from our role in the spreading of a virus. We are fast approaching a point of no return, when humans and nature will not be able to coexist. We are too many, we consume too much, and we want to keep multiplying and improving our living conditions.

Never before has population grown so rapidly—in 1950, five years after the founding of the United Nations, the world population was estimated at around 2.5 billion people. It reached five billion in 1987 and six billion in 1999.[235] In October 2011, the global population was estimated to be seven billion.[236] A global movement, 7 Billion Actions, was launched to mark this milestone. According to a 2022 statement from the UN, "The world's population . . . from the current 8 billion to 9.7 billion . . . in the mid-2080s."[237]

What can we do? The idea of us turning back the clock to reestablish a sort of modern-day Malthusian cycle is absurd, altering our biological traits is equally impossible, and if biology is the master of our destiny on Earth, conditioning our demographic growth, protecting nature to the detriment of mankind—e.g., culling our species—will equally never work. Neither will putting our future in the hands of greedy individuals, i.e., the Techtitans or the Space Barons, who continue to celebrate the model of infinite growth as if that will bring our salvation! It won't. What is needed is a twofold approach: a cultural, existential revolution that will tame our biological instincts and make us seek qualitative instead of quantitative growth, and a new frontier where we will go to find plentiful resources.

The first task is already taking place on Earth. The latter must be developed in space, and specifically in the low Earth orbit.

We have seen that the circular economic model is an important prerequisite for reprogramming our ancestral instincts, for altering Darwin's indelible stamp. We have also acknowledged that, to succeed, this transition must be encouraged, funded, and implemented by the state, the modern version of the prehistoric nest, and for the common good, not for the profit of a few. What remains to be clarified is how we go about the transition.

Australia, for example, has introduced a ban on the export of several waste products. According to the Australian Bureau of Statistics, in 2018–19 the country generated 75 million metric tons of waste. Thirty-two percent, or 1.5 million metric tons of the four million exported, came from five materials subject to the ban: glass, plastic, tires, paper, and cardboard. A further twenty million metric tons—of which about half are organic, masonry, and plastic—end up every two years in landfills in Australia.[238] Recycling these products is a step in the right direction towards a new paradigm of sustainability, as proven by recent statistics: more than 90 percent of all demolition waste in the construction of Sydney's 5.8 hectare Central Park renewal development was recycled, making it one of the largest recycling projects in Australia. Although the Australian government did not invest directly in these projects, the ban on exports of waste opened new business opportunities for companies willing to operate in recycling, i.e., a key component of the circular economy.

The drive towards quantitative growth is also the root cause of food waste, which has a high cost. According to the data collected by Rabobank's 2020 food waste report,[239] 13 percent of Australia's weekly grocery shopping goes to waste. This corresponds to a cost of about 1,043 Australian dollars per year per capita, or 10.3 billion Australian dollars nationally, money literally thrown into the garbage. In 2018–19, the cost of household waste was about six hundred million Australian dollars. If food and garden waste could be reduced, either by composting or anaerobic digestion, large sums of money could be saved, some of the eight metric tons of greenhouse emissions from solid waste in landfills could be reduced, and energy could be produced.[240] These opportunities do exist, as does the technology to make them work. What is needed now is simply a forward-looking state—not a dirigiste state but a state willing to encourage the transition—one with visionary leadership and stable institutions and the trust and responsibility of the population.

The circular economy alone, however, will not solve the pressure that overpopulation places on the Earth's limited resources. Some scientists believe that the only possibility for saving our species and the planet is to tap into the unlimited resources of the cosmos and, in particular, to operate from the low Earth orbit, which, as we shall see, is more easily accessible than higher altitudes. The goal is not only to harvest resources, and to move industrial production and perhaps even food production into space, but to get ready to coexist and cooperate with other governments globally to face new challenges such as climate change in a concerted effort. NASA is already monitoring how cotton roots grow in the absence of gravity in the International Space Station with the idea to help develop new varieties of cotton plants with deeper root systems able to access and absorb water more efficiently from soil in drought-prone areas.[241] Zero gravity research, therefore, can help us improve and maximize crop efficiency and yield on Earth.

Even if many are not aware of it, humanity has already benefitted from research conducted in the International Space Station, ranging from water purification systems to new cures for cancer. The low Earth orbit is already the next rich frontier for our species, one which may offer solutions to our incumbent problems, and it belongs to all of us, not to a handful of billionaires. As we battle against the privatization of our water on Earth, we must also battle against the Space Barons' privatization and industrialization of low Earth orbit. But to do so we must achieve a higher degree of consciousness. We must be able to see ourselves not as citizens, not as consumers, not as users of technology, but as part of a cosmic species that aims at maximizing the reach of human creativity through technological innovation and space exploration. In short, we must take full control of the future.

In the words of the poet T.S. Eliot:

> *We shall not cease from exploration*
> *And the end of all our exploring*
> *Will be to arrive where we started*
> *And know the place for the first time.*

Look up, embrace the stars, and evolve: this should be our motto. Evolve and show ourselves and our leaders that we can modify our nature, that we can stop chasing infinite growth, that we can stop opting for war as the nonsolution we like best, that we can stop being suicidal *AND*, at the same time, that we are willing to venture into the zero gravity frontier because that is where the solutions that we need on Earth are, and we believe so. So those who claim that we have to fix our problems on Earth before we venture into space are partly right; this is indeed our habitat, our home. However, they are wrong about how to go about seeking solutions.

The key question is, can we do it? Having won the battle with nature can we now strike a victory over our own ancestors' imprint? Or will the human biological stamp, once again, write the next chapter of our history and prevent us from going into space?

CHAPTER THIRTEEN

The Space Barons

July 21, 1969, 3:56 a.m., Italy. I am fourteen years old and my parents have just woken me up. Neil Armstrong is about to set foot on the Moon. I rush out of bed and sit in front of the black-and-white TV. I see an astronaut wearing white armor coming down a very small ladder, like those used in swimming pools. He is wearing big boots, a type of platform boots, possibly made of plastic. He is coming down slowly, one step at a time, as if carrying heavy weights inside his space suit. Maybe to offset the lack of gravity on the Moon, I wonder. On his back I see a square container which I assume is for oxygen. Then, when he finally reaches the last step of the ladder, he jumps, landing like a feather on the Moon's surface.

From the open windows the cheers of our neighbors fly into our living room. I look outside and all I see in the darkest hour of the night are the grayish lights of their TV screens shining everywhere. Our neighborhood looks like the Nativity, not of Christ but of mankind, not on Earth but on the Moon, not in December but in July. Everybody is awake. Everybody is up everywhere in the world. We are all watching the Moon landing through a spectacular new machine that never stops mesmerizing us, the television.

It is estimated that in the United States 94 percent of families, and between five hundred and six hundred million people worldwide, witnessed it live.[242] A spectacular event made possible by the launch, the year before, of satellites able to transmit images simultaneously everywhere. The Moon landing was not just an

American phenomenon; it was an epic, global event, an extraordinary achievement for humanity. "One small step for a man, one giant leap for mankind," is how Neil Armstrong summed it up. And he was right. Those Moon images, projected in real time into our homes, expanded our horizon beyond the Blue Planet. We sensed that we were no longer confined to Earth, that we had become a "cosmic" species. The Nativity I thought I was witnessing was the rebirth of humanity.

Despite these promises, the conquest of the Moon did not produce the cosmic revolution that many had anticipated. It did not pave the way for space exploration, nor did it stimulate a new generation of pioneers in search of extraterrestrial treasures. Unlike what happened with the discovery of the Americas, which ushered in the era of exploration of new lands for Europe, space remained essentially inaccessible. And the Moon was retrenched inside its mythical significance, as the Scottish novelist and essayist Andrew O'Hagan pointed out on the fortieth anniversary of the Moon landing: "The Moon we stare up at is in fact more naturally a thing of myth and childhood than of adult ambition."[243] The space race remained locked inside the Cold War dichotomy. It was nothing more than an accessory of the struggle between the two superpowers that the whole planet had been witnessing since Churchill, Roosevelt, and Stalin had redrawn the map of the world at Yalta. The space race was also deeply intertwined with the propaganda of the Cold War. After Armstrong planted the American flag on the Moon, he left a plaque on the lunar lander with the inscription, "We came in peace for all mankind." In the meantime, on Earth, Washington was carpet-bombing Vietnam in a war by proxy with Moscow. The truth is that the Moon landing was never meant to be a Nativity, as I had imagined. Humanity did not experience a cosmic rebirth. On the contrary, humanity sank deeper into the Cold War battle for earthly supremacy.

This outcome was predictable. The first serious foray into space took place with Sputnik, a capsule that the Soviet Union launched in 1957. It was also the Soviets who successfully completed the first Moon landing in 1959 with a space probe, Luna 2, unmanned of course. Later in the year, Luna 3 took the first photos of the dark side of the Moon.[244] To catch up with and surpass Moscow, in 1961 at the height of the Cold War, President John F. Kennedy launched the idea of landing an American astronaut on the Moon. In his opinion, planting the stars and stripes flag on lunar soil would prove once and for all the supremacy of the United States over the Soviet Union: the victory of the free world over the communist world. To get Congress to fund the space program, Kennedy tied it to national security. The space race became a military goal.

Kennedy's words about it are worth rereading:

> . . . if we are to win the battle that is now going on around the world between freedom and tyranny, the dramatic achievements in space which occurred in recent weeks should have made clear to us all, as did the Sputnik in 1957, the impact of this adventure on the minds of men everywhere, who are attempting to make a determination of which road they should take. . . .
>
> First, I believe that this nation should commit itself to achieving the goal, before this decade is out, of landing a man on the Moon and returning him safely to the Earth. No single space project in this period will be more impressive to mankind, or more important for the long-range exploration of space; and none will be so difficult or expensive to accomplish.[245]

Kennedy's words implied that the race to the Moon was part of the much more important battle that was taking place on Earth between the United States and the Soviet Union; even if exceedingly expensive and dangerous, the space race was potentially very rewarding for humanity.

A few years after Kennedy's speech, at the height of the Apollo missions and despite the high costs of the Vietnam War, the lunar project still absorbed 5 percent of the US budget. It is estimated that between $25 billion and $28 billion were spent at the time, equivalent to between $200 billion and $300 billion today.[246] Kennedy and the American presidents who followed him sold space supremacy to the taxpayer as a deterrent against the advance of the Soviet Union and against a nuclear conflict, as if it were enough to plant the American flag on the Moon and wave it in the still, thin lunar atmosphere to finally put an end to the spread of communism. The Moon landing was indeed an extraterrestrial exercise of soft power and national branding for earthly purposes, a strategy that at the time worked well but which, in the long term and in the light of the new space age, appears as what it is: a lost opportunity.

Were Washington and Moscow guilty of terrestrial provincialism? I wonder. Could it be that although they had the technology to venture into space and the will to do so, they had neither the political vision nor the imagination to glimpse the benefits of the cosmos for humanity? During the Cold War, it appears that technology was far ahead of politics, which was conditioned by geopolitical tensions, i.e., by very earthly affairs. If so, the Moon landing was one of the first examples of misunderstanding the Present Future era: technology projected us well into the future but politics prevented us from taking the necessary leap. Because technology and politics were out of sync, neither the United States nor the Soviet Union understood the tremendous potential of the space adventure.

Unsurprisingly, therefore, the enthusiasm of that July night died quickly, gobbled up by the Cold War narrative. And the Blue Planet went back to buzzing with earthly protests about the dichotomy of the two blocks: the hippies and the peace movement, the student uprisings and the anti-Vietnam demon-strations. Those who had a keen interest in the universe and were curious about life beyond Earth retreated to science fiction liter-ature, a rich field of possibilities away from the tensions between the two superpowers. And the space adventure faded away.

In the three years following the first Moon landing, only ten more astronauts set foot on lunar soil.[247] The last one was Eugene Cernan, and, in 1972, the Apollo program was abandoned in favor of the Space Shuttle program, which flew 135 missions until it was ended in 2011.[248] From 1972 onwards, conditioned by terrestrial provincialism, the United States and the Soviet Union focused on Earth's immediate spatial boundaries, i.e., the low Earth orbit (LEO), where both dreamed of locating Star Wars weapons and nuclear shields. LEO is just the vestibule of space, the area con-tained between the atmosphere and the Van Allen belts, i.e., between 150 and 500 miles from Earth.[249] This is where for decades our space adventure has been confined, an area today clogged with satellites and littered with debris, both unquestionable signs of human presence. As discussed in the following chapters, this is also the area where our cosmic adventure could truly take place.

The Space Shuttle's goal was to develop low-cost means to bring humans and goods to LEO to colonize it, primarily for issues of national security, but also for commercial and scientific ventures. And to a certain extent the program has been successful. The Shuttle's fleets were instrumental in building the International Space Station; they docked with the Mir Space Station. Shuttles carried to orbit the Hubble Space Telescope, the Chandra X-ray Observatory, and the interplanetary probes Magellan, Ulysses, and Galileo.[250] Thanks to the Spacelab module, built by the Euro-pean Space Agency, the Shuttle's fleets also carried out scientific experiments in the low Earth orbit that previously had to be per-formed in space stations.

However, the Space Shuttle program did not make LEO commercially manageable, and it did not provide an easily accessible bridge between Earth and LEO because it failed to make the program economically viable. The average cost of a flight was $450 million, most of which was money thrown away because NASA never succeeded in producing a reusable launch system.[251]

They also failed to shorten the turnaround time of spacecraft between flights. The fastest turnaround was fifty-eight days; after the *Challenger* disaster in 1986, it increased to eighty-eight days.[252] The safety of the Space Shuttle was a further problem, which two space tragedies exposed: the explosion of the *Challenger* and the *Columbia* disaster in 2003. Investigations into the *Challenger* explosion showed that the causes had been a series of malfunctions in the Shuttle, apparently well-known problems, which had never been adequately addressed.[253]

The real issue of the Space Shuttle program, anyway, was the absence of any strategic interest in it from the White House after the Cold War ended. President Clinton essentially ditched the Star Wars project, which became a low priority project. Another missed opportunity to improve life on Earth. For years the American space program was left in the hands of scientists-turned-bureaucrats, people with no clear vision or real understanding of its motivation. NASA became just one of the many US state institutions, populated by government employees with PhDs in astrophysics and rocket science acting as civil servants, lacking any commercial sense or commitment to improving the common good.

Even without any guidance from the US administration, NASA never shed its Cold War mentality, which had made the space race central to politics, and kept regarding the space program as a military expense rather than as a potential business, or a valuable asset for the future of humanity. This may well be the main reason why NASA failed to transform the Space Shuttle into an economically viable product and the low Earth orbit into a profitable, valuable sector for the advancement of research and development, i.e., the industry of the future. As a result, in the aftermath of the *Columbia* tragedy, the Bush administration decided to phase out the Space Shuttle program altogether.

The events of 9/11 and the Global War on Terror, which the Bush administration launched in 2001, forcefully revived the importance of the earthly supremacy of the United States as a fundamental pillar of national security. But this time the battle was very much taking place in the Middle East and central Asia, not in space. The war on terror cemented Americans' lack of interest in space; it confirmed that the Moon landing was a milestone of the past, of the Cold War; like the fall of the Berlin Wall, the Moon landing was the unquestionable proof that the free-world model had always been superior to communism.

In July 2011, when the Space Shuttle program was finally shelved, few Americans knew that NASA no longer had a means by which to launch cargo or astronauts into orbit and dock them at the International Space Station. It would take almost a decade for a crewed spaceflight to be launched from American soil. It happened on May 30, 2020, when NASA astronauts Doug Hurley and Robert Behnken reached the International Space Station aboard the SpaceX Crew Dragon spacecraft.[254] The flight was the result of cooperation between NASA and Elon Musk's SpaceX company to build Musk's partially reusable launching system.

To understand the paramount importance of a reusable launching system to provide a bridge between Earth and LEO, let's use a study by Harry Jones of the NASA Ames Research Center. Of the study, Steinar Lag, of the Norwegian consulting firm DNV, says:

> Reusable parts drastically lower the costs of launch, in turn lowering the barrier of access to space. NASA have calculated that commercial launch costs to the International Stations has been reduced by a factor of 4 over the last 20

years. The corresponding number for commercial launch costs to LEO is 20, from the $54,500/kg cost of NASA Space shuttles to $2,720/kg and $1,410/kg for SpaceX's Falcon 9 (2010) and Falcon Heavy (2018).[255]

From 2011 to 2020, NASA relied on Russian rockets, launched from Kazakhstan, to meet its orbital needs. The dependence on Russia to send American astronauts to space cost the American taxpayer large sums of money. As reported by *WIRED* in 2020, "a seat in a Soyuz capsule costs $86 million today, an increase of nearly 400 percent over about a decade and a half."[256] A 2016 report from NASA's Office of Inspector General forecast that by the time Boeing and Elon Musk's SpaceX were ready to fly in 2020, NASA would have ended up paying the Russian space agency Roscosmos more than $3.4 billion.[257]

Although at the beginning of the new millennium space was of little interest to the average American or to the White House, which was attempting to recreate the Cold War hegemony focusing exclusively on terrestrial supremacy, for a very small group of visionaries, who would soon amass huge fortunes in the technology sector, space was the next business frontier, a sector which offered almost unlimited opportunities. For these people, space was the future. Among them: Elon Musk, Jeff Bezos, the Microsoft cofounder Paul Allen, and the British serial entrepreneur and founder of Virgin Atlantic Richard Branson. The *Washington Post* reporter Christian Davenport has named them the Space Barons.

Stepping back to the magical July night of 1969, Elon Musk and Jeff Bezos have both admitted being deeply impressed, even inspired, by the first Moon landing. Growing up during the Cold War, reading science fiction novels, they both dreamed of a cosmic future for humanity. And indeed, some of their visions of our cosmic future seem to have popped out of science fiction novels. In the 1980s, when Bezos was at Princeton, he attended the seminars of physicist Gerard O'Neill, who imagined new settlements in space not too far away from Earth. These settlements would take the shape of huge cylinders and be put in orbit around the Earth. Inside the cylinders, the environment of Earth would be reproduced, including forests, rivers, lakes, and fields.

O'Neill's was a powerful idea, but it was nothing more than a science fiction dream. Though it could be conceptualized and visually represented, it was technologically unfeasible. However, the young Bezos embraced it, most likely because it presented a solution, even if a fantastical one, to something that had been bothering him since he was a child: the limited resources of our planet and humanity's insatiable thirst for growth. The BBC reports that Bezos once told his high school newspaper: "The Earth is finite . . . and if the world economy and population is to keep expanding, space is the only way to go."[258] Many decades and hundreds of billions of dollars later, Jeff Bezos is still clinging to O'Neill's original idea of artificial settlement in space. He envisages residential planets where people would migrate; industrial planets where the polluting activity of the economic model of eternal growth could continue to exist, but far away from Earth and humanity; agricultural planets; planets which replicate regions and cities on Earth, e.g., planets with Swiss villages or sandy white beaches; exclusively recreational planets—who knows, we could even have Las Vegas–type planets. The artificial settlement in space, Bezos believes, will save Earth from climate implosion and transform it into a cosmic park.[259]

Along the same lines, Elon Musk wants to colonize Mars, to make it livable, to save humanity from a third world war. These are very big dreams, that go well beyond earthly and human boundaries, but they are far from new, and perhaps this is the reason why they are so appealing. The idea of humanity's long-term salvation through space dates to the beginning of the twentieth century.

At the beginning of the last century, the discovery of the huge power of the atom triggered the belief that galactic colonization was feasible and that the leap of humanity into the cosmos could prevent its extinction. People like the Russian scientist Konstantin Tsiolkovsky envisioned the colonization of asteroids using nuclear-powered spacecraft. The American engineer Robert Goddard, the inventor of the first liquid-fueled rocket, believed that if humanity could unlock the atom, it could also travel beyond the solar system. Following in the footsteps of these scientists, Elon Musk is convinced that colonizing space will allow humanity to transcend the "Great Filter," the concept that all civilizations in the cosmos face a cut-off point in evolution that extinguishes them, an idea that Robin Hanson, an American professor of economics, first proposed in 1996.[260] Because the life span of an average mammalian species is a million years, if we do nothing to avoid extinction, at some point in the future our time will come.[261]

It is unquestionable that the unlocking of the atom and the Moon landing opened new horizons. Even if some of them at times seemed absurd, they have been instrumental to progress. As George Bernard Shaw pointed out in *Man and Superman*: "The reasonable man adapts himself to the world: the unreasonable one persists in trying to adapt the world to himself. Therefore, all progress depends on the unreasonable man."[262] The Space Barons are part science fiction characters, part unreasonable men attempting to shape the world according to their vision of the future, part modern businessmen whose intuition tells them that space is the next virgin field full of opportunities, and part preachers promoting a new faith that Professor Mary-Jane Rubenstein has defined as "Astrotopia, the dangerous religion of the corporate space race."[263]

As is customary in the businesses on which they built their huge fortunes, i.e., the digital revolution, the Space Barons are selling an idea, a vision of a future in space that they are pursuing without knowing if it is technologically, economically, or even biologically feasible. When they began their space programs, for example, none of them knew (and still don't) if a totally reusable launching system could ever be produced, but they were adamant that they would manufacture it. They operate in the business of the impossible, which becomes probable, and finally, at times, possible, often against all odds. As proven by the Space Shuttle's experience, the initially inconceivable reusable booster technology became a probability and eventually a reality. Without it the economics of space could never have worked. Here is how Elon Musk put it: "If one can figure out how to effectively reuse rockets just like airplanes, the cost of access to space will be reduced by as much as a factor of a hundred. . . That really is the fundamental breakthrough needed to revolutionize access to space."[264] So far, the Space Barons have often achieved the impossible using taxpayer money, i.e., through joint ventures with state-owned organizations such as NASA. They have cleverly sold us the idea that space is accessible, and they have done it using a powerful narrative that has rekindled humanity's interest in the cosmos, a narrative that has reconnected us not only with the magic of the first Moon landing, but with the idea of a cosmic civilization. Predestination, visions, rebirth. These are concepts drenched in religious faith, which the Space Barons project in their messianic special quest, the components of a corporate new religion, Astrotopia, of which they are the chosen ministers. These concepts have also been the main ingredients of their marketing to raise the money required to fund their business ventures in the public and private sector. Richard Branson, for example, funded his Virgin Galactic space program by selling tickets to very rich people eager to become space tourists more than a decade before the first flight took off in December 2018.[265]

People's response to Astrotopia has been enthusiastic. The idea of salvation through space is very appealing in the context of a planet plagued by climate change, overpopulation, anxiety, and disillusionment towards politics; people desperately want to believe in a cosmic destiny to escape terrestrial dissatisfaction. For however absurd it may sound, space tourism is drenched in eschatological escapism.

Naturally, space tourism is accessible only to the very, very rich. Fashion tycoon Yusaku Maezawa has snapped up all the seats on Elon Musk's Starship spacecraft that will take twelve people on a six-day journey around the Moon, scheduled to take place in 2023 at the earliest. That's if SpaceX can pull the trip off. Maezawa has encouraged artists from all over the world to join him. The crew of space travelers is meant to be part of the first lunar voyage since the last US Apollo mission landed on the Moon in 1972. The Starship is also projected to land SpaceX's first crewed flight on Mars.[266]

Space tourism does not add anything to the wealth of humanity. It is yet another badge of exclusivity like the Bored Ape NFTs, and a source of funding. However, space tourism alone would never have been sufficient to bankroll the Space Barons' cosmic adventure. It wouldn't have happened without the involvement of space organizations like NASA. This type of joint venture should not come as a surprise. During the Cold War, the state and the private sector cooperated in many aspects of the space industry. From spy satellites to "the nuclear shield," a select group of private companies have provided the Pentagon, the Department of Defense, and NASA with cutting-edge technology. And they have been well paid. However, during the Cold War, the space sector remained a state monopoly and no proper competition existed among private contractors.

Today, the key question that people everywhere want answered is the following: How feasible is cosmic life for our species? The short answer is not at all, which is very different from what the Space Barons have been telling us. Huge impediments exist to successfully leaping from reality into science fiction. Biology is the first obstacle.

Space sojourns are very challenging for life because our bodies are intimately linked with the gravity, the rotation, and the atmosphere of Earth. Skeletal and vascular system changes—fluid shifting towards the head, alterations in metabolic function and in sensory motor functions, the negative impact of radiation and isolation-related stresses—are just some of the medical issues springing from space travel that have been detected in the six hundred people who have gone into space to date, primarily into the low Earth orbit.

Space tourism may be appealing to those who have big pockets, but that does not mean it is biologically a good idea for periods of days or weeks. Studies have shown that the longer and the further the human body travels away from Earth, the more serious are the health hazards. A NASA report on the bone health of twenty-nine male and six female astronauts over thirty days in space in 2010 showed that they all lost bone mineral density at an average of 1–1.5 percent per month, with some losing 10 percent at their hip and lumbar spines.[267] This is due to weightlessness, which causes a lack of crucial forces, i.e., muscular and gravitational, on the skeleton. The impact on bone density continued for some months after the flights, increasing the risk of fractures.

Astronauts in low Earth orbit, e.g., those working in the International Space Station, experience a constant state of weightlessness. The pull of gravity in LEO is only slightly less than on the Earth's surface, just 10 percent less. However, any object in orbit is in a permanent state of free fall as it rotates around the Earth. This phenomenon occurs because, in orbit, the gravitational force and the centrifugal force balance each other out. This is the reason why spacecraft in orbit remain in orbit and why people inside or outside the spacecraft experience weightlessness, a condition known as microgravity.

Free fall microgravity changes several factors that affect human physiology. For example, microgravity alters the flow and distribution of complex physiological fluids, such as blood and intestinal, lymphatic, and cerebrospinal fluids that are gravity dependent. This phenomenon is well explained in the scholarly article "Human Health during Space Travel: An Overview," in *Neurology India*:

> In microgravity, the heart and blood vessels are relieved of hydrostatic forces exerted on them by blood. The heart becomes rounded, potentially changing its pumping action. Blood is no longer pulled towards the feet. Blood pumped by the heart "floats" forward and remains in the head and upper torso. This causes a redistribution of blood and interstitial fluid towards the upper torso altering the physical shape of the astronaut's body by causing a puffy face, engorged neck veins, an enlarged thorax and reduced leg volume ("puffy face bird leg" syndrome). Physiologic sensors in the upper torso interpret this increase as "too much blood volume" in the body. The body's response is to correct this erroneous perception by decreasing the volume of blood pumped (and work done) by the heart, increasing fluid loss through the kidney and slowing the rate of red blood cell production.[268]

Microgravity is linked to the high incidence of kidney stones in returning astronauts, the development of anemia among them, and the faster rate of muscle atrophy, about 1 percent per week, fifty times the rate of people over fifty-five years of age on Earth. Returning to Earth can be equally challenging for the body's readaptation to earthly conditions: for example, there are risks of urinary retention, space motion sickness, and loss of the senses of smell, taste, and even hearing. In some cases, the alterations caused by space travel—such as eyeball buckling, bone loss, and changes to cardiac architecture—are irreversible.

Even more challenging are the health obstacles to long-term missions. A study conducted by NASA using two identical twins, one on board the International Space Station for 340 days and the other on Earth, produced interesting results. The study isolated five known hazards of long-term space missions: radiation, isolation and confinement, distance from Earth, altered gravity fields, and hostile/closed environments. After twenty-five months of observation, the permanent changes detected included genetic expression level, increased DNA damage from chromosomal inversion, increased number of shortened telomeres (a phenomenon likened to aging), and reduction in cognitive functions. The study emphasizes the negative impact that extended missions have on cognitive performance postflight, which could have serious implications for the safety of the mission. This may imply, for example, that, after landing on Mars, astronauts may not be able to function properly.[269]

Realistically, human missions to LEO and, to a lesser extent, those to the Moon are for now the sole space adventures within our bodies' reach. For periods as long as one year in the low Earth orbit, the negative impact of space upon our bodies can be mitigated and even offset with specific exercises and machines. As Loren Grush in *The Verge* explains:

> The International Space Station is equipped with three machines designed to give astronauts that full-body workout: a bicycle, a treadmill, and a weightlifting machine called ARED, for Advanced Resistive Exercise Device. Each machine is specially designed for space, since normal gym equipment would be useless in microgravity. Lifting weights, for instance, wouldn't do much in space since dumbbells wouldn't weigh anything. So instead, the ARED machine utilizes two canisters that create small vacuums that astronauts can pull against with a long bar. This allows them to do squats, bench presses, dead lifts, and more.[270]

Confinement and even the psychological pressure linked to prolonged missions in space are also big impediments. But they can be mitigated and reduced by building more spacious space-craft and stations. Radiation exposure remains a huge issue; however, it is less serious in LEO than in deep space missions because astronauts are shielded from a significant amount of space radiation by the Earth's magnetic field, which acts like a barrier around our planet.

If biology hinders the realization of the Space Barons' vision of a galactic civilization, physics represents an insurmountable obstacle. Technologically, reproducing in space the conditions of Earth that are essential to the survival of our bodies, what is commonly known as terraforming, is a task which would require centuries and possibly millennia. To understand the importance of this impediment let's analyze the feasibility of the colonization of Mars, promoted by people like Elon Musk.

CHAPTER FOURTEEN

Terraforming

In Kim Stanley Robinson's *Mars* science fiction trilogy, *Red Mars*, *Green Mars*, *Blue Mars*, published between 1992 and 1996, conditions on Earth have deteriorated so much that a group of one hundred people decide to start a voyage to Mars to colonize it. The year is 2026 and technology is sufficiently advanced for them to travel, land, settle on Mars, and start working to alter the highly inhospitable Martian environment to reproduce the conditions of life on Earth. The colonists drill deep holes into the soil to release subsurface heat and they detonate nuclear weapons in the permafrost to start producing flowing water. This process is known as terraforming. Here is how Robinson's publisher summarizes it:

> For centuries, the barren, desolate landscape of the red planet has beckoned to humankind. Now a group of one hundred colonists begins a mission whose ultimate goal is to transform Mars into a more Earthlike planet. They will place giant satellite mirrors in Martian orbit to reflect light to the surface. Black dust sprinkled on the polar caps will capture warmth and melt the ice. And massive tunnels drilled into the mantle will create stupendous vents of hot gases.[271]

Robinson's trilogy is considered by many science fiction readers one of the best accounts of terraforming in this literary genre. The idea that planets can be altered through extraplanetary interventions is indeed a recurring theme in science fiction and many authors have had a go at describing such phenomena. In the 1898 dystopian novel *The War of the Worlds*, H. G. Wells writes that when the Martians invade our planet, they bring with them a red weed. The weed spreads rapidly, killing off Earth's indigenous plants and transforming the environment. In the 1917 science fiction book *A Princess of Mars*,[272] Edgar Rice Burroughs introduces the reader to Barsoom, an arid world made habitable by an "atmosphere factory"; the book and its subsequent ten sequels form the basis for the Disney movie *John Carter*. The stories in Ray Bradbury's 1950 collection, *The Martian Chronicles*, are set on a desert planet crisscrossed with canals built by an alien civilization that distributes water from the polar caps.[273] In the 1952 novel *The Martian Way*, Isaac Asimov, the iconic science fiction writer, describes the terraforming of Mars using ice from Saturn's rings.

Robinson's *Mars* trilogy embraces the idea that because no single technique can alone alter the Martian landscape, the colonists use "synergistic terraforming," i.e., a combination of several technologies, which are applied together—through massive industrial efforts. Terraforming is also a process that takes place simultaneously on the Martian surface and in orbit. Robinson took the concept of synergistic terraforming from a 1991 scientific paper, "Making Mars Habitable," written by the planetary scientist Christopher McKay and published in the journal *Nature*. According to the writer Eric Choi, the article describes

> a two-phase approach in which the planet is first warmed by a massive release of carbon dioxide followed by a modification of the atmosphere to scrub out the carbon dioxide and increase the oxygen content. The estimated time scale for this approach was about one hundred years for the first step and up to one hundred thousand years for the second.[274]

The colonization of Mars is very much part of the idea of cosmic civilization and it should be seen as the first step towards it: if humanity could terraform Mars, then it could replicate the effort all over the galaxy. For the supporters of this belief, terraforming is seen as a necessity. Elon Musk claims that for people like himself it is also a duty they owe to humanity to preserve the human species well beyond its natural life span. "I think we have a duty to maintain the light of consciousness, to make sure it continues into the future," he said in 2014.[275] According to Musk, the reason we have not encountered another civilization, another intelligent species is that none have tried to become a galactic one and, therefore, they have become extinct. Musk sees the universe as a cosmic cemetery, full of "dead, one-planet civilizations." In sharp contrast, the mathematician Olle Häggström developed the "Bullerby scenario," named after the idyllic rural society that the Swedish author Astrid Lindgren described in her children's books published in the late 1940s. This is how Häggström defines the Bullerby scenario:

> Here, humanity settles down into a peaceful and quiet steady state based on green energy, sustainable agriculture, and so on, and refrains from colonization of space and other radical technologies that might lead in that direction.[276]

Other intelligent species in the cosmos may have made the same choice and happily live the life of Bullerby without bothering to go beyond their planet. And this, for Häggström, is precisely why we have not met another intelligent species.

Regardless of the reason why we are still alone in the cosmos, space exploration and sustainability on Earth should not be incompatible, but the temptation to focus on the former while ignoring the latter is strong and therefore of concern to many, including science fiction writers. The author Sim Kern, in a 2021 article in the British newspaper *The Independent*, pointed out that the idea of space salvation is a myth; humanity will not leave behind its messiness, no matter how many light years it travels.[277] Judging by the massive amount of debris in the low Earth orbit, this is a valid point. Naturally, Kern implies that humanity needs to address the issues that threaten our survival on Earth, not look at space as a solution to them.

Focusing on Earth, cleaning up our mess, and then looking at our planet's immediate boundaries in space, i.e., LEO, may well be the only choice we have to save the planet and its inhabitants. Though watching a movie showing Matt Damon living on Mars alone for a year excited many people, terraforming Mars remains technologically unfeasible, so its colonization is confined to Hollywood studios. And Elon Musk's suggestion to nuke the sky over the Martian poles every couple of seconds to create two pulsing suns to warm the planet[278] is just another provocative, outlandish idea from a man who often crosses the boundaries between fiction and reality without major consequences because . . . well, because he is one of the richest people on Earth.

There are in fact several major, major obstacles to terraforming Mars, which are all linked to the phenomena that turned it into such an inhospitable planet in the first place. NASA missions to Mars have helped reconstruct its tragic history. About 3.5 to four billion years ago, when life on Earth first appeared, on the Red Planet there were lakes of liquid water and possibly rivers. The atmosphere was thick and the planet was equipped with a magnetic field that shielded its surface from the Sun's radiation. NASA believes that, at that time, on Mars a variety of organic molecules were present and the conditions for life to emerge were ripe. However, life never materialized for a series of planetary reasons.

Mars probably lost its magnetic field between three to four billion years ago, which implies that the conditions for life to emerge lasted a very short time. Without the magnetic field, solar winds stripped away most of its atmosphere and surface water, turning Mars into a chilly desert. To terraform Mars, we would need to reverse this process. And the first step is to warm up the planet, a task easier said than done.

Elon Musk, as explained above, suggests using nuclear power on the two poles where water is trapped in ice. However, even if one hypothetically succeeded in melting the ice, the water released would not last for very long on the planet in liquid form. The amount of carbon dioxide added to the atmosphere would be insufficient to raise the atmospheric pressure, which is estimated to be 10 to 15 percent of ours, to levels similar to the pressure on Earth. That means that the surface temperature of the planet, which averages -63 degrees Celsius, will only rise by 10 degrees Celsius, not warm enough to keep water in its liquid form.

To warm up Mars to temperatures able to sustain liquid water, terraforming will need to produce a vast amount of carbon dioxide, estimated to be more than the amount humans have released through our entire history on Earth.[279] It is ironic that what threatens the survival of our planet, i.e., the high production of carbon dioxide, is what is needed to terraform Mars. And producing more carbon dioxide on the Red Planet proves to be even harder than reducing it on Earth. Scientists have proposed several scenarios, all sounding closer to science fiction than to reality and not easily feasible: to excavate deep into the Martian crust, though there is no evidence that we can find more carbon dioxide or water there; to introduce heat-trapping gases such as chlorofluorocarbons, but they evaporate quickly and would need to be reintroduced regularly; and to deviate comets and asteroids to hit Mars.

Even if we could generate enough carbon dioxide to make Mars's atmospheric pressure rise enough, we would need oxygen to make it breathable. Not an easy task. NASA experimented with converting Martian carbon dioxide into oxygen using a machine as big as a car battery known as MOXIE. MOXIE works like a tree: it inhales carbon dioxide and exhales oxygen.[280] However, to produce oxygen for the entire planet would be impossible. We do not possess the technology to construct the atmospheric factory of Barsoom, which Edgar Rice Burroughs describes in his books. A better alternative would be to use biology. Some 2.5 billion years ago, photosynthesis by algae converted methane, ammonia, and many other gases present in the Earth's atmosphere into oxygen. However, to reproduce what has happened on Earth, Mars would need a special kind of algae because it has less sunlight than Earth. In 1974, NASA conducted a feasibility study about using algae specifically adapted to the Martian environment and came to the conclusion that it would take millennia to make the atmosphere breathable using this method.[281]

The human race may have succeeded in outliving all very large animals, in surviving against all odds, in creating a unique civilization, even in harnessing Nature, but it is highly unlikely that the age of the Anthropocene will be able to reproduce the miracle of life on Earth on Mars. NASA's 2013 mission MAVEN, which was given the task of studying the atmosphere of the Red Planet, discovered that Mars is losing atmosphere even today.[282] The cause is the absence of a magnetic field. Without it, solar winds will continue stripping Mars of atmosphere and of water. Any changes one introduces to its environment will be short-lived.

The solution would be to create a magnetic field. How? We do not have the technology to alter the core of the planet, but we could create a magnetic field outside Mars. Scientists have come up with the idea of placing an artificial one in a specific point in the solar system, where the pull of gravity of the Sun and of Mars are equal, an area known as L1.[283] Of course, this is only a hypothesis. We do not yet have the technology to create an artificial magnetic field of sufficiently large dimensions, but we could in the future.

Assuming that most of the obstacles to terraforming could be overcome, including the introduction of a magnetic field, transforming Mars into a habitable planet will not be a quick process. It will take centuries, if not millennia. And when completed, we will have a very cold planet by Earth's standards, with very thin air, similar to the atmosphere on top of the Himalayan mountains. Mars is much smaller than Earth and, therefore, has only 38 percent of Earth's gravity, so reproducing our air quality at sea level would be impossible.

If we are serious about colonizing the Red Planet then we should look at para-terraforming Mars, which means creating huge bubbles on its surface where we could recreate Earth's environmental conditions. These bubbles could be massive, encapsulating entire cities; they would be interconnected so people could move among them. Inside the bubbles, there could be forests, rivers, lakes. To create them, however, would require the same effort, on a smaller scale, as terraforming Mars, i.e., crashing several comets into the planet or bombarding the poles with nuclear bombs to free water, introducing algae for photosynthesis, etc.[284] Without a magnetic field and in the absence of a proper atmosphere, the surface of the bubbles will have to withstand solar radiation and the constant bombardment of micro meteors. The time scale of para-terraforming Mars would still be several centuries, probably even millennia.

To manufacture artificial planets, as envisaged by Professor Gerard O'Neill in the 1980s, would take an equally long time and most likely will never happen because it is technologically unfeasible. Jeff Bezos seems to disagree; he believes this type of colonization is possible and within reach in one or two generations.[285] Like Musk, his phenomenal wealth shields him from criticism. Whatever the specific visions of each of the Space Barons, for now they all remain beautiful science fiction dreams. Playing God using technology is not yet possible, not even for them. The two major obstacles remain physics and biology: without a magnetic field, terraforming is impossible; in the absence of the gravity and the rotation of the Earth, our bodies will not last long in space, unless we modify the human body. Do the Space Barons know this?

Of course they do, but they have been very careful in not telling us, and the media has done a very poor job in unmasking their cosmic lies.

Away from the messianic fervor of Astrotopia and the marketing of deep space exploration and space tourism, beyond the images of Mars's colonies or the bucolic pictures of O'Neill's artificial agricultural planets, far, far from the idea of transforming Earth into a cosmic park surrounded by artificial industrial planets, the Space Barons' true business model for the cosmos has never been very different from the one originally developed for the Space Shuttle: to colonize, industrialize, and exploit the low Earth orbit to establish supremacy. NASA's goal was military dominance; the Space Barons' is monopolistic corporate dominance.

Should we be outraged by such a discovery? Should we feel duped by their cosmic propaganda? Yes, we should.

So far, the Space Barons have succeeded in opening LEO to business by cleverly wrapping their earthly marketing in the twentieth century narrative of galactic civilization and applying to it the shining ribbon of the first Moon landing. And we have bought in. This exercise has raised huge, massive sums of money from taxpayers and, through the private space industry, from people willing to venture into space or to invest in the new sector; it has given the Space Barons' private companies access not only to state funding but to public infrastructures, e.g., the joint venture between SpaceX and NASA. But it has not addressed the sustainability issue which threatens our survival. On the contrary, the birth of the space industry in LEO has shifted the emphasis away from key issues such as climate change and food freedom. How? By steering business sponsors and government funding towards a new industry which is believed to be able to generate big profits on Earth. Neither a zero-carbon Earth nor a sustainable agriculture to feed the world is a key feature of the forthcoming space sector envisioned by the Space Barons.

They are not heroes or visionaries, the modern version of great men like Marcus Aurelius or Socrates, or enlightened capitalists like Henry Ford; they are greedy individuals. And this explains why, when sustainability clashes with profitability, the Space Barons use their power and marketing to put profitability over sustainability. The man who believes that we can soon walk on Mars describes as outlandish the idea to harvest the Sun to provide free energy to the entire planet. Instead of encouraging the building of massive structures, space-based solar plants, in LEO, which will orbit around the Earth beaming solar energy for the entire planet, Musk is focused on providing internet from LEO to the entire planet, so he can harvest our precious data. Interestingly, the US military machine disagrees with his criticism and in May 2020 launched Orbital Vehicle 6 carrying a space-based solar power experiment designed by the US Naval Research Laboratory. The aim is to transform solar power into microwave energy and then to transmit it to Earth. Sadly, most likely the new technology will be harnessed to produce a new deadly weapon, not a sustainable alternative energy source. At the time of writing Orbital Vehicle 6 was still in orbit.

Harvesting solar energy from LEO has many advantages, especially if such energy is provided to Earth for free, for humanitarian purposes, outside the capitalist paradigm. Imagine supplying energy to areas hit by natural disasters, like hurricanes, so that hospitals could function even during blackouts. Imagine substituting all fossil fuel with solar energy.

Here is how Peggy Hollinger, who writes for the *Financial Times*, summarizes the importance of solar energy from LEO:

Advocates of space solar power say that it could provide a similar pattern to that of nuclear without requiring or leaving behind radioactive materials. It would function day and night, because a solar station in space would be far enough away to avoid the Earth's shadow.[286]

The key challenges of space-based solar power can be solved in economical ways. Brian Ryan, who works for National Grid, is convinced that it's possible:

> . . . it's estimated that the cost of space-based solar is going to drop to about 3 to 4 pence per kilowatt hour. So this could be half the cost of the electricity that we're providing today. So from a business model perspective this is also incredible. Because you can sell this energy to other countries. You can point it anywhere. So if you don't need it in the UK, why don't you sell it to New Zealand, sell it to Australia, sell it to someplace else around the world?

As long as it remains in the hands of the Space Barons, the industrialization of LEO will harm humanity because it will take place under the umbrella of the economic model of infinite growth, and it will be bent to create monopolistic empires to generate massive profits. Against this background, the Space Barons are not different from the New York City robber barons of 150 years ago, ruthless and greedy individuals who exploited their unique advantages not to better society but to exploit it to enrich themselves.

For decades we have been blind to this reality. Why? Partly because the speed of change is so fast that gathering knowledge and understanding it is often impossible. And partly because the narrative of the new space adventure is as old as the drawings of the hunt of our prehistoric ancestors. The clever marketing of the

Space Barons has won global support by re-proposing old values and concepts, massaging our nostalgia. This technique has worked because at this key juncture, humanity is confused; on the cusp of an epic transition it fears the future and longs for the past. The Space Barons are using the extraordinary speed of technological change and the pandemic of anxiety as leverage to sell us a fantastical cosmic dream, and while doing it they are enslaving us.

CHAPTER FIFTEEN

Space Economics

In 2016, Jeff Bezos suggested that space could be the next internet, a statement that summarizes the business opportunities he and the other Space Barons see in its development. Within a decade, in fact, the space sector is projected to be worth a whopping $3 trillion, and the area where the new industry will be concentrated is the low Earth orbit.[287]

Technological innovation has been the heartbeat of the industrialization of LEO. A major breakthrough came from the miniaturization of space equipment, another innovation that has brought down the cost of accessing space. It is cheaper to launch smaller and lighter spacecraft and satellites than big ones. Here is how the American areo space engineer Robert Zubrin describes the impact of miniaturization:

> We're now seeing micro-spacecraft, 10-kilogram spacecraft, that can do things that previously it took a 1,000-kilogram spacecraft to do. They're much smaller and lighter and therefore much cheaper to launch. They're also cheaper to build. These are million-dollar spacecraft instead of hundreds of millions of dollars. And that's another innovation which will facilitate the opening of space.[288]

Smaller satellites are not only cheaper and faster to produce than traditional ones but some of them are also already manufactured with 3D printers and can be produced with recycled

219

materials. Unlike bigger satellites, micro and nano satellites can be placed nearer to Earth, so they transmit better images and provide faster communications.

Miniaturization, therefore, has contributed to unlocking the economics of LEO, marking the advent of a low-cost space race. As a result, today traditional large satellites coexist with micro and nano satellites, which are also called "smallsats," weighing as little as 20 kg. They already perform a vast spectrum of useful activities on Earth, from monitoring carbon dioxide emissions to telecommunications in remote areas, to the optimization of crops in agriculture and the performance of financial transactions. Their application can improve our living conditions, mitigate and counteract climate change, or speed up the response to natural disasters. As explained by Alén Space:

> Nanosatellites can monitor radio signals transmitted from Earth. This means that in the event of a disaster, they can provide initial information regarding the degree of impact and the most seriously affected areas, allowing for more effective planning of rescue and relief work.[289]

Technological innovation alone, however, would have been insufficient to kick-start the privatization of space. The other key ingredient was strategic join ventures with state institutions. The 2006 contract between SpaceX and NASA, for example, was part of a strategy to encourage private companies to develop low-cost cargo and crew transportation at a time when NASA's budget was seriously squeezed. Thanks to its technological advantage the joint venture generated lucrative private contracts for SpaceX, propelling it into a key position in the space industry. In 2021, SpaceX launched twenty successful flights to take various cargoes into space, an impressive amount of experience to boast over its competitors.[290] From the SpaceX website,[291] anyone can now book a payload of up to 830 kg of cargo to be brought into orbit, for a price as low as one million dollars, depending on the weight of the cargo. The first flight of this "Rideshare" program was launched on January 24, 2021, with a record-breaking 143 satellites on board.[292]

Only a few other private companies, which also operate in conjunction with NASA as a partner or a client, have benefitted from this type of joint venture and are today able to offer transport facilities for cargoes to low Earth orbit to other private companies. Nanoracks, for example, is a private in-space service company, which uses containers compatible with the International Space Station to distribute hundreds of small satellites with a single launch.[293] Through joint ventures in the private sector, Nanoracks has built the Bishop Airlock, which has become a permanent addition to the International Space Station.[294] Here is Jeffrey Manber's summary of Nanoracks' activities:

> . . . at Nanoracks we have customers from over 30 countries. As I said, we're investing in different platforms. We work everything from biopharma to satellite deployments. We've deployed over 280 satellites from the space station. We've coordinated over 1,000 projects.[295]

A further consequence of the privatization of the space industry has been the sprouting of a cottage industry on Earth. The Swedish Space Corporation provides ground staff and specialist expertise to give access to satellite data to companies operating in low Earth orbit, which do not want to invest in creating their own network on the ground.[296]

Unlike deep space traveling, inaccessible for now due to the biological constraints of the human body, the industrialization of LEO is within our reach. The human body, we have seen, can withstand one-year missions in the low Earth orbit providing the correct exercises are performed regularly, the psychological impact is monitored, and the area of confinement is sufficiently spacious. High finance seems to share this optimism. In 2020, venture capitalists raised a record $8.7 billion to finance low Earth orbit related companies.[297] As with the digital revolution, Wall Street giants are willing to bankroll the privatization of space. In April 2021, Goldman Sachs sent a note to customers stating that the mining of asteroids "may be more realistic than has been perceived to date."[298] The mining, of course, will have to be performed by robots.

The miniaturization of space equipment could well be the spinning jenny of the industrial revolution of LEO. As explained by Surfeo, a business development service for the defense and aerospace industries in Europe:

> Traditional satellites that used to be the size of a bus are now the size of a washing machine for micro-satellites and a shoebox for nano-satellites. With these new-scale models, the change is brutal for the space industry, which is now entering the era of mass production.[299]

Elon Musk's Starlink, a satellite internet constellation operated by SpaceX, has already launched more than 2,000 satellites and applied to launch 40,000 more. Jeff Bezos's Project Kuiper has identical objectives and plans to put in orbit its own constellation of internet satellites. OneWeb, which is owned by the UK government and the Indian multinational company Bharti Enterprises, wants to build a constellation of broadband satellite internet services. Countries like Canada and China have plans to build similar, much bigger constellations. By 2030, according to the Satellite Industry Association, there could be more than 100,000 commercial spacecraft in orbit.

Expanding the internet is the primary aim of the Space Barons. And why not? They are entrepreneurs constantly on the lookout for the next business venture. They have become immensely rich in a relatively short period of time exploiting the digital revolution: Bezos with Amazon and Musk with several start-ups beginning with PayPal. The Space Barons could be regarded as the great-grandchildren of the industrialists who orchestrated the Industrial Revolution. However, unlike their capitalist ancestors, who had to operate in conjunction with the working class, the capitalism of the Space Barons does not face the constraint of the labor force. In the Present Future, technology has replaced a large number of workers with machines and artificial intelligence, even more so in space than in cyberspace. As capitalism expands in the cosmos, the absence of the dichotomy between capital and labor could become a problem for democracies and for humanity in general, leading to ever greater inequalities, abuses, and even wars.

Leaving the economic colonization of LEO in the hands of the Space Barons, their institutional partners such as NASA, and the tiny private space sector is a mistake we may end up paying for with our freedom and our lives and the lives of our children and grandchildren. No common good will come from the race to accumulate cosmic profits selling connectivity to the masses in order to harvest their brains. Just to mention one of the many negative consequences: the environmental impact of the proliferation of satellite activity in LEO. Matthias Maurer, a German astronaut, explains the danger of polluting the low Earth orbit: "It makes me very, very sad to see we are repeating in space what we have done on the planet's surface. . . . People think space is so big, if I leave trash here no one cares."[300] Perhaps this is what the author Sim Kern referred to when they wrote that humanity must address the issues that threaten our survival on Earth before thinking of venturing into space. The industrialization and commercialization of LEO could represent a major leap into the future. It could also contribute to resolving the forthcoming scarcity of resources and alteration of the climate, but to maximize these benefits we must offset all the shortcomings. Turning LEO into a cosmic junkyard is not an option, but to a certain extent this has already happened. Antony David, the Technology Editor at TechTribe Oxford, writes:

> Of the nearly 9,000 satellites that have been launched, it is estimated some 5,000 remain in orbit of which 1,950 are still active. There have been around 500 collisions or explosions that have created smaller pieces of debris. Around 34,000 of these pieces are thought to be greater than 10 cm in size, 900,000 between 1 cm and 10 cm and 130 million smaller than 1 cm. A small fleck of paint hitting the very thick window of a space shuttle very nearly penetrated it. The energy of a small object impacting at speeds of more than 10 km/sec is huge.[301]

Space debris travels at a speed almost ten times faster than a bullet, which means that it covers the distance between London and Moscow in ten minutes. At such speeds, even tiny pieces of debris can cause serious damage through a collision that, in turn, produces more debris. Because LEO is a finite resource, exactly as Earth is, filling it with debris will eventually make it inaccessible: imagine the risk for spacecraft to cross a junkyard of flying debris to reach the Moon, or to place a new satellite in orbit; imagine the danger for astronauts working outside space stations.

Unsurprisingly, the Space Barons are not interested in cleaning up LEO; neither are their state partners. Cleaning up LEO is just as unappealing as cleaning up Earth; it is not part of the "cosmic dream," it does not feed the "nostalgia" that marketing sells daily.

In the absence of legislation requiring companies and governments to clean up their own junk in space, a few start-ups have begun to do exactly that. They spotted a business opportunity. Astroscale is one of them. Headquartered in Japan, the company was set up in 2013 by a group of firms that specialize in space debris removal. Both the European Space Agency and the UK Space Agency have invested in Astroscale's cleaning business. In 2021, the company completed an experimental mission into low Earth orbit, one of the first demonstrations of large-scale debris removal technology from orbit.[302] By 2030, the Astroscale cleaning system is expected to be fully operational.

Even if Astroscale and similar companies succeed in providing an efficient cleaning system for debris in LEO, why would people pay to have their space junk removed when there are no enforceable rules to keep space clean? As was the case during the Industrial Revolution, the industrialization of LEO is taking place in the absence of regulations and laws. Space legislation is presently a very gray area, including in terms of ownership.

Unlike on Earth, where a sovereign nation can grant companies mining concessions, or a person can sell the right to exploit land they own, no one in space has any legal claim. The Outer Space Treaty, signed at the UN in 1967, explicitly prohibits individual nations, or individuals, from claiming sovereignty over celestial bodies.

In the absence of international regulations governing exploration, ownership, and exploitation in space, some nations have produced their own laws, which are not universal but biased in favor of their own country and citizens. In 2015, Congress granted ownership of space materials to US companies that mine or collect them under the Space Act. Of course, the Space Act only applies to US companies. In 2015, Luxembourg commissioned a study to define private property in space. The report, completed in 2016, noted that, "While legal uncertainty remains, in the current legal and regulatory framework, space mining activities are not prohibited,"[303] and concluded that Luxembourg should pass legislation giving miners the right to claim and retain extraterrestrial ownership. Subsequently, Luxembourg produced similar legislation to Congress for companies registered in the principality.

Without proper international treaties upheld by all states with ventures in space, without international institutions like the World Trade Organization, the industrialization of LEO could transform the Earth's orbit into a modern Wild West ruled by the Space Barons, and eventually a cosmic junkyard, something very dangerous for humanity and for the planet. Or LEO could become the arena in which the superpowers battle for earthly supremacy.

Military exercises in LEO are already taking place and their aim is to show strength to other nations. In November 2021, Russia fired a missile at the inoperative Cosmos 1408 satellite five hundred kilometers above Earth, which produced new clouds of junk. In 2007, China shot down an old weather satellite, Fengyun-1C, flying at an altitude of 863 km, which is estimated to have increased traceable debris in LEO by 25 percent. The following year, the US brought down a failing reconnaissance satellite flying at an altitude of 247 km; 99 percent of the debris was pulled into the Earth's atmosphere within months. The US, China, India, and Russia regularly test their new weapons in LEO, smashing old, obsolete satellites. Though, in April 2022, the US became the first nation to declare a ban on antisatellite weapon tests,[304] all other countries are still conducting military exercises in LEO.

From the launch of Sputnik in 1957, space has been one of the peripheral battlegrounds of the Cold War. Though technology has projected us well into the future, politics has prevented us from taking the necessary leap to exploit space for the common good instead of using it to achieve earthly supremacy. The privatization of space has not changed this scenario: space remains a terrain where earthly battles take place. In the forthcoming confrontation among earthly powers, the low Earth orbit is going to be central to the wars by proxy on Earth.

The new world order may spring from the outcome of the conflict that the United States and China have already begun fighting in LEO and beyond. Could we be fast approaching a Zero Gravity War? If so, this conflict will be the manifestation of the darker side of this era and possibly the prelude to our extinction.

For now, partly thanks to the Space Barons' activity, Washington has maintained the upper hand over Beijing, both in terms of technology and budget. According to a 2021 SpaceTech Analytics report, out of more than ten thousand "space-focused" private companies worldwide, more than 52.1 percent are based in the United States and only 2.7 percent in China. In terms of investment, also, the government of the United States spends much more than the Chinese: $41 billion versus $6 billion per year, respectively.[305] However, China is rapidly morphing into a phenomenal contender in the quest for space dominance. At the end of 2021, it became the world leader in terms of space launches, with an impressive fifty-three successes out of fifty-six attempts. In the same year, the US managed forty-eight launches out of fifty-one attempts, with SpaceX behind thirty-one of those.[306]

China's very ambitious plans include missions to finish the Tiangong space station, to set up a manned base on the Moon, to continue the robotic exploration of Mars, to explore the solar system further (including asteroids, Jupiter, and wider interstellar space) and to improve its launch capabilities. The new leadership, which came into power in 2012 with the election of Xi Jinping, has been instrumental in boosting China's space adventure. It has increased the funding allocated for the space program and outlined its roadmap in the directive "Document 60." This indicates China's greater interest in commercial space operations and the granting of permission to Chinese private space companies, such as LinkSpace, i-Space, and Galactic Energy, to join the space industry.[307]

China's space ambitions are as old as the space race between the United States and the Soviet Union. In 1957, the launch of the world's first satellite, Sputnik, greatly impressed Mao Zedong, who started a cooperation with Moscow to put Chinese satellites in space. However, Communist China's tumultuous history, and its effort to develop economically, hindered Mao's space dream. Though China managed to launch its first satellite in 1970, until the end of the nineties, the Chinese space program only managed to deliver a few satellites into orbit, using modified ballistic missiles.[308] The breakthrough came in 2003, when China sent its first astronaut, Yang Liwei, into space in the Shenzhou 5 spacecraft, very similar to the Russian Soyuz spacecraft. The launch made China the third nation to have independent spaceflight capabilities. To stress its entry into the space race, Beijing coined a new name for its astronauts, who were no longer called cosmonauts, as the Russians were, or astronauts, as the Americans were, but taikonauts, from the Chinese word for universe and the Greek word for sailor.

In May 2021, China became the third nation in history, after the Soviet Union and the United States, to land a mission on Mars.[309] In 2021, in an official document—"China's Space Program: A 2021 Perspective"—Beijing reiterated the objective of its space program:

> In the next five years, China will . . . start a new journey towards [being] a space power. The space industry will contribute more to China's growth as a whole, to global consensus, and common effort with regard to outer space exploration and utilization, and to human progress.[310]

Beijing has selected four clear steps to achieve its goal: improve launching ability; establish a firm presence in the low Earth orbit with a space station; land on the Moon and establish a presence there; and, finally, explore the further solar system. Let's revisit some of these objectives to understand the true potential of China in space.

China has four operational launch sites: in Jiuquan, Taiyuan, Xichang, and Wenchang.[311] Construction is planned of a new

$3 billion launch facility in Ningbo, Zhejiang Province, which will be capable of one hundred launches per year to meet the increasing commercial launch demand. Ningbo enjoys a favorable latitude and geography,[312] which are of paramount importance for launching spacecraft. The vicinity to the equator of Cape Canaveral in Florida and of Ningbo in China allows for more efficient entry into space, while their positions on the coast are conducive to a "soft" landing in case of a failure.[313]

China is also building its own space station in LEO. In 2011, the US Congress passed the Wolf Amendment, which bars NASA from collaborating with China, so China has never had a presence on the International Space Station. So it decided to build its own.[314] As the International Space Station looks to be decommissioned before the 2030s,[315] and China is making rapid progress with the construction of its own space station, the ban appears to have been a bad decision.

In April 2021, China launched Tianhe, the station's first module, and it launched two more modules in 2022 to complete a three-module space station. At the end of 2022, the Shenzhou 15 mission commenced a six-month rotation program on the station, and China aims to keep Tiangong continuously crewed for the next ten years.[316] In 2023, the Xuntian space telescope, to be used for astronomical research, will be added to the space station, and there are plans for a further three modules in the future. Although China has offered places in the station to international partners, Tiangong is under the full control of Beijing. Among the commercial uses of the station, there is the construction of a massive solar plant to provide space power to Earth by 2030.[317]

China's ambitions beyond LEO are equally high. In 2019, China became the first nation to land a spacecraft on the "dark side" of the Moon. The mission collected and returned lunar rock samples to Earth. However, it also had a greater scope.[318] Beijing teamed up with Russia to build the International Lunar Research

Station (ILRS), which, although planned for 2035, could be ready as early as 2027.[319] The station seems to be a response to the US's Artemis Accords, the international treaty signed by twenty-three countries to return to the Moon.[320] Russia has refused to sign the accords because it considers them "US-centric," and China cannot sign them because of the Wolf Amendment. Thus, China, with the help of Russia, aims to beat or better the US Artemis Accords in establishing a permanent lunar base to exploit the Moon's resources and its commercial and tactical benefits.

Since May 2021, when China landed a mission on the surface of Mars, their orbiter, Tianwen-1, and their rover, Zhurong, have been carrying out research on the possibility of life on Mars.[321] The mission's architect, Zhang Rongqiao, has said the mission has been successful, but that it was only a "first step" for China. In interviews and in their 2021 document, China reveals some exciting new goals to follow the US on some of their own deep space exploration missions. These would include missions to bring back samples from Mars and images of Jupiter and its moons, to land on and bring back samples from asteroids and comet belts, to study the heliosphere (the region surrounding the Sun where solar wind has an effect), and even to reach the boundary of our solar system.[322]

On Earth and in space, this technological era, the Present Future, unravels against an increasingly unstable background. The turmoil that the speed of change of technological innovation triggers in the individual is the mirror image of the disorder that the velocity of transformation prompts in politics. Blinded by anxiety, drenched in nostalgia, faithfully committed to the model of infinite economic growth, and conditioned by the imprint of our ancestors, humanity and politics seem unaware of the empowering of technology and refuse to embrace the epochal change that will allow us to leap into a better future. Instead of using our technological innovation to fight, as a species, the common enemy of extinction, we use our remarkable conquests to undermine and fight each other no differently from how we would have as prehistoric tribes—except with unimaginably destructive modern weaponry.

Unaware of the consequences of these failures on the part of our governments, our societies, and, above all, ourselves, we are sleepwalking towards dystopia, unless someone or something manages to wake us up in time.

GLOSSARY

"A Cypherpunk's Manifesto"
A document written by Eric Hughes in 1993, explaining the importance of anonymity in online commercial transactions, considered to be one of the conceptual foundations of future cryptocurrencies.

AAA rating
A credit assessment used by credit rating agencies, indicating that a bond has a high level of creditworthiness and a very low risk of default.

Algorithmic (algo) trading
The use of automated trading techniques wherein buy and sell orders on financial instruments are executed by computers without the need of human input.

Analog computer
A device in which continuously variable physical quantities, such as electrical potential, fluid pressure, or mechanical motion, are represented in a way analogous to the corresponding quantities in the problem to be solved, i.e., the inner mechanisms are an 'analog' or model of the problem at hand.

Angel investor
A wealthy individual who provides seed capital to support a start-up business in the early stage of development, usually in exchange for convertible debt or ownership equity.

Anthropocene
Proposed current geological epoch, in which humans are the primary cause of permanent planetary change.

Apollo missions
A series of missions conducted by NASA between 1961 and 1972, aimed at landing humans on the Moon and bringing them back safely to Earth.

Arms Export Control Act
A US legislation that controls the export of defense-related articles and services.

Artemis Accords
An international treaty signed by twenty-three countries with the goal to return to the Moon, led by the United States.

Artificial general intelligence (AGI)
The hypothetical ability of a computer program to understand, learn, adapt, and implement knowledge in a range of intellectually demanding tasks, matching or even surpassing human intelligence.

Artificial intelligence (AI)
A branch of computer science that involves the development of machines and software able to perform tasks normally requiring human intelligence, such as visual perception and speech.

Artificial planets
Hypothetical large-scale space habitats, envisioned by Gerard O'Neill and others, capable of housing human societies outside Earth.

Asperger's syndrome
A type of pervasive developmental disorder which is classified as a part of the autism spectrum. The main characteristics of a person with Asperger's are difficulties in social interaction and nonverbal communication, alongside restricted and repetitive patterns of behavior and interests.

Astroscale
A private orbital debris removal company headquartered in Tokyo, Japan, founded in 2013 by IT entrepreneur Mitsunobu "Nobu" Okada.

Atmosphere factory
A hypothetical facility capable of producing a breathable atmosphere on a planet that currently lacks one.

Autotelic experience
A state of mind where the self and the task performed become one, often associated with flow.

Axie Infinity
A blockchain-based trading and battling game that is partially owned and operated by its players.

Axie Infinity Shards (AXS)
A governance token for the Axie Infinity game, which can be used to participate in key governance votes and earn rewards.

Bailout
An act of giving financial assistance to a failing business or economy to save it from collapse. Generally used with reference to government support for private companies.

Bishop Airlock
A commercial airlock module developed by Nanoracks, used on the International Space Station for deploying CubeSats and other small payloads from the station.

Bitcoin
A type of digital currency in which encryption techniques are used to regulate the generation of units of currency and verify the transfer of funds, operating independently of a central bank.

Bitcoin exchanges
Digital marketplaces where traders can buy and sell bitcoins using different fiat currencies or altcoins.

Bitcoin mining
The process by which new bitcoins are entered into circulation, and also a critical component of the maintenance and development of the blockchain ledger.

BlackNet
A concept envisioned by Tim May for an unregulated online market where anything could be bought or sold without tracking and surveillance.

Blockchain
A decentralized and distributed digital ledger that records transactions across multiple computers in such a way that the registered transactions cannot be altered retroactively, without the alteration of all subsequent blocks.

Bretton Woods agreement
An agreement in 1944 that overhauled the world's international monetary system and established the International Monetary Fund and the World Bank.

Business cycle
The fluctuations in economic activity that an economy experiences over a period of time. It can be divided into expansions, peaks, recessions, troughs.

Central bank
A national bank that provides financial and banking services for its country's government and commercial banking system, controlling the nation's money supply.

Centrifugal force
The force that draws a rotating body away from the center of rotation, caused by the inertia of the body.

Chainalysis
A blockchain data research company providing data, software, services, and research trying to connect cryptocurrency transactions to real-world activity.

Chatbot
A software application used to conduct an online chat conversation via text or text-to-speech, in lieu of providing direct contact with a live human agent.

"China's Space Program: A 2021 Perspective"
An official document outlining China's objectives in space for the next five years, including an emphasis on exploration and utilization of outer space.

Chlorofluorocarbons (CFCs)
Types of compounds that contain carbon, chlorine, and fluorine. They are known for their role in the depletion of the stratospheric ozone layer but are also powerful greenhouse gases.

Cipher
In cryptography, a cipher is a method for performing encryption or decryption.

Clipper chip
A chip with an encryption device, proposed by the US government, that would have allowed the government to have access to the keys.

Cold War
The period of political tension and military rivalry between the United States and the Soviet Union, and their respective allies, from the end of World War II until the early 1990s, although the term is often used to refer to the entire post-war era.

Collateralized debt obligations (CDOs)
A type of structured asset-backed security (ABS). CDOs are constructed from a portfolio of fixed-income assets and sliced into tranches that have different risk levels.

Co-location
The practice used by certain algorithmic traders of placing servers inside the same building as the stock exchange to gain faster access to the market.

Commodities
A raw material or primary agricultural product that can be bought and sold on financial markets. In the context of Bitcoin, it is often debated whether cryptocurrencies should be considered commodities.

Commodity Futures Modernization Act
Legislation signed by Bill Clinton in 2000, marking the beginning of financialization.

Consensus mechanism
The method through which a blockchain network reaches consensus on the contents of a blockchain. It sets the rules and procedures that need to be followed by all network nodes to validate new transactions and add them to the blockchain.

Credit default swaps
A financial derivative or contract that allows an investor to "swap" or offset his or her credit risk with that of another investor.

Crypto anarchy
The use of cryptographic software to evade prosecution and harassment while sending and receiving information over computer networks.

Crypto winter
A term used in the cryptocurrency market to describe the period following the bursting of a speculative bubble, characterized by a

bear market where the prices of cryptocurrencies fall for a prolonged period.

Cryptocurrency
A digital or virtual form of currency that uses cryptography for security and operates independently of a central bank. Cryptocurrencies use blockchain technology to gain decentralization, transparency, and immutability.

Cryptography
The practice and study of securing information and communications through the use of codes, so that only those for whom the information is intended can read and process it.

CryptoKitties
A blockchain-based virtual game developed by Axiom Zen that allows players to purchase, collect, breed, and sell various types of virtual cats.

CryptoPunks
One of the first NFTs on the Ethereum blockchain. They are 10,000 unique collectible characters with proof of ownership stored on the Ethereum blockchain.

Cyberpunk
A subgenre of science fiction set in a dystopian futuristic setting, typically featuring advanced technological and scientific achievements, such as artificial intelligence and cybernetics, juxtaposed with a degree of breakdown or radical change in the social order.

Cyberspace
The interconnected digital world of computer networks, internet, and online spaces.

Cypherpunks
A movement and community that advocates for the widespread use

of strong cryptography and privacy-enhancing technologies as a way to social and political change.

Dark web
The part of the World Wide Web that is only accessible by means of special software, allowing users and website operators to remain anonymous or untraceable.

Darknet
A private network where connections are made only between trusted peers, often used for illegal activities.

Decentralization
The process by which the activities of an organization, particularly those regarding planning and decision-making, are distributed or delegated away from a central, authoritative location or group.

Decentralized finance (DeFi)
A financial system that operates without intermediaries like banks, using cryptocurrency-based software programs.

Default
Failure to repay a debt including interest or principal on a loan or security.

Deflationary currency
A type of currency that increases in value over time, in contrast to inflationary currency which tends to lose value over time. Bitcoin is often referred to as a deflationary currency due to its finite supply.

Depository Trust & Clearing Corporation (DTCC)
A centralized clearing and settlement institution that facilitates the clearing and settlement of securities trades in the United States.

Difficulty adjustment
A feature of the Bitcoin network that automatically adjusts the dif-

ficulty level of mining new blocks, based on the network's overall speed. The goal is to ensure that new blocks are added approximately every ten minutes.

Digital addresses
These are unique identifiers which allow information or cryptocurrencies to be sent and received. They function like email addresses or URLs.

Digital fingerprint
The unique identifier associated with a particular piece of digital art.

Digitization of money
The process of converting physical forms of money (like cash or coins) into digital forms.

Document 60
A directive issued by the Chinese government indicating China's greater interest in commercial space operations and the granting of permission to Chinese private space companies to join the space industry.

Double entry scheme
A system in accounting where every transaction is recorded in two different accounts, the debit account and the credit account. The total amount debited will always equal the total amount credited.

Double-spending
A potential flaw in a digital cash scheme in which the same single digital token can be spent more than once, due to the digital information being easily replicated.

Economy of scale
The cost advantages that enterprises obtain due to their scale of operation, with cost per unit of output generally decreasing with increasing scale.

e-Gold
A digital currency that allowed the instant transfer of gold ownership from 1996 to 2009, before it was outlawed for fostering illegal activities.

Encryption
The process of converting information or data into a code to prevent unauthorized access.

Ether (ETH)
A cryptocurrency native to the Ethereum platform. Ethereum is a blockchain-based software platform.

Ethereum
An open-source blockchain-based platform used to create and share businesses, applications, and services.

Exchange traded funds (ETFs)
Investment funds traded on stock exchanges, representing a basket of securities.

Fandom
A community or subculture composed of fans often characterized by a feeling of camaraderie with others who share a common interest.

Fannie Mae (Federal National Mortgage Association)
A government-sponsored enterprise in the United States that provides liquidity to the mortgage market by buying mortgages from lenders and selling them to investors.

Federal Reserve
The central banking system of the United States, which regulates the US monetary and financial system.

Fiat currency / fiat money
Currency that a government has declared to be legal tender, but it is not backed by a physical commodity. The value of fiat money is

derived from the relationship between supply and demand rather than the value of the material from which the money is made.

Financial deregulation
The process of removing governmental regulations from financial institutions. This process allows these institutions more freedom in how they conduct their operations.

Financial engineering
The application of mathematical methods to the solution of problems in finance. It involves the design, development, and implementation of innovative financial instruments and processes.

Financialization
The increasing influence of finance on the overall economy.

Fixed exchange rate
A system under which the exchange rate for converting one currency into another is fixed by the government or a central bank.

Flow
A state of mental immersion and focus during an activity, as defined by Professor Mihály Csíkszentmihályi.

flOw
A video game designed to facilitate a state of flow in players, based on Csíkszentmihályi's theory.

Gas flaring
The process of burning off unwanted gas that is released during industrial processes, particularly oil extraction.

Generation Z
The generation born between the mid-1990s and early 2010s.

Genesis block
The first block of data that is processed and validated to form a new blockchain, often referred to as 'block 0' in the blockchain.

Ginnie Mae (Government National Mortgage Association)
A US government corporation within the US Department of Housing and Urban Development (HUD) that guarantees the timely payment of principal and interest on mortgage-backed securities (MBS) backed by federally insured or guaranteed loans.

Gold standard
A monetary system where a country's currency or paper money has a value directly linked to gold. With the gold standard, countries agreed to convert paper money into a fixed amount of gold.

Golden parity
The fixed amount of gold that a currency is worth.

***Grand Theft Auto* series**
A popular video game series known for its realistic simulation of various aspects of life, including the stock market.

Great Depression
The deepest and longest-lasting economic downturn in the history of the Western industrialized world, lasting from 1929 to 1939.

Halving effect
A mechanism within the Bitcoin system where the reward for mining a new block gets halved after every 210,000 blocks. This process continues until all 21 million Bitcoins are released.

Hash
A function that converts an input of letters and numbers into an encrypted output of a fixed length. Hash functions are used in cryptocurrencies and NFTs to verify the integrity of data.

Hedge funds
Investment funds that pool capital from accredited individuals or institutional investors and generate returns exploiting different instruments including derivatives and leverage.

Heliosphere
The region surrounding the Sun where solar wind has an effect.

Herd mentality
A phenomenon (often see in financial markets) in which individuals follow the majority behavior or thinking, even if this leads to irrational actions.

High frequency trading (HFT)
Trading conducted by machines with high-speed performance.

High street banking system
The major or mainstream banks that have a large number of physical locations in a country or region.

Hubble Space Telescope
A space-based observatory launched in 1990 that has provided some of the most detailed images of distant galaxies, nebulae, and other astronomical phenomena.

Hyman Minsky
An American economist noted for his research on financial crises, specifically on what has been named as the "Minsky moment"—a sudden, major collapse of asset values.

Hyperinflation
An extremely high and typically accelerating inflation. It quickly erodes the real value of the local currency, as the prices of all goods increase.

Industrial revolution of LEO
This phrase signifies the rapid development and commercialization of low Earth orbit, compared to the Industrial Revolution on Earth during the eighteenth and nineteenth centuries. The miniaturization of space equipment is seen as a driving force in this transformation.

Inflation
The rate at which the general level of prices for goods and services is rising, and subsequently, purchasing power is falling.

Influencers
Individuals who have a significant following and influence on social media platforms.

Institutional investors
Entities that pool money to purchase securities, real property, and other investment assets. Institutional investors include banks, insurance companies, pensions, hedge funds, REITs, investment advisors, endowments, and mutual funds.

Interest rates
The proportion of a loan that is charged as interest to the borrower, typically expressed as an annual percentage of the loan outstanding.

International Lunar Research Station (ILRS)
A proposed scientific research facility on the lunar surface, initiated by Russia and China.

International Space Station (ISS)
A modular space station in low Earth orbit. It is a multinational collaborative project involving five participating space agencies: NASA, Roscosmos, JAXA, ESA, and CSA.

Joint ventures
In the context of space industry, this refers to collaborative efforts between private companies and state institutions like NASA. These joint ventures often aim to develop specific technologies or capabilities.

L1 (Lagrange Point 1)
A point in space where the gravitational forces of two large bodies, such as Earth and the Moon, or Mars and the Sun, equal the centrifugal force felt by a smaller object, such as a satellite.

Large language model (LLM)
Machine-learning models that have been trained on a large corpus of text data. They're designed to generate humanlike text based on the input they're given.

Lehman Brothers
An American investment bank whose bankruptcy in 2008 was a major event in the global financial crisis.

Leverage
The use of borrowed money to increase the potential return (but also the potential loss) of an investment.

Leverage limits
Restrictions on the amount of debt a financial institution can take on relative to its equity.

Libertarianism
A political philosophy that advocates minimal state intervention in the lives of citizens and prioritizes individual liberty.

Liberty Dollar
A private currency launched in 1998 by Bernard von NotHaus, which was eventually shut down by US authorities.

Low Earth orbit (LEO)
An orbit around Earth with an altitude between 160 kilometers (99 mi) and 2,000 kilometers (1,200 mi). It is the most commonly used area for satellite deployments.

Luna 2 and Luna 3
Spacecraft launched by the Soviet Union as part of the Luna program. Luna 2 was the first man-made object to reach the Moon in 1959, while Luna 3 captured the first photographs of the Moon's far side later that year.

Malthusian loop
Thomas Malthus suggested that while technological advances could increase a society's supply of resources, such as food, and thereby improve the standard of living, the abundance of resources would enable population growth, which would eventually bring the supply of resources for each person back to its level prior to its original level.

Manhattan Project
The US research and development project during World War II that produced the first nuclear weapons.

Markets in crypto assets
Legal frameworks or legislations dealing with the handling, trading, and potential regulation of cryptocurrency markets.

Martian permafrost
Permanently frozen soil found on Mars. Permafrost on Earth contains water, but on Mars, it can contain carbon dioxide as well.

MAVEN (Mars Atmosphere and Volatile Evolution)
A mission developed by NASA to study the Martian atmosphere while orbiting Mars. Tasked with determining how the planet's atmosphere and water, presumed to have once been substantial, were lost over time.

Memes
Viral images, videos, or phrases that are widely shared and imitated on the internet.

Memex
An adjustable microfilm viewer with a large transparent screen. It was seen as a prototype of the kind of information retrieval systems we now use every day on the internet.

Metaverse
A virtual-reality space where users can interact with a computer-generated environment and other users. It's a collective virtual shared space, created by the convergence of virtually enhanced physical reality and physically persistent virtual reality.

Microfilm
A film bearing a miniature photographic copy of printed or other graphic matter, usually of a document, newspaper or book pages, etc., made for a library or archive.

Microgravity
The condition of very weak gravity, typically found in space, in which people or objects appear to be weightless.

Micrometeors
Small particles from space that enter the Earth's atmosphere and burn up, often seen as "shooting stars" in the night sky.

Micro-spacecraft
This term refers to exceptionally small spacecraft, often weighing just a few kilograms. These devices are capable of performing many of the same functions as much larger spacecraft, but at a fraction of the cost and size.

Millennials
The generation born between the early 1980s and mid-1990s.

Miniaturization
In the context of space technology, miniaturization refers to the trend towards making space equipment smaller and lighter. This includes satellites and spacecraft, which are becoming increasingly compact, reducing the cost of launching them into space.

Moderator
A person who monitors and manages online discussions or forums, ensuring that the conversation remains productive and respectful.

Modern Monetary Theory (MMT)
An economic theory that emphasizes the role of governments in controlling the economy's money supply, arguing that governments should use their power to regulate the economy, create full employment, and control inflation.

Monetary sovereignty
A concept where a state has the exclusive right to regulate its own currency, including controlling its money supply.

Monetization of the debt
The process by which the government converts its debt into money, typically by having the central bank purchase government bonds.

Monetization models
Strategies used to generate revenue from a product, service, or platform.

Money laundering
The process of making large amounts of money generated by a criminal activity appear to have come from a legitimate source.

Money supply
The total quantity of money in circulation within an economy, including cash, coins, and checking and savings account deposits.

Monopoly
An economic situation where a single entity or company exclusively provides a particular product or service, restricting competition.

Mortgage-backed security (MBS)
A type of asset-backed security that is secured by a mortgage or collection of mortgages. Investors buy these securities, which gives them the right to collect the interest and principal payments on the mortgages.

Mortgages
A loan secured by the collateral of specified real estate property, that the borrower is obliged to pay back with a predetermined set of payments.

MOXIE (Mars Oxygen In-Situ Resource Utilization Experiment)
A technology demonstration on the Mars 2020 mission that produced oxygen from Martian atmospheric carbon dioxide.

Nano satellites (Nanosats)
These are a specific type of small satellite, typically weighing between one and ten kilograms. Despite their size, they can perform many of the same functions as larger satellites.

Nanoracks
This is a private in-space service company that provides hardware and services for the satellite deployment, research, and education market.

NASA
The National Aeronautics and Space Administration, the US government agency responsible for the nation's civilian space program and for aeronautics and aerospace research.

National debt
The total debt owed by the central government of a country to creditors within and outside the country.

National Defense Research Committee (NDRC)
A committee formed in 1940, the task of which was to gather research of interest to the military and inform the armed forces about new technologies that could be applied to the war machine.

National Securities Clearing Corporation (NSCC)
A subsidiary of the Depository Trust & Clearing Corporation (DTCC) that provides clearing, settlement, risk management, and central counterparty services for securities transactions in the United States.

Neil Armstrong
An American astronaut who was the first person to walk on the Moon during the Apollo 11 mission in 1969.

Neural network architecture
A computational model used in machine learning which is designed to simulate the behavior of human brain neurons.

NFTs (Non-fungible tokens)
Unique digital assets created using blockchain technology. Unlike cryptocurrencies, NFTs are not interchangeable as each has a unique identifier that proves its authenticity and ownership.

Occupy Wall Street
A protest movement that emerged in 2011 to challenge social and economic inequality.

Office of Scientific Research and Development (OSRD)
An institution created during WWII to coordinate the scientific research for military operations, including the Manhattan Project.

OneCoin
This was a major cryptocurrency scam perpetrated by Ruja Ignatova, who defrauded investors of billions of dollars by selling them a non-existent cryptocurrency.

Online trading platforms
Tools or software offered by brokerage firms that allow investors to buy and sell assets, such as stocks, through the internet.

Open-source software
A type of software whose source code is released under a license in which the copyright holder grants users the rights to study, change, and distribute the software to anyone and for any purpose.

Options
Financial instruments used to hedge against potential losses in investments or to speculate on financial instruments exploiting leverage.

Orbital Vehicle 6
A spacecraft equipped with highly classified experimental technology, including a space-based solar power experiment.

Outer Space Treaty
Signed at the UN in 1967, this treaty explicitly prohibits individual nations, or individuals, from claiming sovereignty over celestial bodies.

Para-terraforming
The concept of creating habitable environments, like enclosed ecosystems or "bubbles," on the surface of a non-Earth-like planet.

Payload
This term refers to the cargo carried by a spacecraft. It could include anything from satellites to scientific equipment or supplies for the International Space Station (ISS).

Peer-to-peer system
A decentralized communications model in which each party has the same capabilities and either party can initiate a communication session.

Physiological fluids
The liquids in the human body that perform various functions, including but not limited to blood, lymph, and cerebrospinal fluid.

Pretty Good Privacy (PGP)
An encryption program providing cryptographic privacy and authentication for data communication.

Private keys
These are secret, alphanumeric passwords used that allow individuals to access their digital wallets or conduct transactions on the blockchain.

Project Kuiper
This is a project by Amazon to launch a constellation of low Earth orbit satellites that will provide broadband internet connectivity to unserved and underserved communities around the world.

Promotion code
A sequence of letters or numbers that lets customers receive a discount or benefit on products or services.

Proof of stake
A type of algorithm by which a cryptocurrency blockchain network aims to achieve distributed consensus by asking users to prove ownership of a certain number of tokens.

Proof of work
A form of cryptographic zero-knowledge proof in which one party (the prover) proves to others (the verifiers) that a certain amount of computational effort has been expended.

Public debt
The total debt owed by the central government of a country to creditors within and outside the country.

Public-key cryptography
A cryptographic system in which each user has a pair of keys, a public key, which is known to the public, and a private key, which is known only to the user. The public key is used to encrypt messages, and the private key is used to decrypt them.

Quantitative easing
A monetary policy whereby a central bank prints money to buy government bonds or other financial assets, with the aim of stimulating the economy.

Rai stones
Large, circular stone disks carved out of limestone, used in the island of Yap in the Micronesia as a form of currency.

Rehypothecation
The practice of using collateral for a loan to secure another loan.

Reinforcement learning with human feedback (RLHF)
A process of training AI models where the model learns from the feedback provided by humans over time, modifying its actions to become more accurate in its tasks.

Repurchase agreement (repo)
An agreement to sell a security and to buy it back at a certain date in the future. It is used as a form of short-term borrowing, primarily in fixed-income securities.

Robinhood app
A mobile trading platform that allows users to buy and sell stocks.

Satoshi Nakamoto
The pseudonymous person or group of people who developed Bitcoin, authored the Bitcoin white paper, and created and deployed Bitcoin's original reference implementation.

Second Life
An online virtual world, introduced in 2003, where users can create a virtual representation of themselves (an avatar) and interact with other users.

Shenzhou 5 spacecraft
The spacecraft that carried China's first astronaut, Yang Liwei, into space in 2003.

Short position
A financial technique where a trader borrows stocks from another and sells them, hoping to rebuy them at a lower price in the future.

Short sellers
Speculators who bet against the stock of weak companies, profiting from their decline.

Short squeeze
A sudden upward move in the prices of a stock, causing losses for short sellers.

Silk Road
An online black market on the dark web, best known for selling illegal drugs. It used Bitcoin as its primary form of currency.

Single-key model
A cryptographic system where a single code is used to both encrypt and decrypt messages. Also referred to as symmetric encryption, as opposed to public-key, asymmetric cryptography.

Smallsats
This term is used as a collective name for small satellites, which include both micro and nano satellites.

Smart contract
A computer protocol intended to digitally facilitate, verify, or enforce the negotiation or performance of a contract.

Smooth Love Potion (SLP)
A token in the *Axie Infinity* game that players can earn as rewards and use for various purposes within the game.

Solar radiation
Radiant energy emitted by the Sun, particularly electromagnetic energy.

Solar winds
Streams of charged particles, including protons and electrons, that are ejected from the upper atmosphere of the Sun.

Space Act
A US law passed by Congress in 2015 granting ownership of space materials to US companies that mine or collect them.

Space Barons
Refers to the influential entrepreneurs who are investing heavily in the development and commercialization of space, such as the leaders of SpaceX, Blue Origin, and Virgin Galactic.

Space debris
Refers to defunct human-made objects in space, including old satellites, spent rocket stages, and fragments from disintegration, erosion, and collisions. This debris poses potential threat to active satellites and the International Space Station.

Space probe
An unmanned spacecraft, carrying instruments, that is sent to gather information about the cosmos or celestial bodies.

Space race
The competition between the Soviet Union and the United States during the Cold War to achieve superior spaceflight capability.

Space Shuttle program
A NASA program that ran from 1981 to 2011, which used reusable spacecraft to transport crew and cargo to and from Earth's orbit.

SpaceTech Analytics report
A report providing information about global trends, investment activity, and emerging growth areas in the space industry.

SpaceX
A private American aerospace manufacturer and space transportation company founded by Elon Musk in 2002.

SpaceX Rideshare program
This is a service provided by SpaceX that allows other organizations to send payloads into space aboard SpaceX rockets. It has made space access more affordable for a variety of organizations.

Sputnik
The first artificial satellite to orbit the Earth, launched by the Soviet Union in 1957.

Stagflation
A condition of slow economic growth and relatively high unemployment accompanied by rising prices, or inflation.

Star Wars project
Officially known as the Strategic Defense Initiative (SDI), this was a proposed missile defense system intended to protect the United States from attack by ballistic strategic nuclear weapons during the Reagan administration in the 1980s.

Starlink
A satellite internet constellation being deployed by SpaceX to provide satellite internet connectivity.

Starship spacecraft
A fully reusable spacecraft currently under development by SpaceX, intended to carry both crew and cargo for interplanetary missions.

Subprime crisis
The financial crisis that occurred in 2008, primarily caused by the collapse of the subprime mortgage market and excessive leverage in the financial system.

Subprime mortgages
Home loans given to borrowers who have a higher chance of defaulting, often due to poor credit history or other financial challenges.

Synergistic terraforming
The application of a combination of several technologies to alter a planet's environment. It implies a massive, cooperative effort.

Synthetic financial instruments
Financial products that replicate the returns of other financial assets without owning them.

Taikonauts
The term used by China for its astronauts, derived from the Chinese word for universe and the Greek word for sailor.

Technocapitalism
A term that describes changes in capitalism associated with the emergence of new technology sectors, the power of corporations, and new forms of organization.

Telomeres
The protective caps on the end of chromosomes which shorten over time. The shortening of telomeres is associated with aging, cancer, and a higher risk of death.

Terraforming
The hypothetical process of deliberately modifying the atmosphere, temperature, surface topography, or ecology of a planet, moon, or other body to be similar to those of Earth in order to make it habitable by terrestrial organisms.

Tiangong space station
A permanently crewed space station constructed by China that operates in low Earth orbit.

Tianwen-1
A Chinese Mars mission involving an orbiter, a lander, and a rover to explore the Martian surface.

TikTok
A social media platform that allows users to create and share short videos, often used for marketing and influencing.

Tranches
A portion, slice, or block of a deal or structured financing arrangement. In the context of CDOs and ABSs, these are slices of the debt obligation that are tiered based on the risk of default.

Unbacked cryptoassets
Cryptoassets that are not backed by any physical asset or other assurance of value.

Universal basic income (UBI)
A governmental public program for a periodic payment delivered to all on an individual basis without a means test or work requirement.

US Naval Research Laboratory
The corporate research laboratory for the United States Navy and the United States Marine Corps and conducts a wide range of

basic scientific research, applied research, technological development and prototyping.

Venture capitalists
Investors who provide capital to start-ups or small companies with high growth potential.

Virtual reality
An artificial environment that is created with software and presented to the user in such a way that the user suspends belief and accepts it as a real environment.

Volatility
A statistical measure of the dispersion of returns for a given security or market index. Bitcoin and other cryptocurrencies have experienced bouts of outsized price volatility.

Wolf Amendment
An amendment passed by the US Congress in 2011, which bars NASA from collaborating with China.

Zero Gravity War
Hypothetical conflict involving space-faring nations with military objectives or operations in space.

Zhurong
The rover component of the Tianwen-1 Mars mission, currently conducting research on the Martian surface.

NOTES

1. Borwin Bandelow and Sophie Michaelis, "Epidemiology of Anxiety Disorders in the 21st Century," *Dialogues in Clinical Neuroscience* 17, no. 3 (Spring 2015): 327–335, https://www.tandfonline.com/doi/full/10.31887/DCNS.2015.17.3/bbandelow

2. Terrance Bell, "The History of Steel: From Iron Age to Electric Arc Furnaces," Thought Co., August 21, 2020. https://www.thoughtco.com/steel-history-2340172.

3. *Encyclopedia Britannica Online*, "Bessemer process," accessed August 27, 2019, https://www.britannica.com/technology/Bessemer-process.

4. Haruki Murakami, *1Q84* (New York: Knopf Doubleday, 2011).

5. Nienke Krook, "These Are The Best Quotes on Outer Space You Need To Know," The Space Tester, August 21, 2020, https://www.thespacetester.com/best-quotes-on-outer-space.

6. Cale Tilford et al, "How Green Is Your Electric Vehicle?" *Financial Times*, October 5, 2021, https://ig.ft.com/electric-car/.

7. "Introducing ChatGPT," OpenAI, November 30, 2022, https://openai.com/blog/chatgpt#OpenAI.

8. Jamie Bartlett, "Cypherpunks Write Code," American Scientist, excerpted from Bartlett's *The Dark Net: Inside the Digital Underworld* (New York: Melville House, 2015).

9. Timothy C. May, "The Cyphermonicon," Nakamoto Institute, September 10, 1994, https://nakamotoinstitute.org/static/docs/cyphernomicon.txt.

10. Bartlett, "Cypherpunks Write Code."

11. Timothy C. May, "Re: Blacknet Worries," Cypherpunks Mailing List, February 20, 1994. https://mailing-list-archive.cryptoanarchy.wiki/archive/1994/02/e6a43588522aa402985d90327d9c5f277b55752676f702030c4920b87f635a1b/.

12. Fred Turner, "Taking the Whole Earth Digital," *From Counterculture to Cyberculture: Stewart Brand, The Whole Earth Network,and the Rise of Digital Utopianism* (University of Chicago Press, 2006), 103–141.

13. Eric Hughes, "A Cypherpunk's Manifesto," Activism.net, March 9, 1993, https://www.activism.net/cypherpunk/.

14. Matt Macfarland, "Why Shades of Asperger's Syndrome Are the Secret to Building a Great Tech Company," *Washington Post*, April 3, 2015, https://www.washingtonpost.com/news/innovations/wp/2015/04/03/why-shades-of-aspergers-syndrome-are-the-secret-to-building-a-great-tech-company/.

15. Xische Reports, "Birth of a Bitcoin," Medium, February 12, 2018, https://medium.com/xische-reports/birth-of-bitcoin-9fb451e00886.

16. Will Binns,"Bitcoin.org is 10 Years Old!" Bitcoin.org, August 16, 2018, https://bitcoin.org/en/posts/ten-year-anniversary.

17. Daniel Garrahan, "Cryptocurrencies: How Regulators Lost Control," November 16, 2021, video for Financial Times Film, 26:46, https://www.ft.com/video/c461153e-5588-44cd-a73d-cea30afaa05d.

18. Jamie Redman, "A Deep Dive Into Satoshi's 11-Year Old Bitcoin Genesis Block," Bitcoin. com, January 3, 2020, https://news.bitcoin.com/a-deep-dive-into-satoshis-11-year-old-bitcoin-genesis-block/.

19. Joe Hall, "Not a Minor Adjustment: Bitcoin Mining Difficulty Soars 13.5% to New ATH," Cointelegraph, October 10, 2022, https://cointelegraph.com/news/not-a-minor-adjustment-bitcoin-mining-difficulty-soars-13-5-to-new-ath.

20. John Caroline, "Bitcoin Halving 2024: What You Need to Know," Coinspeaker, September 9, 2022, https://www.coinspeaker.com/guides/bitcoin-halving-2024-what-you-need-to-know/.

21. "Bitcoin Price Index," Cointelegraph, accessed Nov. 29, 2021, https://cointelegraph.com /bitcoin-price.

22. "Bitcoin Price Index," Cointelegraph.

23. At the beginning of 2022, coinmarketcap.com, one of the most authoritative crypto monitoring systems, listed 9,266 different cryptocurrencies, a few with a market cap of hundreds of billions of dollars, while many were worth just a few hundred thousand dollars.

24. Garrahan, "Cryptocurrencies: How Regulators Lost Control."

25. Satoshi Nakamoto, "Bitcoin: A Peer-to-Peer Electronic Cash System," United States Sentencing Commission, 2018, PDF, https://www.ussc.gov/sites/default/files/pdf/training /annual-national-training-seminar/2018/Emerging_Tech_Bitcoin_Crypto.pdf.

26. Garrahan, "Cryptocurrencies: How Regulators Lost Control."

27. Shaurya Malwa, "'Elon Musk' Twitter Scams Rake in 580,000 of Bitcoin," Decrypt, January 15, 2021, https://decrypt.co/54271/elon-musk-twitter-scams-rake-in-580000-of-bitcoin.

28. María Luisa Paúl, "Former 'Cryptoqueen' Is Now One of 10 Most-Wanted Fugitives," *The Washington Post*, July 1, 2022, https://www.washingtonpost.com/nation/2022/07/01 /cryptoqueen-ruja-ignatova-fugitive/.

29. US Department of Energy, "National Defense Research Committee: (1941-1947)," The Manhattan Project, n.d., https://infinite.mit.edu/video/mit-science-reporter%E2%80%94 looking-back-bomb-excerpt.

30. "MIT Science Reporter—'Looking Back on the Bomb' (Excerpt)," InfiniteMIT, 2016, original video 1963, 2:46, https://infinite.mit.edu/video/mit-science-reporter%E2%80%-94looking-back-bomb-excerpt.

31. An analog computer is a device "in which continuously variable physical quantities, such as electrical potential, fluid pressure, or mechanical motion, are represented in a way analogous to the corresponding quantities in the problem to be solved," i.e., the inner mechanisms are an "analog" or model of the problem at hand. (Erik Gregersen, *Encyclopedia Britannica Online*, s.v. "analog computer," n.d., https://www.britannica.com/ technology/analog-computer/additional-info#history.)

32. In his article, Bush described a theoretical machine he called a "memex," which was to enhance human memory by allowing the user to store and retrieve documents linked by associations. This associative linking was very similar to what is known today as hypertext. (Vannevar Bush, "As We May Think," *The Atlantic*, July 1945, https://www.theatlantic. com/magazine/archive/1945/07/as-we-may-think/303881/.)

33. Bernard von NotHaus, "REAL Money Is Inflation Proof: Your Liberty Dollar Solution," Liberty Dollar, n.d., http://www.libertydollar.org.

34. US Department of Justice, "Digital Currency Business E-Gold Pleads Guilty to Money Laundering and Illegal Money Transmitting Charges," 08-635, July 21, 2008, https://www. justice.gov/archive/opa/pr/2008/July/08-crm-635.html.

35. Tim Hume, "How FBI Caught Ross Ulbricht, Alleged Creator of Criminal Marketplace Silk Road," CNN, October 5, 2013, https://edition.cnn.com/2013/10/04/world/americas /silk-road-ross-ulbricht/index.html.

36. Tom Robinson, "How Law Enforcement Tracked Down $3.6 Billion in Bitcoin," interview by Laura Shin, *Unchained*, podcast, 35:00, February 11, 2022, https://unchainedpodcast .com/how-law-enforcement-tracked-down-3-6-billion-in-bitcoin/.

37. Sean Foley, Jonathan R. Karlsen, and Tālis J. Putniņš, "Sex, Drugs, and Bitcoin: How Much Illegal Activity Is Financed through Cryptocurrencies?" *Oxford Business Law Blog*, February 19, 2018, https://blogs.law.ox.ac.uk/business-law-blog/blog/2018/02/sex-drugs-and-bitcoin-how-much-illegal-activity-financed-through.

38. Gertrude Chavez-Dreyfuss, "Cryptocurrency Crime in 2021 Hits All-Time High in Value—Chainalysis," Reuters, January 6, 2022, https://www.reuters.com/markets/us /cryptocurrency-crime-2021-hits-all-time-high-value-chainalysis-2022-01-06/.

39. "Proof of work" and "proof of stake" are the two major consensus mechanisms crypto-currencies use to verify new transactions, add them to the blockchain, and create new tokens. Proof of work, first pioneered by Bitcoin, uses mining to achieve those goals. Proof of stake—which is employed by Cardano, the ETH2 blockchain, and others— uses staking to achieve the same things. ("What is 'Proof of Work' or 'Proof of Stake,'?" Coinbase, n.d., https://www.coinbase.com/learn/crypto-basics/what-is-proof-of-work -or-proof-of-stake.)

40. "'Proof of Work' or 'Proof of Stake,'?" Coinbase.

41. "What Is the Environmental Footprint of Bitcoin?" University of Cambridge Judge Business School, September 27, 2002, https://www.jbs.cam.ac.uk/insight/2022/ what-is-the-environmental-footprint-of-bitcoin/.

42. Hass McCook, "Comparing Bitcoin's Environmental Impact . . ." Medium, April 22, 2021, https://hassmccook.medium.com/comparing-bitcoins-environmental-im-pact-f56b18014f64.

43. McCook, "Comparing Bitcoin's Environmental Impact . . . ."

44. "Bitcoin Mining Map," University of Cambridge Judge Business School, n.d., https:// ccaf.io/cbnsi/cbeci/mining_map.

45. "What Is the Environmental Footprint of Bitcoin," University of Cambridge Judge Business School.

46. "Crusoe," Crusoe, n.d., https://www.crusoeenergy.com/emissions-reduction.

47. Nic Carter, "Noahbjectivity on Bitcoin Mining: A Response to Noah Smith," Medium, March 29, 2021, https://medium.com/@nic__carter/noahbjectivity-on-bitcoin-min-ing-2052226310cb.

48. CuriosityStream, "The Blockchain Revolution," YouTube video, 21:13, December 19, 2020, https://www.youtube.com/watch?v=OwnFf5oZil8.

49. Quartz, "Bitcoin, Blockchains, and the Future of Money," YouTube video, 11:26, October 25, 2017, https://www.youtube.com/watch?v=A-L2Mol5dEY.

50. Curiosity Stream, "The Blockchain Revolution."

51. "What is OpenAI?—Its History and How ChatGPT Is Changing the World," Taskade, n.d., https://www.taskade.com/blog/openai-chatgpt-history/.

52. Essentially, the neural network architecture tries to mirror the structure of the human brain, with neurons being replaced by "nodes" and connections between neurons replaced by "channels." Each channel is assigned a weight (between 1 and 0); think of this as the strength of that particular connection. To illustrate, imagine a neural network that is being trained to identify whether the shape it is given is a square, circle, or triangle. It is given an image of a square and it gives an output ("square," "circle," or "triangle"). If it is correct, it increases the weight on the connections it just used, meaning it will more easily identify a square as a square in the future. If it is wrong, it readjusts its weights according-ly so that next time, it will be closer to the correct answer (see video below). This iterative process allows a neural network to learn and become better at its function every time it sees a new example or piece of data. (Simplilearn, "Neural Network in 5 Minutes/ What

Is a Neural Network/ How Neural Networks Work," YouTube video, 5:44, June 19, 2019, https://www.youtube.com/watch?v=bfmFfD2RIcg.)

53. Christina Criddle and Tim Bradshaw, "Investors Seek to Profit from Groundbreaking 'Generative AI' Start-ups," *Financial Times,* n.d., https://www.ft.com/content/9c5f7154-5222-4be3-a6a9-f23879fdod6a.

54. Microsoft uses OpenAI's AI models, such as GPT-4, Codex, and DALL-E, in its cloud services and products like GitHub Copilot, Power BI, Microsoft Teams Premium, Viva, and the Bing chatbot.1 The partnership aims to leverage Microsoft's expertise in software engineering with OpenAI's cutting-edge research in AI to develop new AI technologies and bring them to market through Microsoft's cloud platform, Azure. The investment is intended to give Microsoft access to some of the most popular and advanced artificial intelligence systems. (Tom Warren, "ChatGPT Is Now Available in Microsoft's Azure OpenAI Service," The Verge, https://www.theverge.com/2023/3/9/23632312/microsoft-azure-openai-chatgpt-feature-available.)

55. Frederic Lardinois, "Microsoft's New Bing Was Using GPT-4 All Along," TechCrunch, March 14, 2023, https://techcrunch.com/2023/03/14/microsofts-new-bing-was-using-gpt-4-all-along.

56. Stephen Ornes, "The Unpredictable Abilities Emerging from Large AI Models," Quanta Magazine, March 16, 2023, https://www.quantamagazine.org/the-unpredictable-abilities-emerging-from-large-ai-models-20230316/.

57. Robert Frank, "Crypto Investor Who Bought Beeple's NFT for $69 Million Says He Would Have Paid Even More," CNBC, March 30, 2021, https://www.cnbc.com/2021/03/30/vignesh-sundaresan-known-as-metakovan-on-paying-69-million-for-beeple-nft.html.

58. "Beeple's Opus," Christie's, n.d., https://www.christies.com/features/Monumental-collage-by-Beeple-is-first-purely-digital-artwork-NFT-to-come-to-auction-11510-7.aspx?sc_lang=en&lid=1.

59. "Beeple's Opus," Christie's.

60. Elizabeth Howcroft and Ritvik Carvalho, "How a 10-Second Video Clip Sold for $6.6 Million," Reuters, March 1, 2021, https://www.reuters.com/business/media-telecom/how-10-second-video-clip-sold-66-million-2021-03-01/.

61. "What Is 'Proof of Work' or 'Proof of Stake,'?" Coinbase.

62. "Natively Digital: A Curated NFT Sale/Lot 2/Kevin McCoy: *Quantum*," Sotheby's, https://www.sothebys.com/en/buy/auction/2021/natively-digital-a-curated-nft-sale-2/quantum.

63. Simply Explained, "NFT's Explained in 4 Minutes!" YouTube video, 3:33, June 8, 2021, https://www.youtube.com/watch?v=FkUn86bH34M.

64. Because of the speed of technological change, in several countries the taxation of NFTs has not been fully developed and many gray areas exist; for example, if NFTs are regarded as collectibles, the taxation levy is different from if they are regarded as financial assets.

65. Joanna Ossinger, "Crypto Whale behind $69 Million NFT Sees 'Huge Risk' for Traders," Bloomberg, April 6, 2021, https://www.bloomberg.com/news/articles/2021-04-06/crypto-whale-behind-69-million-nft-sees-huge-risk-for-traders?sref=WYbI89jw#xj4y7vzkg.

66. Megan Brobrowsky, "Jack Dorsey Tweet NFT Once Sold for $2.9 Million, Now Might Fetch Under $14,000," *The Wall Street Journal,* April 16, 2022, https://www.wsj.com/articles/jack-dorsey-tweet-nft-once-sold-for-2-9-million-now-might-fetch-under-14-000-11650110402?mod=article_inline.

67. Taylor Locke, "Millionaire Artist Beeple: This Is the Very Important Thing 'I Think People Don't Understand' about Buying NFT's," CNBC, March 26, 2021, https://www.cnbc.com/2021/03/26/digital-artist-beeple-common-misunderstanding-about-nfts.html.

68. Andrew Steinwold, "The History of Non-fungible Tokens (NFT's)," Medium, October 7, 2019, https://medium.com/@Andrew.Steinwold/the-history-of-non-fungible-tokens-nfts-f362ca57ae10.

69. Daniel Van Bloom, "Why This CryptoPunk NFT Sold for $532 Million. Sort Of," CNET, December 19, 2021, https://www.cnet.com/personal-finance/crypto/why-this-cryptopunk-nft-sold-for-532-million-sort-of/.

70. "The Inside Story of the CryptoKitties Congestion Crisis," Consensys, February 20, 2018, https://consensys.net/blog/news/the-inside-story-of-the-cryptokitties-congestion-crisis/.

71. Consensys, "The Inside Story of the CryptoKitties."

72. Shoshanna Delventhal, "Bitcoin Is a $15,000 Beanie Baby, Says John Oliver," Investopedia, March 13, 2018, https://www.investopedia.com/news/bitcoin-15000-beanie-baby-says-john-oliver/.

73. Paul Vigna, "NFT Sales Are Flatlining," *The Wall Street Journal*, May 3, 2022, https://www.wsj.com/articles/nft-sales-are-flatlining-11651552616.

74. Vigna, "NFT Sales Are Flatlining."

75. Miles Kruppa, Christina Criddle, and Tim Bradshaw, "Bored Ape Start-up in Investment Talks with Andreessen Horowitz," *Financial Times*, n.d., https://www.ft.com/content/acc635d6-bb05-4af6-b4da-b8462c06466d.

76. "What Is an NFT (Non-fungible Token)?" Kraken, n.d., https://www.kraken.com/learn/what-are-non-fungible-tokens-nft.

77. Eva Szalay, "Decision to Use the Tokens to Back Crypto Deals Highlights Boom in Digital Collectibles Market," *Financial Times*, n.d., https://www.ft.com/content/ce600e79-93cf-40c8-928c-e9bbd66072c7.

78. Christian Davies and Song Jung-a, "South Korean Crypto Exchange Plans 'Eco-Friendly' NFTs for K-Pop Fans," *Financial Times*, https://www.ft.com/content/bb8c5995-c6d7-43c5-a12e-381901be231Christian.

79. Davis and Jung-a, "South Korean Crypto Echange Plans 'Eco-Friendly' NFTs."

80. Davis and Jung-a.

81. Yuga Labs (@yugalabs), Twitter, January 3, 2022, 3:27 p.m., https://twitter.com/yugalabs/status/1478100705542131713.

82. Sky Mavis, https://www.skymavis.com/.

83. Joshua Brustein, "A Billion-Dollar Crypto Gaming Startup Promised Riches and Delivered Disaster," Bloomberg, June 10, 2022, https://www.bloomberg.com/news/features/2022-06-10/axie-infinity-axs-crypto-game-promised-nft-riches-gave-ruin?sref=WYbI89jw.

84. Second Life is an online platform based on users creating avatars and interacting with one another. ("Second Life," Linden Research, Inc., n.d., https://secondlife.com.)

85. Merijn Knibbe, "Everyone Can Create Money," *WEA Commentaries* 7, no. 4 (August 2017): 2–5, https://www.worldeconomicsassociation.org/newsletterarticles/everyone-can-create-money/.

86. Sandra Kollen Ghizoni, "Creation of the Bretton Woods System," Federal Reserve History, accessed August 16, 2020, https://www.federalreservehistory.org/essays/bretton-woods-created.

87. As dictionary.com explains: "The origin of the word fiat in English is connected to the origin of the world itself. Taken from the Latin meaning 'let it be done,' this word appears in the Latin translation of Genesis, the first book of the Bible, when God proclaimed 'let there be light' (fiat lux)." ("Lexical Investigations: Fiat," Dictionary.com, August 13, 2013, https://www.dictionary.com/e/fiat/.)

88. Sandra Kollen Ghizoni, "Nixon Ends Convertibility of U.S. Dollars to Gold and Announces Wage/Price Controls," Federal Reserve History, n.d., https://www.federalreserve-history.org/essays/gold-convertibility-ends.

89. Jean Folger, "What is stagflation? Understanding the economic phenomenon that stifled growth through the 1970s," ed. Jasmine Suarez, *Business Insider*, July 6, 2022, https://www.businessinsider.com/personal-finance/stagflation?r=US&IR=T.

90. —Congress passed the Depository Institutions Deregulation and Monetary Control Act in 1980, which served to deregulate financial institutions that accept deposits while strengthening the Fed's control over monetary policy.
—Restrictions on the opening of bank branches in different states that were in place since the McFadden Act of 1927 were removed under the Riegle-Neal Interstate Banking and Branching Efficiency Act of 1994.
—The Gramm-Leach-Bliley Act of 1999 repealed significant aspects of the Glass-Steagall Act as well as of the Bank Holding Company Act of 1956, both of which had served to sever investment banking and insurance services from commercial banking. From 1999 onwards, a bank could now offer commercial banking, securities, and insurance services under one roof.

91. "Ginnie Mae at 50," Ginna Mae, n.d, https://www.ginniemae.gov/newsroom/publications /Documents/ginnie_at_50.pdf.

92. Kimberly Amadeo, "The Cause of the Subprime Mortgage Crisis," The Balance, January 29, 2022, https://www.thebalancemoney.com/what-caused-the-subprime-mortgage-crisis-3305696.

93. Jeffrey Chang and David Wessel, "What is the Repo Market and Why Does It Matter?" The Brookings Institution, January 28, 2020, https://www.brookings.edu/blog/up-front/2020/01/28/what-is-the-repo-market-and-why-does-it-matter/.

94. John Mullin, "The Repo Market is Changing (and What Is a Repo, Anyway?)" Federal Reserve Bank of Richmond, 2020, https://www.richmondfed.org/publications/research /econ_focus/2020/q1/federal_reserve.

95. Adam Davison, "How AIG Fell Apart," Reuters, September 18, 2008, https://www.reuters.com/article/us-how-aig-fell-apart-idUSMAR85972720080918.

96. The Investopedia Team, "What Is Quantitative Easing (QE), and How Does It Work?" Investopedia, August 03, 2022, https://www.investopedia.com/terms/q/quantitative-easing.asp.

97. Edward Roe, "Modern Monetary Theory: Changing the Questions?" Ruffer, March 2, 2020, https://www.ruffer.co.uk/en/thinking/articles/the-ruffer-review/2020-03-modern -monetary-theory.

98. Alan Kohler, "'The Money Story' Told by a Father of MMT," Eureka Report, August 4, 2020, https://www.eurekareport.com.au/investment-news/the-money-story-told-by-a -father-of-mmt/148340.

99. Margaret Thatcher, "Speech to Conservative Party Conference," (speech), Margaret Thatcher Foundation, October 14, 1983, https://www.margaretthatcher.org/docu-ment/105454.

100. Kohler, "'The Money Story.'"

101. Kohler, "'The Money Story.'"

102. ECP Balance Sheet (graph), taken from "The ECB's Policy of Printing Money Will Not Lead to Wealth Creation. Instead, It Will Inevitably Lead to Inflation Far above 6% across Europe," London School of Economics and Political Science, May 29, 2012.

103. Zach Helfand, "The Economist Who Believes the Government Should Just Print More Money," The New Yorker, August 20, 2019, https://www.newyorker.com/news/news-desk/ the-economist-who-believes-the-government-should-just-print-more-money.

104. Emily Stewart and Rebecca Heilweil, "War in the Time of Crypto," Vox, March 15, 2022. https://www.vox.com/recode/22955381/russia-ukraine-bitcoin-donation-war-crypto.

105. Stewart and Heilweil, "War In the Time of Crypto."

106. Stop-losses is a mechanism built into the stock market to stop trading when prices reach a designated dangerously low level.

107. Gillian Tett, "The Goldilocks Crisis May Have Arrived for Crypto," Financial Times, May 19, 2022, https://www.ft.com/content/7e0e2e24-cb4c-4694-be86-5cad9fc26d3e.

108. Martin Arnold, "Crypto Links with Banks Pose Threat to Financial Stability, Says ECB," *Financial Times*, May 24, 2022, https://www.ft.com/content/5124fe2d-0f37-4173-89ba-fe9812e09e67?shareType=nongift.

109. "The Block," The Block, n.d., https://www.theblockcrypto.com.

110. Arnold, "Crypto Linked with Banks."

111. Stephen Kahl, "Germany to Allow Institutional Funds to Hold Up to 20% in Crypto," Bloomberg, July 30, 2021, https://www.bloomberg.com/news/articles/2021-07-30/germany-to-allow-institutional-funds-to-hold-up-to-20-in-crypto#xj4y7vzkg.

112. Bjarke Smith-Meyer, "Brussels Agrees on Crypto Rulebook for the EU," *Politico*, July 1, 2022, https://www.politico.eu/article/brussels-agrees-on-crypto-rulebook-for-the-eu/.

113. "eBay's StumbleUpon Acquisition: Confirmed at $75 Million," TechCrunch, May 30, 2007, https://techcrunch.com/2007/05/30/ebays-stumbleupon-acquisition-confirmed-at-75-million/.

114. "Akami Acquires Red Swoosh," ResponseSource, accessed June 2022, https://pressreleases.responsesource.com/news/30748/akamai-acquires-red-swoosh/.

115. Fox Business, accessed June 2022, https://www.foxbusiness.com/markets/startups-great-recession.

116. Marc Vartabedian, "Initial Uber Investor First Round Capital Banked on UberCab," *The Wall Street Journal*, April 11, 2019, https://www.wsj.com/articles/initial-uber-investor-first-round-capital-banked-on-ubercab-11555027586.

117. Fox Business.

118. Connie Loizos, "A Peek inside Sequoia Capital's Low-Flying, Wide-Reaching Scout Program," TechCrunch, June 7, 2019, https://techcrunch.com/2019/06/07/a-peek-inside-sequoia-capitals-low-flying-wide-reaching-scout-program/.

119. Gené Teare, "Lessons from 2008: How the Downturn Impacted Funding Two to Four Years Out," Crunchbase News, March 24, 2020, https://news.crunchbase.com/startups/lessons-from-2008-how-the-downturn-impacted-funding-two-to-four-years-out/.

120. Amazon web services provide on-demand cloud computing platforms and APIs to individuals, companies, and governments, on a metered, pay-as-you-go basis.

121. Harry Davis et al., "Uber Broke Laws, Duped Police and Secretly Lobbied Governments, Leak Reveals," *The Guardian*, July 11, 2022, https://www.theguardian.com/news/2022/jul/10/uber-files-leak-reveals-global-lobbying-campaign.

122. Nathaniel Meyersohn, "After the Crisis, Silicon Valley Overtook Wall Street as the Place to Be," CNN Business, June 7, 2018, https://money.cnn.com/2018/06/07/news/economy/wall-street-silicon-valley-google-goldman-sachs/index.html.

123. Bobby Allyn, "Google Workers Speak Out about Why They Formed a Union: 'To Protect Ourselves,'" NPR Up First, January 8, 2021, https://www.npr.org/2021/01/08/954710407/at-google-hundreds-of-workers-formed-a-labor-union-why-to-protect-ourselves.

124. Stephen Rodrick, "'How Many Women Were Abused to Make That Tesla?'" *Rolling Stone*, September 19, 2022, https://www.rollingstone.com/culture/culture-features/tesla-sexual-harassment-lawsuit-investigation-elon-musk-1234590697/.

125. "Gig Economy," Quit Genius, n.d., https://www.quitgenius.com/hr-glossary/gig-economy.

126. Government of the United Kingdom, Department for Business, Energy, and Industrial Strategy, *The Characteristics of Those In The Gig Economy: Final Report*, Katriina Lepanjuuri, Robert Wishart, and Peter Cornick, 2018, PDF, https://assets.publishing.service.gov.uk/government/uploads/system/uploads/attachment_data/file/687553/The_characteristics_of_those_in_the_gig_economy.pdf.

127. Sam Knight, "How Uber Conquered London." *The Guardian*, April 27, 2016, https://www.theguardian.com/technology/2016/apr/27/how-uber-conquered-london.

128. Knight, "How Uber Conquered London."

129. Mary-Ann Russon, "Uber Drivers Are Workers Not Self-Employed, Supreme Court Rules," BBC News, February 19, 2021, https://www.bbc.com/news/business-56123668.

130. Bowdeya Tweh and Andrew Gainer-Dewar, "Why Google Workers Formed a Union," interview by Kate Linebaugh and Ryan Knutson, *The Wall Street Journal Podcast*, January 11, 2021, 15:37, https://www.wsj.com/podcasts/the-journal/why-google-workers-formed-a -union/50fc530f-d1db-4e43-a1a5-d2ee96b6e2b7.
131. Ross LaJeunesse, "I Was Google's Head of International Relations. Here's Why I Left," Medium, January 2, 2020, https://medium.com/@rossformaine/i-was-googles-head-of-international-relations-here-s-why-i-left-49313d23065.
132. Allyn, "Google Workers Speak Out."
133. Ben Gilbert and David Rosenthal, "The Best Acquisitions of All Time," *Acquired*, podcast, March 17, 2020, 1:50:37, https://www.acquired.fm/episodes/acquired-top-ten-the-best-acquisitions-of-all-time.
134. BI India Bureau, "Top 10 Smartest Acquisitions of All Time," Business Insider India, August 3, 2022, https://www.businessinsider.in/business/news/biggest-profitable-merger-and-acquisitions-of-all-time-in-world/slidelist/93322654.cms.
135. Gilbert and Rosenthal, "The Best Acquisitions of All Time."
136. BI India, "Top 10 Acquisitions."
137. Gilbert and Rosenthal, "The Best Acquisitions of All Time."
138. Alison L. Deutsch, "WhatsApp: The Best Meta Purchase Ever?" Investopedia, March 29, 2022, https://www.investopedia.com/articles/investing/032515/whatsapp-best-facebook-purchase-ever.asp.
139. Stephen Hutcheon, "The Untold Story about the Founding of Google Maps," Medium, February 10, 2015, https://medium.com/@lewgus/the-untold-story-about-the-founding-of-google-maps-e4a54430aec92.
140. Ben Gilbert and David Rosenthal, "Google Maps," *Acquired*, podcast, April 26, 2019, 1:41:13, https://www.acquired.fm/episodes/google-maps.
141. Wikipedia, s.v. "C++," March 6, 2023, https://en.wikipedia.org/wiki/C%2B%2B#History.
142. A geospatial data visualization company (with investment from the CIA) whose marquee application suite, EarthViewer, emerged as the highly successful Google Earth application in 2005 while other aspects of its core technology were integrated into Google Maps. (Andrew Orlowski, "Google Buys CIA-Backed Mapping Startup," The Register, October 28, 2004, https://www.theregister.com/2004/10/28/google_buys_keyhole/.)
143. "Google Acquires ZipDash" Mergr, September 1, 2004, https://mergr.com/alphabet-acquires -zipdash.
144. Bill Kilday, "The Little Known Story of How Google Earth Helped Save More than 400 Lives after Hurricane Katrina," Linkedin, excerpt from Kilday's *Never Lost Again: The Google Mapping Revolution That Sparked New Industries And Augmented Our Reality*, (New York: Harper Business, 2018), June 1, 2018, https://www.linkedin.com/pulse/little -known-story-how-google-earth-saved-more-than-400-kilday.
145. Chris Welch, "Steve Jobs Added Google Maps to the Original iPhone Just Weeks before Unveiling," https://www.theverge.com/2012/9/29/3428380/steve-jobs-apple-google-maps-original-iphone.
146. The DARPA Grand Challenge is a prize competition for American autonomous vehicles, funded by the Defense Advanced Research Projects Agency, the most prominent research organization of the United States Department of Defense.
147. Michael Arrington, "Whispers about Stealth Startup Vutool," TechCrunch, March 28, 2007, https://techcrunch.com/2007/03/28/whispers-about-stealth-startup-vutool/.
148. Haaretz, "Waze Workers Get $1.2M Each From Google Deal," Forward, June 13, 2013, https://forward.com/news/breaking-news/178580/waze-workers-get-12m-each-from-google-deal/.
149. Richard Dawkins, *Unweaving the Rainbow* (Boston: Mariner Books, 2000).
150. Gerardus Mercator's "most famous work, the Mercator projection, is a geographical chart where the spherical globe is flattened into a two-dimensional map, with latitude and lon-

gitude lines drawn in a straight grid." ("Gerardus Mercator," *National Geographic*, n.d., https://education.nationalgeographic.org/resource/gerardus-mercator/.)

151. Tom Holland, "*A History of the World in Twelve Maps* by Jerry Brotton—Review," *The Guardian*, August 24, 2012, https://www.theguardian.com/books/2012/aug/24/history-world-twelve-maps-review.

152. Thomson Reuters, "Ukraine Berates Apple for Identifying Crimea as Part of Russia in Apps," CBC, November 27, 2019, https://www.cbc.ca/news/science/apple-crimea-1.5375793.

153. "Mappa Mundi," Mappa Mundi, n.d., https://www.themappamundi.co.uk/.

154. Jesse Walker, "Cartography for the Masses," *Reason*, June 28, 2007, https://reason.com/2007/06/28/cartography-for-the-masses/.

155. Evan Ratliff, "Google Maps Is Changing the Way We See the World," *Wired*, June 26, 2007, https://www.wired.com/2007/06/ff-maps/.

156. "In-Q-Tel Announces Strategic Investment in Keyhole," In-Q-Tel, https://www.iqt.org/news/in-q-tel-announces-strategic-investment-in-keyhole/.

157. John Herrman, "How Google and Bing Maps Control What You Can See," BuzzFeed News, March 1, 2013, https://www.buzzfeednews.com/article/jwherrman/how-google-and-bing-maps-control-the-world.

158. Robert F. Worth, Mark Mazzetti, and Scott Shane, "Drone Strikes' Risks to Get Rare Moment in Public Eye," *The New York Times*, February 5, 2013, https://www.nytimes.com/2013/02/06/world/middleeast/with-brennan-pick-a-light-on-drone-strikes-hazards.html?hp=&pagewanted=all&_r=0.

159. Ratliff, "Google Maps Is Changing the Way We See the World."

160. Ratliff, "Google Maps Is Changing the Way We See the World."

161. Wikipedia, s.v. "Terravision (computer game)," Wikipedia, https://en.wikipedia.org/wiki/Terravision_(computer_program).

162. "Michael Jones . . . and Brian McClendon . . . were employed at SGI during the period that ART+ COM was developing Terravision. . . . Mr. McClendon was employed by Keyhole and Mr. Jones served on its Board of Directors." (ART+COM Innovationpool GmbH. v. GOOGLE INC, First amended complaint, C.A. No. 14-cv-217-RGA, March 13, 2014. https://www.ipwatchdog.com/wp-content/uploads/2017/10/ARTCOM-amended-complaint.pdf.)

163. Joachim Sauter, Pavel Mayer, Axel Schmidt, and Gerd Grüneis.

164. Gilles Babinet, "The End of Nation States? Part 1: Technology-Induced Sovereignty Transfers," Institut Montaigne, November 27, 2018, https://www.institutmontaigne.org/en/blog/end-nation-states-part-1-technology-induced-sovereignty-transfers.

165. Italo Calvino, *Invisible Cities* (Orlando: Harcourt), 87.

166. Chris Humble, "Facebook Announces Apollo, a New NoSQL Database for On-line Low Latency Storage," InfoQ, June 13, 2014, https://www.infoq.com/news/2014/06/facebook-apollo/.

167. Isabelle Amurao, "The Politics of Facebook in the Philippines," *Asia Times*, May 4, 2022, https://asiatimes.com/2022/05/the-politics-of-facebook-in-the-philippines/.

168. Rochel Ellen Bernido, "Marcos Jr. Benefited from Facebook—Study," Rappler, May 10, 2022, https://www.rappler.com/nation/elections/ferdinand-marcos-jr-benefited-facebook-disinformation-study/.

169. Rahul Bhatia, "The Inside of Facebook's Biggest Setback," *The Guardian*, May 12, 2016, https://www.theguardian.com/technology/2016/may/12/facebook-free-basics-india-zuckerberg.

170. Yifan Yu et al., "Losing Face: the Perils of Facebook's Asia strategy," *Financial Times*, n.d., https://www.ft.com/content/2776c841-e907-43a4-851f-ed372305b389.

171. Mihály Csíkszentmihályi, *Flow: The Psychology of Optimal Experience* (New York: Harper Perennial).

172. Mihály Csíkszentmihályi, *Flow*.

173. Christine Byrd, "(Don't) Just Go with the Flow," UCI School of the Humanities News, April 19, 2021, https://www.humanities.uci.edu/news/dont-just-go-flow.

174. Daniel Huang, "Young, Poor and Looking to Invest? Robinhood Is the App for That," *The Wall Street Journal*, January 6, 2015, https://www.wsj.com/articles/BL-MBB-31486.

175. Matthew Johnston, "Robinhood IPO: What You Need to Know," Investopedia, July 29, 2021, https://www.investopedia.com/assessing-the-robinhood-ipo-5187047.

176. "Congress Passes Commodity Futures Trading Commission," US Congress, December 15, 2000, https://www.cftc.gov/sites/default/files/opa/press00/opa4479-00.htm.

177. "High Frequency Trading (HFT)," Nasdaq, https://www.nasdaq.com/glossary/h/high-frequency-trading.

178. Matteo Aquilina, Eric Budish, and Peter O'Neill, "BIS Working Papers No 955: Quantifying the High-Frequency Trading 'Arms Race,'" Bank for International Settlements, August 2021, https://www.bis.org/publ/work955.pdf.

179. High frequency trading places thousands or millions of winning trades each day, but generally earns a tiny profit of a few cents on each trade. In a bull market, human beings don't care about losing a few cents to a machine for trades where they can make thousands or millions of dollars. But each time the market moves down, strategists and market commentators blame the "algos," high frequency computers, for their losses. As with kids playing video games, they never accept a defeat, it is never their fault: it is always because of a computer glitch. (Interview with a trader.)

180. "What Risks Are There in ETFs?" etf.com, https://www.etf.com/etf-education-center/etf-basics/what-risks-are-there-in-etfsmake.

181. Martin Arnold, "Crypto Links with Banks Pose Threat to Financial Stability, Says ECB," *Financial Times*, May 24, 2022, https://www.ft.com/content/5124fe2d-0f37-4173-89ba-fe9812e09e67?shareType=nongift.

182. "r/wallstreetbets," Reddit, https://www.reddit.com/r/wallstreetbets/.

183. David J. Lynch, "The GameStop Stock Craze Is about a Populist Uprising against Walls Street. But It's More Complicated than That," *The Washington Post*, February 1, 2021, https://www.washingtonpost.com/business/2021/02/01/gamestop-origins/.

184. Theron Mohamed, "GameStop Millionaire Keith Gill Is Testifying before Congress on Thursday. Meet the Investor Who Upended Wall Street with cat Memes, Reaction GIFs, and Fundamental Analysis," Markets Insider, February 18, 2021, https://markets.businessinsider.com/news/stocks/gamestop-investor-deepfuckingvalue-roaring-kitty-reddit-stocks-wall-street-2021-1-1030022004.

185. Brandon Kochkodin, "How WallStreetBets Pushed GameStop Shares to the Moon," Bloomberg, January 25, 2021, https://www.bloomberg.com/news/articles/2021-01-25/how-wallstreetbets-pushed-gamestop-shares-to-the-moon?leadSource=uverify%20wall.

186. Lynch, "The Game Stop Stock Craze."

187. Elijah Brasley (@eli.brazy), "Guess I'm just different [] #stocks #investing #forex #bitcoin," TikTok, January 19, 2021, https://www.tiktok.com/@elijah.brasley/video/6919585048119282949.

188. Olga Kharif, "Discord Bans WallStreetBets for Allowing Hateful Speech," Bloomberg, January 27, 2021, https://www.bloomberg.com/news/articles/2021-01-28/wallstreetbets-banned-from-discord-for-allowing-hateful-speech.

189. Kate Rooney, "A Controversial Part of Robinhood's Business Tripled in Sales Thanks to High Frequency Trading Firms," CNBC, April 18, 2019, https://www.cnbc.com/2019/04/18/a-controversial-part-of-robinhoods-business-tripled-in-sales-thanks-to-high-frequency-trading-firms.html.

190. *Robinhood, 2021 Annual Report*, 78, https://s28.q4cdn.com/948876185/files/doc_financials/2021/ar/HOOD-2021-Annual-Report.pdf.

191. ColdFusion, "Reddit vs Wallstreet—GameStop, The Movie," February 4, 2021, YouTube video, https://www.youtube.com/watch?v=YFQ-v1jCpF0.

192. Matt Egan, "Robinhood CEO Details 3:30 am Call to Put Up $3 Billion," CNN Business, February, 1, 2021, https://www.cnn.com/2021/02/01/investing/robinhood-gamestop -vlad-tenev/index.html.

193. Ortenca Aliaj and James Fontanella-Khan, "Gabe Plotkin's Melvin Capital to Wind Down Funds," *Financial Times*, n.d., https://www.ft.com/content/74ee1f19-1cdc-4cb8 -941e-7d035cf86faf.

194. "Fossil Gas, Liquefied: What LGN Is and Why It Is a Looming Climate Disaster," Global Witness, October 11, 2021, https://www.globalwitness.org/en/blog/fossil-gas-liquefied- what-lng-and-why-it-looming-climate-disaster/.

195. "Fossil Gas, Liquefied," Global Witness.

196. "Total Delivers Its First Carbon Neutral LNG Cargo," TotalEnergies, October 20, 2020, https://totalenergies.com/media/news/communiques-presse/total-delivers-its-first-carbon- neutral-lng-cargo.

197. Stephen Stapczynski, Akshat Rathi, and Godfrey Marawanyika, "How to Sell 'Carbon Neutral' Fossil Fuel That Doesn't Exist," Bloomberg, August 11, 2021, https://www. bloomberg.com/news/features/2021-08-11/the-fictitious-world-of-carbon-neutral-fossil- fuel.

198. "Carney, Antonioli Agree That Carbon Credits Are Vital for Getting the World Net Zero," Verra, March 29, 2022, https://verra.org/carney-antonioli-agree-that-carbon-cred- its-are-vital-for-getting-the-world-to-net-zero.

199. Henry Sanderson, "Congo, Child Labour and Your Electric Car," *Financial Times*, n.d., https://www.ft.com/content/c6909812-9ce4-11e9-9c06-a4640c9feebb.

200. Cale Tilford et al., "How Green Is Your Electric Vehicle," *Financial Times*, October 5, 2021, https://ig.ft.com/electric-car/.

201. "Environmental Costs," Costs of War, Watson Institute International and Public Affairs, Brown University, https://watson.brown.edu/costsofwar/costs/social/environment.

202. "LNG versus Pipeline Gas: How Do Lifecycle Emissions Compare," Wood Mackenzie, June 25, 2017, https://www.woodmac.com/news/editorial/lng-pipeline-gas-emissions/.

203. "About Us," Sphera, https://sphera.com/about-us/.

204. "The U.S. Shale Revolution" Energy and Security, Strauss Center, The University of Texas at Austin, https://www.strausscenter.org/energy-and-security-project/the-u-s-shale-revolu- tion.

205. "Overexposed," Global Witness, April 23, 2019, https://www.globalwitness.org/en/cam- paigns/oil-gas-and-mining/overexposed/.

206. University of Houston Energy Fellows, "Russia-Ukraine War Reinforces LNG's Role in Global Energy Security," *Forbes*, April 19, 2022, https://www.forbes.com/sites/uhenergy/2022/04/19/ russia-ukraine-war-reinforces-lngs-role-in-global-energy-security/?sh=7e97819c6c02.

207. James Sandy, "Carbon Capture: The Hopes, Challenges, and Controversies," *Financial Times*, April 5, 2022, video, https://www.ft.com/video/25df7aa2-e414-484f-ac2f- 63e06644fcb1.

208. Sandy, "Carbon Capture: The Hopes, Challenges, and Controversies."

209. "Apple Expands the Use of Recycled Materials across Its Products," Apple, April 19, 2022, https://www.apple.com/uk/newsroom/2022/04/apple-expands-the-use-of-recycled-mate- rials-across-its-products/.

210. "Leading a Sustainable Revolution: Ford and HP Collaborate to Transform 3D Waste into Auto Parts, An Industry First," Ford Media Center, March 25, 2021, https://media. ford.com/content/fordmedia/fna/us/en/news/2021/03/25/leading-a-sustainable-revolution. html.

211. "Homepage," Twelve, https://www.twelve.co/technology.

212. Ed Ballard, "Tech Startups Race to Rate Carbon Offsets," *The Wall Street Journal*, January 25, 2022, https://www.wsj.com/articles/tech-startups-race-to-rate-carbon-offsets- 11643115605?mod=article_inline.

213. "Carbon Capture Startup Sees Its New Tech as a Profitable Investment," Bloomberg, July 1, 2021, video, https://www.bloomberg.com/news/videos/2021-07-01/carbon-capture-startup-sees-its-new-tech-as-a-profitable-investment-video?sref=WYbI89jw.

214. Tom Hannen et al., "Space-Based Solar Power 'Could Be Deployed in 10 Years,'" *Financial Times*, November 23, 2021, video, https://www.ft.com/video/2f48b8e4-bb5a-4d90-b267-e33d9a59804c.

215. Bruce Riedel, "75 Years after a Historic Meeting on the USS Quincy, US-Saudi Relations Are in Need of a True Re-think," Brookings Institution, February 10, 2020, https://www.brookings.edu/blog/order-from-chaos/2020/02/10/75-years-after-a-historic-meeting-on-the-uss-quincy-us-saudi-relations-are-in-need-of-a-true-re-think/.

216. "Oil and Petroleum Products Explained: Oil Imports and Exports," US Energy Information Administration, last updated November 2, 2022, https://www.eia.gov/energyexplained/oil-and-petroleum-products/imports-and-exports.php.

217. The US would lose its position as largest oil producer in 1976. It would become once again the global leader in 2018. (Data is Beautiful, "Oil Production by Country," September 2, 2019, YouTube video, https://www.youtube.com/watch?v=GQokbIsuTUw.)

218. "1950s Interstate Highway Promotional Film 'We'll Take the High Road' 62784," Periscope Film, May 9, 2018, YouTube video, https://www.youtube.com/watch?v=xTPgbePibWg.

219. Kimberly Amadeo, "Oil Price History—Highs and Lows Since 1970," The Balance, April 13, 2022, https://www.thebalance.com/oil-price-history-3306200.

220. Bill Bonner, "Why We Should Be Measuring the Quality of Stuff and Not the Quantity," *Business Insider*, July 30, 2015, https://www.businessinsider.com/economists-quality-over-quantity-2015-7?r=US&IR=T.

221. English translation mine. (Giorgia Colucci, "Altro che lotta alla deforestazione: nel 2021 distrutti 11,1 milioni di ettari ai Tropici: una superficie pari a quella dei boschi italiani," *il Fatto Quotidiano*, May 2, 2022, https://www.ilfattoquotidiano.it/2022/05/02/altro-che-lotta-alla-deforestazione-nel-2021-distrutti-111-milioni-di-ettari-ai-tropici-una-superficie-pari-a-quella-dei-boschi-italiani/6576743/.)

222. Evannex, "More on Tesla Co-founder Straubel's Redwood Battery Supply Chain," InsideEVs, September 28, 2021, https://insideevs.com/news/536979/tesla-straubel-redwood-materials-battery/.

223. International Energy Agency, *Global EV Outlook 2019: Scaling-up the Transition to Electric Mobility* (Paris: OECD Publishing), https://doi.org/10.1787/35fb60bd-en.

224. Amanda Quick, "Tapping into the Topic of EV Battery Waste," Web Bike World, May 27, 2021, https://motorbikewriter.com/tapping-into-the-topic-of-ev-battery-waste/.

225. "Lithium," Trading Economics, https://tradingeconomics.com/commodity/lithium.

226. "Electric Vehicle Battery Costs Soar," Institute for Energy Research, April 25, 2022, https://www.instituteforenergyresearch.org/renewable/electric-vehicle-battery-costs-soar/.

227. "It's Such a Big Deal to Manufacture Batteries That They Already Reach for Rubbish," Li-Cycle, May 12, 2022, https://li-cycle.com/in-the-news/its-such-a-big-deal-to-manufacture-batteries-that-they-already-reach-for-rubbish/.

228. Laura Lander et al., "Financial Viability of Electric Vehicle Lithium-ion Battery Recycling," *iScience* 24, no. 7 (2021), https://doi.org/10.1016/j.isci.2021.102787.

229. James D. Watson, *Darwin: The Indelible Stamp* (Philadelphia: Running Press, 2005).

230. Edward O. Wilson, "The Social Conquest of Earth," The Long Now Foundation, April 20, 2012, video, 1:32:15, https://longnow.org/seminars/02012/apr/20/social-conquest-earth/.

231. Edward O. Wilson, "The Social Conquest of Earth."

232. SPGAP2, which causes delayed maturation of the frontal lobe and protracted childhood of humans, facilitating learning from adults.

233. Edward O. Wilson, "The Social Conquest of Earth."

234. Hannah Ritchie, Fiona Spooner, and Max Roser, "Biodiversity," Our World in Data, 2022, https://ourworldindata.org/extinctions.
235. Max Rosner et al., "World Population Growth," Our World in Data, 2013, https://ourworldindata.org/world-population-growth.
236. "The World Population at 7 Billion," United States Census Bureau, October 31, 2011, https://www.census.gov/newsroom/blogs/random-samplings/2011/10/the-world-population-at-7-billion.html.
237. "Global Issues: Population," The United Nations, 2022, https://un.org/en/global-issues/population.
238. Australian Circular Economy Briefing, "Key Sectors That Will Catalyse the Australian Circular Economy," Circular Australia, 2021, https://circularaustralia.com.au/key-sectors-that-will-catalyse-the-australian-circular-economy/.
239. "Foodwaste," Rabobank, 2021, https://www.rabobank.com.au/foodwaste/.
240. "Machinery of Government (MoG) Changes to Our Department from 1 July 2022," Australian Government, Department of Industry, Science, and Resources, July 1, 2022, https://www.industry.gov.au/data-and-publications/australias-emissions-projections-2020.
241. Ajwal Dsouza and Thomas Gram, "Space Agriculture Boldly Grows Food Where No One Has Grown Before," University of Guelf News, July 12, 2022, https://news.uoguelph.ca/2022/07/space-agriculture-boldly-grows-food-where-no-one-has-grown-before/.
242. Tiffany Hsu, "The Apollo 11 Mission Was Also a Global Media Sensation," *The New York Times*, July 15, 2019, https://www.nytimes.com/2019/07/15/business/media/apollo-11-television-media.html.
243. Andrew O'Hagan, "Goodbye Moon," *London Review of Books* 32, no. 4 (February 25, 2010).
244. Miriam Cosic, "The Moon and Mankind," *The Australian*, July 19, 2019.
245. Michele Ostovar, "The Decision to Go to the Moon: President John F. Kennedy's May 25, 1961 Speech before a Joint Session of Congress–NASA," NASA (blog), September 29, 2023, https://www.nasa.gov/history/the-decision-to-go-to-the-moon/.
246. "How Much Did the Apollo Program Cost?" The Planetary Society, 2020, https://www.planetary.org/space-policy/cost-of-apollo.
247. Adam Mann, "The Apollo Program: How NASA Sent Astronauts to the Moon," Space.com, June 25, 2020, https://www.space.com/apollo-program-overview.html.
248. Brian Dunbar and Sarah Loff, "Space Shuttle Era," NASA, August 3, 2017, https://www.nasa.gov/mission_pages/shuttle/flyout/index.html.
249. "Low Earth Orbit," The European Space Agency, February 3, 2020, https://www.esa.int/ESA_Multimedia/Images/2020/03/Low_Earth_orbit.
250. "Building the International Space Station," The European Space Agency, https://www.esa.int/Science_Exploration/Human_and_Robotic_Exploration/International_Space_Station/Building_the_International_Space_Station3.
251. Doug Adler, "Why Did NASA Retire the Space Shuttle?" Astronomy, November 12, 2020, https://astronomy.com/news/2020/11/why-did-nasa-retire-the-space-shuttle.
252. Adler, "Why Did NASA Retire the Space Shuttle?"
253. Peter Beaumont, "NASA Chiefs 'Repeatedly Ignored' Safety Warnings," *The Guardian*, February 2, 2003, https://www.theguardian.com/science/2003/feb/02/spaceexploration.usnews3.
254. Michael Sheetz, "SpaceX Launches Two NASA Astronauts to Space for the First Time in Historic US Mission," CNBC, May 30, 2020, https://www.cnbc.com/2020/05/30/spacex-launches-two-nasa-astronauts-to-space-for-the-first-time.html.
255. Harry W. Jones, "The Recent Large Reduction in Space Launch Cost," NASA Ames Research Center, 48th International Conference on Environmental Systems, July 8–12, 2018, Albuquerque, New Mexico.

256. Daniel Oberhaus, "The US Hitches Its Final Ride to Space from Russia—for Now," *Wired*, April 8, 2020, https://www.wired.com/story/the-us-hitches-its-final-ride-to-space-from-russia-for-now/.

257. "NASA's Commercial Crew Program: Update on Development and Certification Efforts," NASA Office of Inspector General, Office of Audits, September 1, 2016, https://oig.NASA.gov/audits/reports/FY16/IG-16-028.pdf.

258. Richard Fisher, "The Long-Term Quest to Build a 'Galactic Civilization,'" BBC News, July 21, 2021, https://www.bbc.com/future/article/20210721-the-quest-for-a-galactic-civilisation-that-saves-humanity.

259. "Blue Origin 2019: For the Benefit of Earth," Blue Origin, May 9, 2019, YouTube video, 51:27, https://www.youtube.com/watch?v=GQ98hGUe6FM.

260. Robin Hanson, "The Great Filter—Are We Almost Past It?" September 15, 1998, https://mason.gmu.edu/~rhanson/greatfilter.html.

261. Fisher, "The Long-Term Quest to Build a 'Galactic Civilization.'"

262. George Bernard Shaw, *Man and Superman* (Cambridge: Cambridge UP, 1905), 238.

263. Mary-Jane Rubenstein, *Astrotopia: The Dangerous Religion of the Corporate Space Race* (Chicago: Chicago UP, 2022).

264. Steinar Lag, "Technology Outlook 2030: Reusable Rockets: Revolutionizing Access to Outer Space," DNV, https://www.dnv.com/to2030/technology/reusable-rockets-revolutionizing-access-to-outer-space.html.

265. Mike Wall, "Ticket Price for Private Spaceflights on Virgin Galactic's SpaceShipTwo Going Up," Space.com, April 30, 2013, https://www.space.com/20886-virgin-galactic-spaceshiptwo-ticket-prices.html.

266. "Fly Me to the Moon: Japanese Billionaire Plans Space Voyage," DW, March 3, 2021, https://www.dw.com/en/fly-me-round-the-moon-japanese-billionaire-offers-out-of-this-world-trip/a-56754753.

267. Jean D. Sibonga et al., "Risk of Early Onset Osteoporosis Due to Space Flight," Human Research Program, NASA, May 9, 2017, https://humanresearchroadmap.nasa.gov/evidence/other/Osteo.pdf.

268. Krishna Kandarpa, Victor Schneider, and Krishnan Ganapathy, "Human health during space travel: An overview," *Neurology India* 67, no. 8 (2019), https://www.neurologyindia.com/article.asp?issn=0028-3886;year=2019;volume=67;issue=8;spage=176;epage=181;aulast=Kandarpa.

269. Francine E. Garrett-Bakelman et al., "The NASA Twins Study: A Multidimensional Analysis of a Year-Long Human Spaceflight," *Science* 364, no. 6436 (Spring 2019), https://doi.org/10.1126/science.aau8650.

270. Loren Grush, "How Do Astronauts Exercise in Space?" The Verge, December 23, 2019, https://www.theverge.com/2017/8/29/16217348/nasa-iss-how-do-astronauts-exercise-in-space.

271. Kim Stanley Robinson, *Red Mars* (New York: Spectra, 1993).

272. Edgar Rice Burroughs, *A Princess of Mars* (Chicago: A.C. McClurg & Company, 1917).

273. Ray Bradbury, *The Martian Chronicles* (New York: Doubleday, 1950).

274. Eric Choi, "Making Mars a Nicer Place," *The Space Review*, September 10, 2012, https://www.thespacereview.com/article/2152/1.

275. Dante D'Orazio, "Elon Musk Believes Colonizing Mars Will Save Humanity," The Verge, October 4, 2014, https://www.theverge.com/2014/10/4/6907721/elon-musks-believes-colonizing-mars-will-save-humanity.

276. Olle Häggström, "The Bullerby Scenario," *Häggström hävdar* (blog), January 15, 2016, http://haggstrom.blogspot.com/2016/01/the-bullerby-scenario.html.

277. Sim Kern, "Jeff Bezos Is Sending Us All a Frightening Message with His Colonial Space Flight," *Independent*, July 19, 2021, https://www.independent.co.uk/voices/bezos-musk-branson-space-billionaires-b1886741.html.

278. Loren Grush, "Elon Musk Elaborates on His Proposal to Nuke Mars," The Verge, October 2, 2015, https://www.theverge.com/2015/10/2/9441029/elon-musk-mars-nuclear-bomb-colbert-interview-explained.
279. Jatan Mehta, "Can We Make Mars Earth-Like through Terraforming?" The Planetary Society, April 19, 2021, https://www.planetary.org/articles/can-we-make-mars-earth-like-through-terraforming.
280. MOXIE is a short, snappy name for a tool that helps lead to human footprints on Mars. It helps humans explore Mars by making OXygen. It works "In situ" (in place) on the Red Planet, and it is an "Experiment." ("Moxie," NASA Science, Mars: 2020 Mission Perseverance Rover, https://mars.nasa.gov/mars2020/spacecraft/instruments/moxie/.)
281. Mehta, "Can We Make Mars Earth-Like through Terraforming?"
282. "MAVEN, Studying How Mars Lost Its Atmosphere," The Planetary Society, n.d., https://www.planetary.org/space-missions/maven.
283. J. L. Green et al., "A Future Mars Environment for Science and Exploration," Planetary Science Vision 2050 Workshop, 2017, https://www.hou.usra.edu/meetings/V2050/pdf/8250.pdf.
284. "Could We Terraform Mars?" PBS Space Time, September 16, 2019, video, 19:36, https://www.youtube.com/watch?v=FshtPsOTCP4.
285. "Blue Origin 2019: For the Benefit of Earth," Blue Origin.
286. Hannen et al., "Space-Based Solar Power."
287. Peggy Hollinger and Sam Learner, "How Space Debris Threatens Modern Life," Financial Times, June 8, 2022, https://ig.ft.com/space-debris/.
288. Robert Zurin and Bernin Zóka, "The Future of Space," Cato Policy Report, January/February 2020, https://www.cato.org/sites/cato.org/files/2020-02/cpr-v42n1-5.pdf.
289. "A Basic Guide to Nanosatellites," Alén Space, https://alen.space/basic-guide-nanosatellites.
290. "Upcoming - Galaxy 33 (15R) & 34 (12R)," Space Stats, https://www.spacexstats.xyz/#launchhistory-per-year.
291. "Smallsat Rideshare Program," SpaceX, https://www.spacex.com/rideshare/.
292. Rachel Jewett, "SpaceX Launches Record Rideshare Mission Carrying 143 Satellites," Via Satellite, January 24, 2021, https://www.satellitetoday.com/launch/2021/01/24/spacex-launches-record-rideshare-mission-carrying-143-satellites/.
293. "Homepage," Nanoracks, https://nanoracks.com.
294. "Expanding the Market in Low-Earth Orbit," Houston We Have a Podcast, NASA, April 30, 2021, transcript, https://www.nasa.gov/johnson/HWHAP/expanding-the-market-in-low-earth-orbit.
295. "Expanding the Market in Low-Earth Orbit," Houston We Have a Podcast.
296. "The Economics of Space," Deloitte, 2020, https://www2.deloitte.com/content/dam/Deloitte/uk/Documents/consultancy/deloitte-uk-economics-of-space.pdf.
297. Peggy Hollinger, "Investors Join Space Race with Record Funding," Financial Times, https://www.ft.com/content/bdbe37cf-8d23-467c-89a5-abeae23de73f.
298. Jim Edwards, "Goldman Sachs: Space-Mining for Platinum Is 'More Realistic than Perceived," Business Insider, April 6, 2017, https://www.businessinsider.com/goldman-sachs-space-mining-asteroid-platinum-2017-4?r=US&IR=T.
299. "The Miniaturization of Satellites and Launchers: The Advent of the Low-Cost 'New Space,'" Surfeo, 2022, https://surfeo.eu/the-miniaturization-of-satellites-and-launchers-the-advent-of-the-low-cost-new-space/.
300. Hollinger and Learner, "How Space Debris Threatens Modern Life."
301. Anthony David, "Harwell's Astroscale Aims to Solve Space Debris Cleanup," TechTribe Oxford, August 3, 2019, https://oxford.techtribe.co/astroscale-aims-to-solve-space-debris-cleanup/.
302. "Astroscale's ELSA-d Mission Successfully Completes Complex Rendezvous Operation," Astroscale, May 4, 2022, https://astroscale.com/astroscales-elsa-d-mission-successfully-completes-complex-rendezvous-operation/.

303. Paul Zenners, "Luxembourg's New Space Law Guarantees Private Companies the Right to Resources Harvested in Outer Space in Accordance with International Law." Luxembourg Ministry of the Economy press release, November 11, 2016. https://space-agency. public.lu/dam-assets/press-release/2016/2016_11_11PressReleaseNewSpacelaw.pdf.

304. Hollinger and Learner, "How Space Debris Threatens Modern Life."

305. John Koetsier, "Space Inc: 10,000 Companies, $4T Value . . . and 52% American," *Forbes*, May 22, 2021, https://www.forbes.com/sites/johnkoetsier/2021/05/22/space-inc-10000-companies-4t-value--and-52-american/?sh=74da35c855ac.

306. Eric Berger, "The World Just Set a Record for Sending the Most Rockets into Orbit," Ars Technica, January 3, 2022, https://arstechnica.com/science/2022/01/thanks-to-china-and-spacex-the-world-set-an-orbital-launch-record-in-2021/.

307. Neel V. Patel, "China's Surging Private Space Industry is Out to Challenge the US," *MIT Technology Review*, January 21, 2021, https://www.technologyreview.com/2021/01/21/1016513 /china-private-commercial-space-industry-dominance/.

308. "How China's Space Programme Went from Launching Satellites to Building Its Own Space Station," *South China Morning Post*, July 29, 2021, YouTube video, https:// www.youtube.com/watch?v=vUR60ECbf8A&list=TLPQMjEwNTIwMjLeLGDc_ b6ZoQ&index=3.

309. Berger, "The World Just Set a Record for Sending the Most Rockets into Orbit."

310. "China's Space Program: A 2021 Perspective," China National Space Administration, January 2022, http://english.scio.gov.cn/node_8027953.html.

311. "Xiangshan," Google Maps, https://www.google.com/maps/place/Xiangshan,+Ning-bo,+Zhejiang,+China/@26.3019187,117.2988545,5.26z/data=!4m5!3m4!1s0x-3452718c3485a4c5:0x96c3dd6f0bd33d59!8m2!3d29.4766499!4d121.86932.

312. "China Begins Construction of Its Fifth Rocket Launch Site," Reuters, April 7, 2021, https://www.reuters.com/article/us-space-exploration-china-idUSKBN2BV0CF.

313. Karen Rowan, "Why Do Rockets Launch from Florida?" Live Science, May 30, 2020, https://www.livescience.com/32721-why-are-rockets-launched-from-florida.html.

314. Anthony Bouchard, "Why China Was Banned from the International Space Station," Labroots, February 11, 2020, https://www.labroots.com/trending/space/16798/chi-na-banned-international-space-station.

315. Heather Muir, "NASA Wants to Destroy the International Space Station—Here's Why," Inverse, March 5, 2022, https://www.inverse.com/science/destroy-the-iss.

316. Andrew Jones, "China Lays Out Big Plans for its New Tiangong Space Station," Space. com, May 3, 2022, https://www.space.com/china-big-plans-tiangong-space-station.

317. Andrew Jones, "China Aims for Space-Based Solar Power Test in LEO in 2028, GEO in 2030," *SpaceNews*, June 8, 2022, https://spacenews.com/china-aims-for-space-based-solar-power-test-in-leo-in-2028-geo-in-2030/.

318. Andrew Jones, "Watch China's Chang'e 5 Spacecraft Land on the Moon in This Amazing Video," Space.com, December 2, 2020, https://www.space.com/china-chang-e-5-moon-landing-lunar-sample-video.

319. Patel, "China's Surging Private Space Industry."

320. "The Artemis Accords: Principles for a Safe, Peaceful, and Prosperous Future," NASA, October 13, 2020, https://www.nasa.gov/specials/artemis-accords/index.html.

321. "Tianwen-1 and Zhurong, China's Mars Orbiter and Rover," The Planetary Society, n.d., https://www.planetary.org/space-missions/tianwen-1/.

322. Andrew Jones, "Russia Joins China's Mission to Sample an Asteroid and Study a Comet," Space.com, April 22, 2021, https://www.space.com/russia-joins-china-asteroid-comet-mis-sion. Andrew Jones, "China to Launch a Pair of Spacecraft Towards the Edge of Solar System," *SpaceNews*, April 16, 2021, https://spacenews.com/china-to-launch-a-pair-of-spacecraft-towards-the-edge-of-the-solar-system/.

INDEX

1Q84 (Murakami), 7

A

acquisitions in tech industry, 121–126
activism, 17
Acton, Brian, 112
addiction, 145
agriculture, development of, 183–184
AIG (American International Group),
    92–93
Alén Space, 220
algae, 212
algorithms ("algos"), 152
Allen, Paul, 23, 198
Altman, Sam, 61
Amazon rainforest, 179
Amazon web services, 269n120
analog computers, 45–46, 264n31
anarchism, 17
anonymity
    in cryptography, 18–21
    of Nakamoto, 47–50
    in online transactions, 21–22
    privacy and, 22
    in web surfing, 18
Anthropocene, age of, 8
anxiety, pandemic of, 3–4, 6–7, 11
Apollo project, 137–138
Apple
    acquisitions, 127
    Ukrainian maps, 129
Arms Export Control Act (1976), 20

Armstrong, Neil, 191–192
Arnold, Martin, 153
art
    as investment, 68–69
    as non-fungible, 67
    smart contracts via NFTs, 74–75
ART+COM, 131–132
Artemis Accords (US), 230
artificial intelligence, 8, 13, 24
    blockchain and, 59–60
    OpenAI, 61–62, 266n54
    in space exploration, 10–11
artificial planets, 213–214
"As We May Think" (Bush), 45
Asimov, Isaac, 208
Asperger's syndrome, 23–24
Assange, Julian, 16–17, 18
Astroscale, 224–225
Astrotopia, 200–202
atom, unlocking of, 200
atomic bomb(s), 43–45
Australia
    food waste, 188
    waste export ban, 187–188
Axie Infinity, 79
AXS (Axie Infinity Shards), 79

B

Ballard, Ed, 174
Bank Holding Company Act (1956),
    268n90
Bankman-Fried, Sam, 4, 105